WIRRAL AT WAR

MIKE ROYDEN

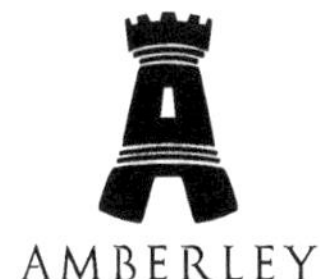

AMBERLEY

First published 2022

Amberley Publishing
The Hill, Stroud
Gloucestershire, GL5 4EP

www.amberley-books.com

British Library Cataloguing in Publication Data.

A catalogue record for this book is available from the British Library.

ISBN 978 1 4456 7522 0 (print)
ISBN 978 1 4456 7523 7 (ebook)

Typesetting by SJmagic DESIGN SERVICES, India.
Printed in the UK.

Contents

PART 1

THE FIRST WORLD WAR

Chapter 1

Mobilisation for War

MOBILISATION

4th Battalion, Cheshire Regiment

All members of the Battalion are hereby warned to report themselves at once at their Company Headquarters in Marching Order with Kit Bags packed. Any man who fails to appear will be treated as a deserter and proceeded against according to the ARMY ACT.

H. E. Patersall, Captain and Adjutant, 4th Battalion, Cheshire Regiment,

Headquarters, Grange Road West, Birkenhead

This stark announcement appeared prominently on the front page of the *Birkenhead News* on Saturday 8 August, but by then the war was already four days old, the Cheshire company of Royal Engineers had been urgently recalled from camp in Aberystwyth, and mobilisation was already underway across the country. First to be called upon were the serving regulars, followed by the trained reservists and part-time territorials. But this was woefully inadequate; just 450,000 professionals, 900 trained staff officers and some 250,000 reservists. This was tiny compared to the conscripted armies on the continent – and badly equipped. Anyone thinking at that stage that the war would be over by Christmas were out of their minds.

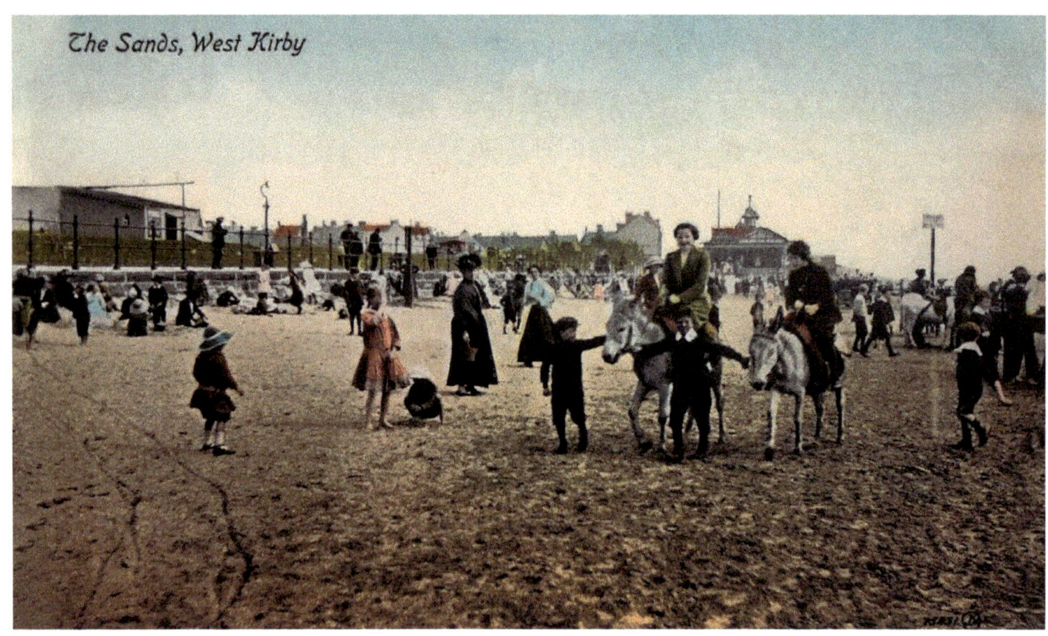

The Sands, West Kirby.

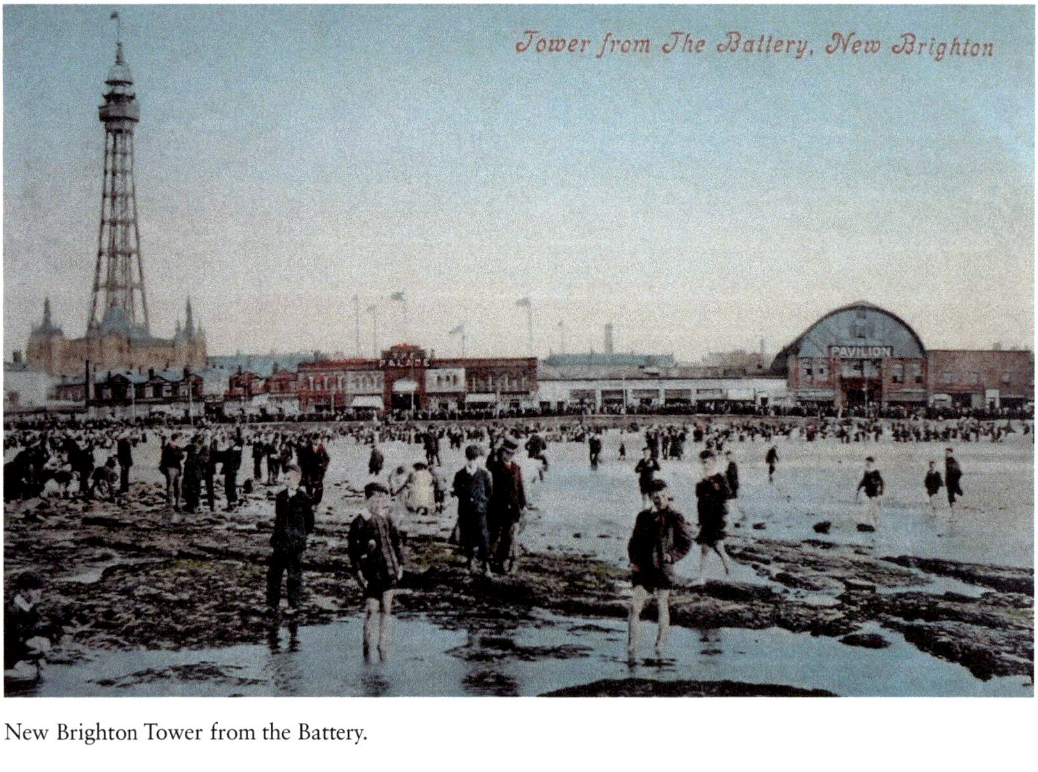

New Brighton Tower from the Battery.

COMPANY SERGEANT-MAJOR 133 JAMES EDWARD WILLIAMS, 1/4TH BATTALION, CHESHIRE REGIMENT (T. F.)

Born in Birkenhead on 31 November 1884, William was educated at Cathcart Street School before serving twelve years with the Cheshire Regiment. After demobilising, he became a bricklayer with his father, John, and joined the Army Reserve. He married Margaret on Christmas Eve 1905 at St Mary's Birkenhead, and had three children, John (1907), Charles (1912), and Lillian (1915), while living at 7 Woodland Terrace in the town. Called up on the outbreak of war, he returned to the 4th Cheshires Territorial Unit at their headquarters in Grange Road, Birkenhead, from where they were moved to camps at Shrewsbury and Church Stretton, then on to Northampton by the end of August. In December they were at Cambridge, but by March 1915 they were in Bedford, training and preparing for an expedition to India. However, on 2 July orders were changed, and the 1/4ths were to be part of the Mediterranean Expeditionary Force campaign destined for Gallipoli, and they left Devonport for Alexandria on the 14th. Arriving at Suvla Bay, Gallipoli, on 9 August, they were swiftly involved in operations and casualties quickly escalated. Within just a few days of landing, James was killed in action on 18 August 1915, while pushing forward to establish front-line trenches. He has no known grave, and like many other Cheshires who lost their lives in the Gallipoli campaign, James is remembered on the Helles Memorial.

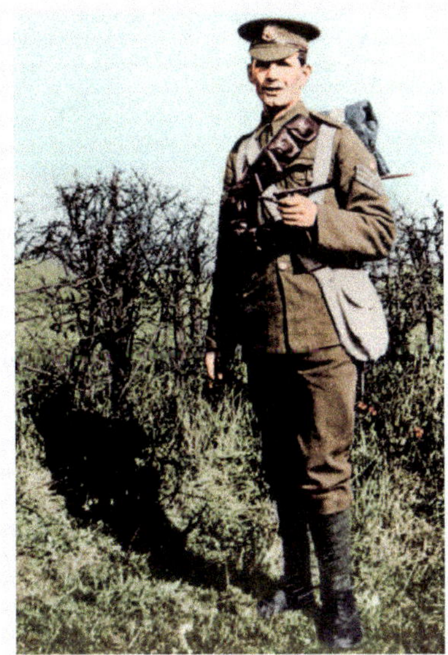

Company Sergeant-Major 133 James Edward Williams, 1/4th Battalion, Cheshire Regiment. (T. F.)

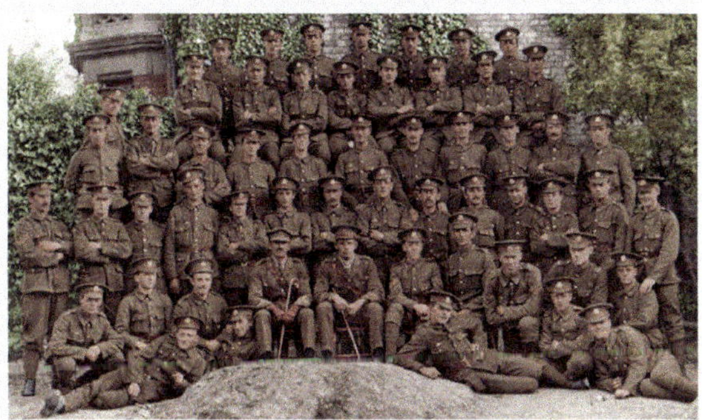

Men of B Company, 1/4th Cheshire Regiment during training. Company Sergeant-Major James Edward Williams can be seen front right, sitting on a chair.

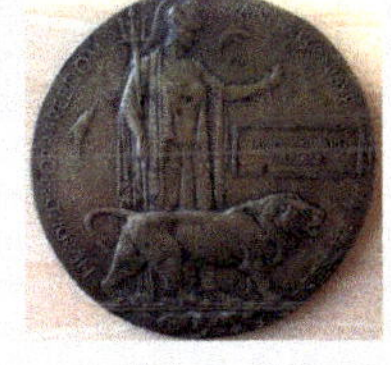

The 'memorial penny' of Company Sergeant-Major James Edward Williams.

(Photos and family history – Richie Gillham, great-grandson of Sergeant J. E. Williams)

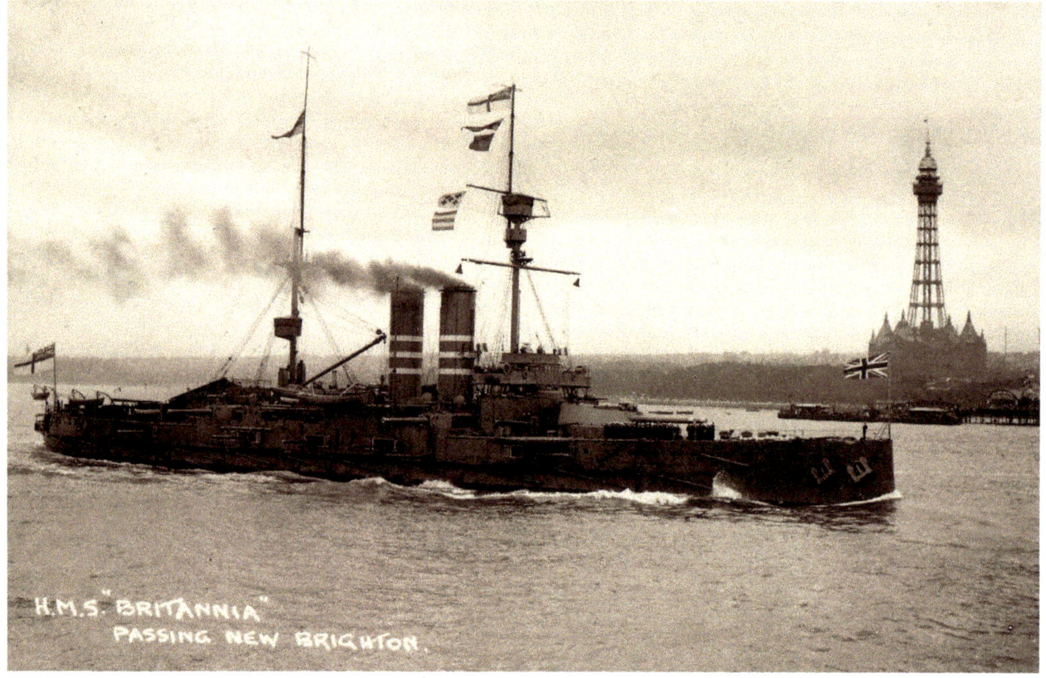

HMS *Britannia*, a pre-dreadnought class battleship, passing New Brighton as she leaves the Mersey. Built at Portsmouth Dockyard and completed in 1906, she later served on patrol and convoy escort duties in the Atlantic, where on 9 November 1918, just two days before the end of the war, she was torpedoed by a German submarine off Cape Trafalgar and sank with the loss of fifty men.

On 6 August, Parliament sanctioned an increase in Army strength of 500,000 men; days later Lord Kitchener, the newly appointed Secretary of State for War, issued his first call to arms.

This was for 100,000 volunteers, aged between nineteen and thirty, at least 1.6 m (5'3") tall and with a chest size greater than 86 cm (34 inches). Worried that the take-up would be sluggish, General Henry Rawlinson initially suggested that men would be more willing to join up if they could serve with people they already knew – people they worked with, or friends and neighbours.

Lord Derby was the first to put the idea into practice, announcing in late August that he intended to raise a battalion in Liverpool, comprised solely of local men. Within days, Liverpool had enlisted enough men to form three battalions, and by November it was four. The idea of the 'Pals Battalions' had quickly come to fruition, and spread with haste to other towns and organisations across the country.

WALLASEY SCENE
ENTHUSIASTIC SEND-OFF FOR VOLUNTEERS

A cheering crowd such as not been seen since the Royal visit to Wallasey, and seldom before, congregated in Central Park, Liscard, this morning to witness the assembly and departure of the local contingent for Lord Derby's 'Battalion of Pals,'

The crowd formed an immense square, in the centre of which, the recruits were marshalled and drilled by Captain Fry, R.N. manager of the Wallasey Ferries, the band for the Lancashire Sea Training Homes, meanwhile, played inspiring airs.

As fresh groups of men arrived on the ground and joined those already at drill, the crowd broke into round after round of cheering, this being especially enthusiastic when a company of thirty young engineers in their overalls arrived.

The Wallasey contingent had been recruited largely through the efforts of Messrs J Bushell and Wilson, energetic Liscard tradesmen, to whom all praise is due.

Among those present in the park were, the Mayor (Alderman T.V. Burrows), the chairman of the Watch Committee (Alderman Edwin Peace), the chairman of the Works Committee (Alderman Parkinson), and the Chief Constable (Mr. P. Barry).

While the recruits were assembling in the park, the boys from Sommerville Council Schools, who were drawn up in line near the gates, sang patriotic songs. They carried Union Jacks, which they waived vigorously as the men for Liverpool marched along their ranks, led by the Navy League Band, and marched off along Church Street on their way to Seacombe Ferry.

All along the route they were heartily cheered, and again on the boat, where the men sang lustily while crossing, finishing at the Liverpool Landing Stage with '*Rule Britannia*' and '*God Save the King*', all the steamers meanwhile tooting a noisy '*Hip-hip-hip-hurrah*'. Still headed by the Navy League Band, the Wallasey contingent, numbering 160 strong, marched off up Dale Street to St George's Hall.

Liverpool Echo, 31 August 1914

While hundreds of Wirral volunteers headed over the water to join the Pals, many more trekked to their local recruiting hall to join the Cheshires. In Port Sunlight for example, a meeting was called for the Lever Brothers factory workers at Gladstone Hall, where it was announced:

In view of the present grave crisis, the directors desire to make it known to all employees that they hope and respect that all men between the ages of 19 and 35 will offer their services to their King and country. The situations of each will be kept open for them against their return. In the case of married men on weekly pay, the practice already adopted of making an allowance of half-wages will apply, and similarly in the case of unmarried men the present practice of considering any special case where immediate dependants are left behind also apply. The time during which employers are thus serving their King and country will be counted in calculating their length of service with the company for the purpose of co-partnership, long service awards, employers' benefit fund etc. Time allowance will be made to those requiring to visit recruiting stations during working hours, provided application is made beforehand to the head of department.

The news that General Sir Henry Mackinnon had sanctioned the raising of a Wirral battalion in which all the recruits from Port Sunlight would be kept together was greeted with thunderous applause at this crowded meeting. Local

MP Mr Gershom Stewart, who played an active part in the raising of the battalion, attended the meeting and delivered a rousing address. He spoke of the grave danger with which the nation was confronted, and his desire to raise a battalion of a thousand Wirral men, whom he hoped 'would do everything to uphold the glorious traditions of the 22nd Cheshires'. He understood that from those works alone he could depend upon 500 men (a voice came from the crowd: 'A thousand if necessary!'), and with such a prospect in view, he felt certain that the ranks would be full in no time. He hoped that by the time they were fit and ready, the Germans would have had enough of British pluck and determination, but whatever happened, he could rely upon them doing their duty and behaving like men and like British soldiers (*more applause*). He assured them that everything would be done to secure men being combined in one regiment so that they would drill, work, and if necessary, fight together. What wasn't mentioned in the euphoria of the moment of course, was that many would inevitably die together too.

At the close of the meeting, which was 'characterised by scenes of unparalleled enthusiasm', the Gladstone Hall was opened as a recruiting depot, and well over 500 men – 'most of them of sturdy stature and full of vim and vigour' – formed a

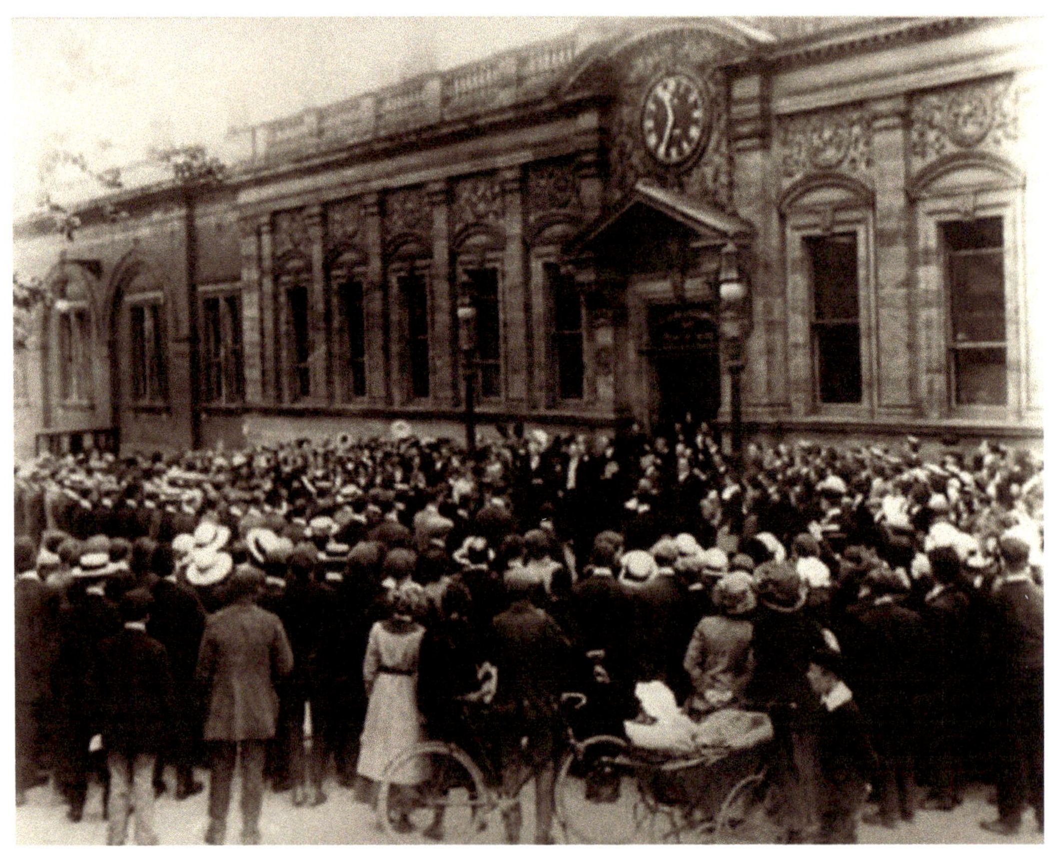

Port Sunlight volunteers parade at the factory before departure.

queue for the purpose of medical examination and enrolment. (*Birkenhead News,* 2 Sep 1914)

[This battalion was known as the 13th (Service) Battalion of the Cheshire Regiment – the Wirral Battalion. The men were moved to Chester by October 1914 and attached to 74th Brigade in the 25th Division. By December 1914 they were in billets, training in Bournemouth. Following another move to Aldershot in May 1915, they landed in France on 25 September 1915. The Battalion was disbanded in France on 16 February 1918.]

To the south, Ellesmere Port, in 1914 still little more than a village centred around a slowly expanding canal port where the Shropshire Union Canal terminated at the Mersey, was gearing up to witness the departure of local men. By 5 August, reservists and territorials had already left for Chester with their departing menfolk being given a rousing send-off with marching bands, church services, and cheering onlookers at crowded stations. Local newspapers described the streets as 'impassable', while the Salvation Army band gathered at the entrance to the station and played selections of popular music and stirring hymns. Further recruitment drives continued through that first month and beyond, and newspapers refer more than once to the 'Glorious 514' from Ellesmere Port. The reason for this name seems to be the numbers of the first batch of brave volunteers from the Port, particularly the married men who volunteered in the initial phase, when the priority was for single men. The 'Glorious 514' appears to have been the name for the Port's own 'Pals'.

Of course, when reading the newspapers of the war, it helps to be mindful of the potential element of propaganda in the reportage, as recruitment meetings were not without opposition. In Birkenhead during one such meeting, the speaker was constantly heckled by Richard Henderson of Conway Street. While those around

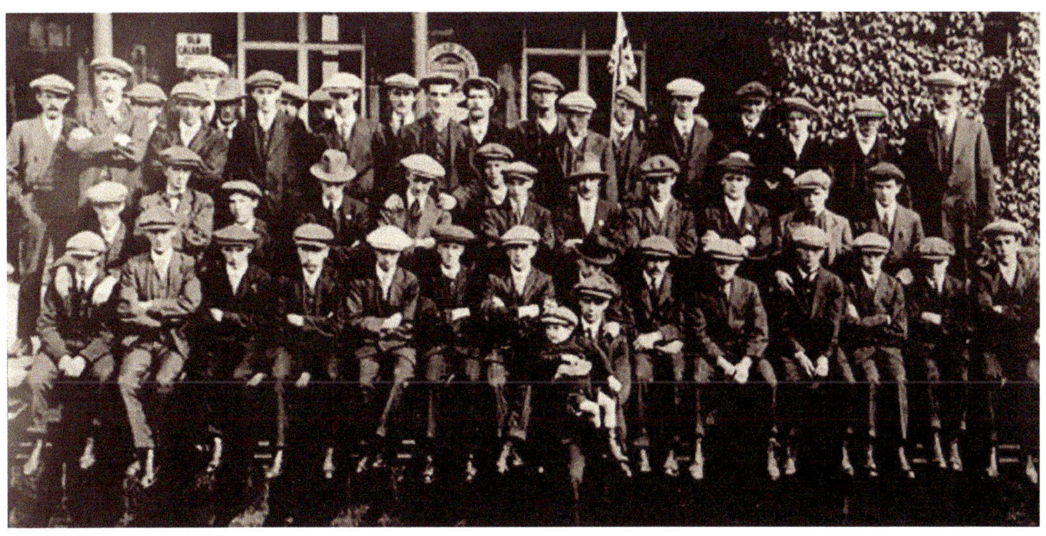

Little Sutton volunteers at the village station, September 1914.

him remonstrated with him regarding his outspoken behaviour, he protested, 'It's all bloody fine for you to stand there asking us to go to the front, but who the bloody hell are going to keep our wives and families while we are out there?' Not all would have the guarantees and support offered by the directors at Lever's factory. This outburst didn't go down well with those around him, and as they turned on him, he became 'violent and struck out right and left among the crowd'. The police moved in and escorted him away, later charging him with disorderly conduct.

In Little Sutton a man was taken into custody for his own safety as a crowd gathered around a mission hall where he was speaking. Later he appeared in the county police court, charged with 'unlawfully using words calculated to create discontent or disaffection, or to incite people to turmoil or disorder, and bring the Government into hatred and contempt'. The accused was George Dempsey, a local preacher, and while busy handing out his leaflets, he began to persuade anyone who would listen that 'Germany was justified in doing what she had done and the British deserved all they got', and, 'the war was caused by the wickedness going on in Paris and it was bound to be crushed; if Britain had a thousand more Dreadnoughts she could not win when Christ was on top'. As locals began to take more notice of him, he was now surrounded by around twenty bystanders and it seemed a riot was about to break out, when he fled the scene. Later that Sunday evening, he was speaking at the local mission house when a crowd of around 600 began to gather outside. There was a deafening

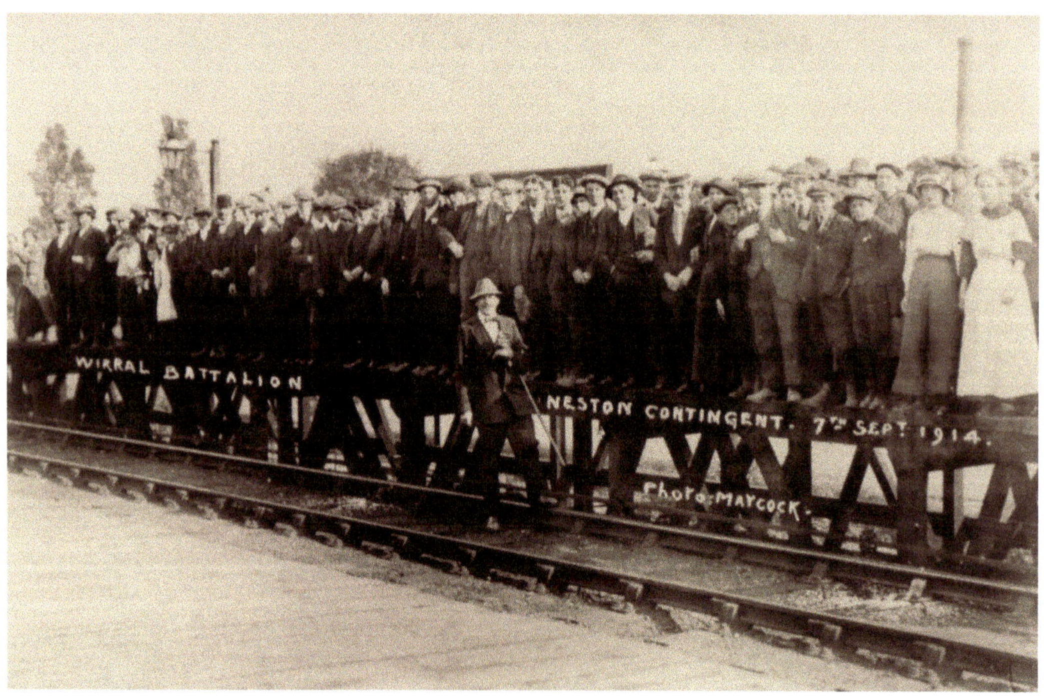

Neston volunteers leaving for Chester to join the Cheshire Regiment, 7 September 1914.

sound of children banging tin cans and throwing stones, while the onlookers shouted 'Turn him out!' and sang the National Anthem and 'Rule Britannia'. Dempsey eventually appeared, but faced with such a hostile crowd he began to recant, all to no avail, while the incensed gathering threatened to lynch him. A policeman arrived on the scene in the nick of time, taking him into custody initially for his own safety. In court, Dempsey sincerely apologised and claimed he had been 'misunderstood'. He was warned that such conduct could see him sent to the Assizes charged with sedition, but he was discharged with a caution and told to be more careful in the future. [NB. given the population of Little Sutton at the time, it is likely the local press added a zero to the numbers gathered outside the mission. The pro-war reportage was often blatant propaganda, especially after controls placed upon the press and proprietors under the Defence of the Realm Act.]

The recruiting officers were now reaching out to the local villages throughout the Wirral, 'scouring for volunteers'. After a series of village meetings, Bromborough sent thirty men, ten came from Willaston, and fifty-one from Little Sutton. Captain Field, who spoke at the meetings, commented that he was 'delighted with the physique of the men recruited'. The local news further reported that 'he intends to beat up the same places again shortly, and is confident of more good "bags". That Little Sutton should have sent 51 recruits has especially pleased and astonished Captain Field in view of so small a population.' A small but creditable number in relation to the tiny population, which adds to the theory of likely exaggeration in the Dempsey angry mob issue.

Meanwhile, in Neston:

NESTON AND THE WAR

The war call has told heavily upon the male population of Neston, the Territorials of the Deeside company being embodied, the reservists called out, and almost every home, suburban and cottage alike, has sent a son or sons to the front. Four young ladies of the Red Cross detachment have volunteered their services and been accepted. Others, held by home ties, are preparing meetings etc., for consideration of work to be done, sewing, knitting etc. Prayers and hymns for peace were conspicuous in the church services on Sunday, and great excitement prevails. The panic rush on provision shops, which has not been confined to larger towns, but was conspicuous in the locality, appears to be subsiding, and a more harmonious feeling prevails. It is felt that a real patriotic spirit should be shown in this direction, and in the matter of economy the classes should stand together, shoulder to shoulder.

Chester Chronicle, 8 August 1914

By the end of the first month of the war it was reported,

NESTON'S RESPONSE

It is calculated that from the various homes in Neston and neighbourhood, some fifty persons are now with the various forces. It is highly pleasing to note that some twenty boys, who have during the past six or seven years have passed through Captain Coventry's hands in the Boys Brigade, are now serving their country as members of the Regular Army, Territorial Force and new Army. It will be remembered that King George specially complimented Captain Coventry on the fine appearance and soldierly bearing of his boys at Hooton Station in his recent visit. So widely scattered are the local patriots and so well guarded their present whereabouts, that it is difficult to establish a complete list at the moment. Seven Reservists have gone from the village, and one is in Ireland. Others are at the front, and Territorials are everywhere training at their appointed centres.

Interesting letters are being received. Two choristers from St Michael's Mission Church have been keenly missed, but they write regularly to Captain Scholey and Miss Jackson, expressing appreciation of the calm strength of Christian teaching. One vivid narrative describing a service in their new quarters said when the preacher touched on their great patriotism and readiness, if need be, to pass into the great unknown 'strong men sobbed with tense emotion, but were unflinching in devotion to their country'. These youths expressed their preparedness to be absent at least some fourteen months. All the residents think of them as they sing on Sundays that God may 'guard and bless our Fatherland', and special services continue to be very impressive. It is possible that a list of local soldiers and Red Cross workers may be published next week.

Chester Chronicle, 29 August 1914

Yet not all was efficient in the early organisation of the recruits, as such huge numbers were clearly causing difficulties for the authorities, as this article bears witness:

BIRKENHEAD RECRUITS DEPART

The town's meeting on Friday night yielded only 20 recruits. The raising of the standard height has all but stopped recruiting in Birkenhead. This is what the Government want, for there is not sufficient accommodation for all the volunteers, and fresh arangements will have to be made for the half million who are coming on.

On Monday afternoon 150 recruits left the town under Major Strachan for Chester. Some were men who had been previously at Chester and had had to return because there was no room for them; others were men who had recently joined and been passed into the Reserve, receiving 3s a day and being liable to be called up at ten days' notice. Instead of ten days, the men only got one, and Major Strachan was the first to protest against the Government's breach of their own undertaking. Even the one day's notice was not posted to the men; they had to find out by calling at the recruiting offices, 76 Market Street, where the notice was posted on the window, and so suddenly was the call, that the muster was rather disorderly, and the attempt to call the roll and to form ranks in the public street was greatly impeded by a curious crowd and by wheeled traffic. The men evidently belonged to all classes, and some wore straw hats, others felt or caps, and one man a railway guard, had come off duty only a few minutes before, and had no time to change his uniform or to get rid of his 'bait' tin. Nevertheless, they were in the highest spirits, and marched gaily to Woodside Railway Station [near the Mersey Ferry] accompanied by wives, sweethearts, and friends, who clung to them and waved farewell, and among the spectators many raised their hats in salute to the brave fellows. The same scenes were repeated inside the railway station and the cheering kept up until the train was out of sight.

The addition of three inches to the height is debarring many otherwise eligible candidates. Men have been rejected because they were an inch short, who have been through the South African War and who were thought good enough for the Boers, though they had had no previous war experience, who are not thought good enough and big enough for the Germans. Much also depends on the way volunteers are received at the recruiting offices whether they will join, and having been kicked about from pillar to post from the door in Market Street to the door in Argyle Street, they have been noticed to walk away disgusted, vowing they will never come again; but from Major Strachan himself, applicants receive the utmost courtesy, the difficulty being that he is often called away to Chester and having been deprived of his assistant, Captain Field, now at Tidworth [training camp], cannot always give personal attention to applicants.

Birkenhead Advertiser & Wallasey Guardian, 16 September 1914

This issue of height was taken very personally in the Wirral. The army may well have laid down the criteria of 5 feet 3 inches for minimum height, but this was

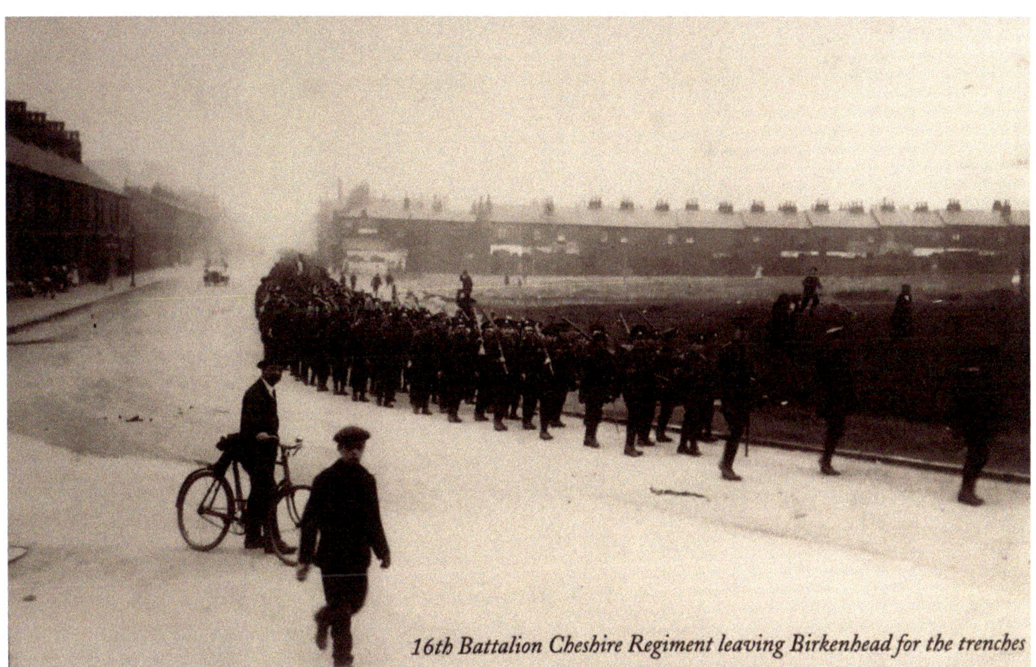

16th Battalion Cheshire Regiment leaving Birkenhead for the trenches

Birkenhead Bantams.

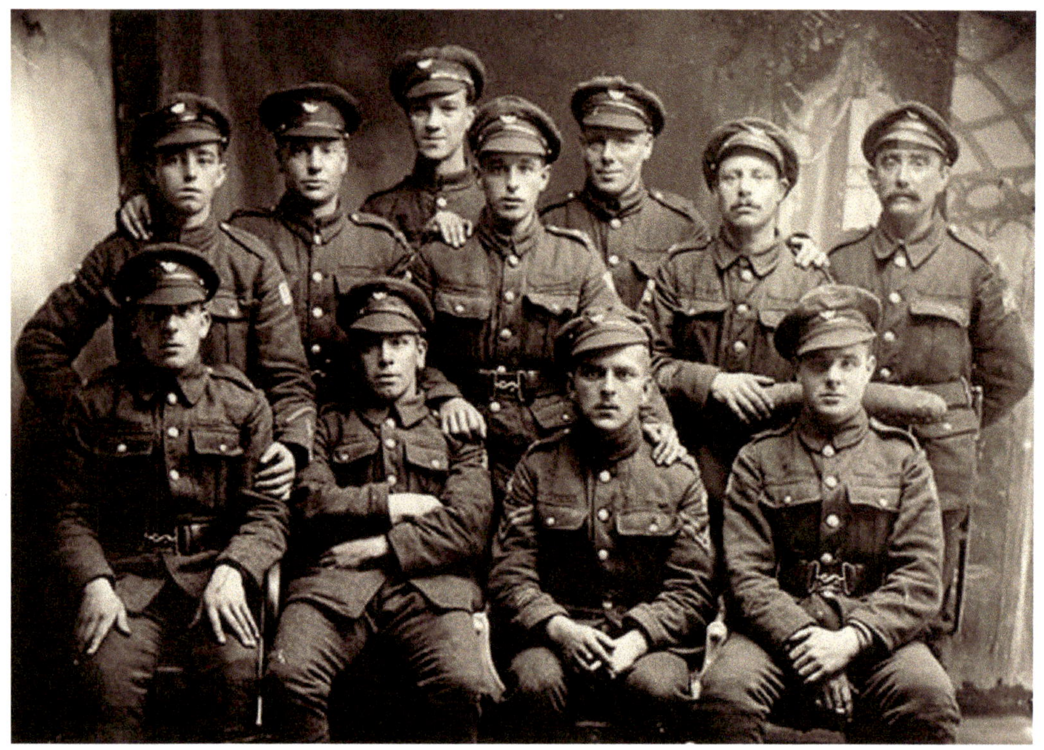

Neston Bantams.

causing a great deal of local disquiet from those men who felt they were fit enough and were being turned away for what they felt was an unjust reason. Crookenden, in his *History of the Cheshire Regiment*, tells the story of four Durham miners who had been rejected from every recruiting office, and had made their way to Birkenhead. They were put through the medical and found to be otherwise physically fit, but were again rejected being under the height limit. One of the miners became so incensed that he threw off his coat and offered to fight any man there, as proof of his suitability as a soldier. It took six men to eventually calm him down and remove him from the premises. This story, and those of other local men going through the same humiliating experience, reached the ears of local MP Alfred Bigland, who petitioned Kitchener and the War Office for permission to establish a unit for those under size. Permission was granted, and the first Bantam regiment in the country was established in Birkenhead. The story of the four miners is not recounted in Bigland's version when he published his memoirs in 1922, and instead he attributed the recruitment office rumpus to a rejected local man. But then, given how feelings ran high on rejection, both could be true. Whatever the catalyst, news spread across the country that a Bantam regiment was now signing up recruits, and men from far and wide headed for Birkenhead. By the end of November 1914, 3,000 had signed on. They were taken to the hearts by locals and they were honoured with enamel 'BBB' badges – Bigland's Birkenhead

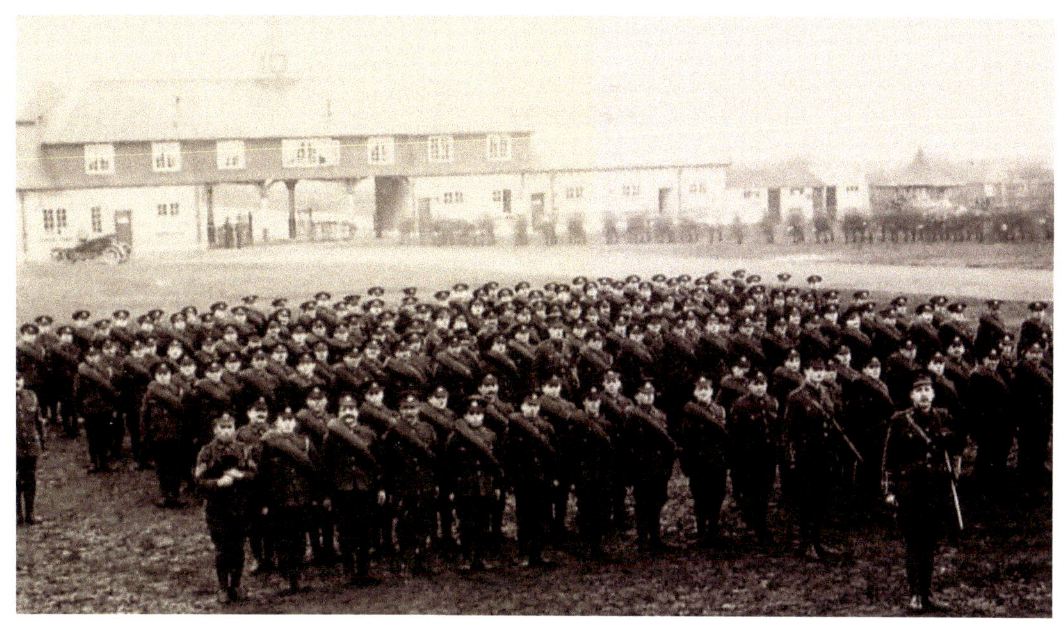

15th Battalion Cheshire Regiment (Bantams) on parade, Bebington Showground, early 1915.

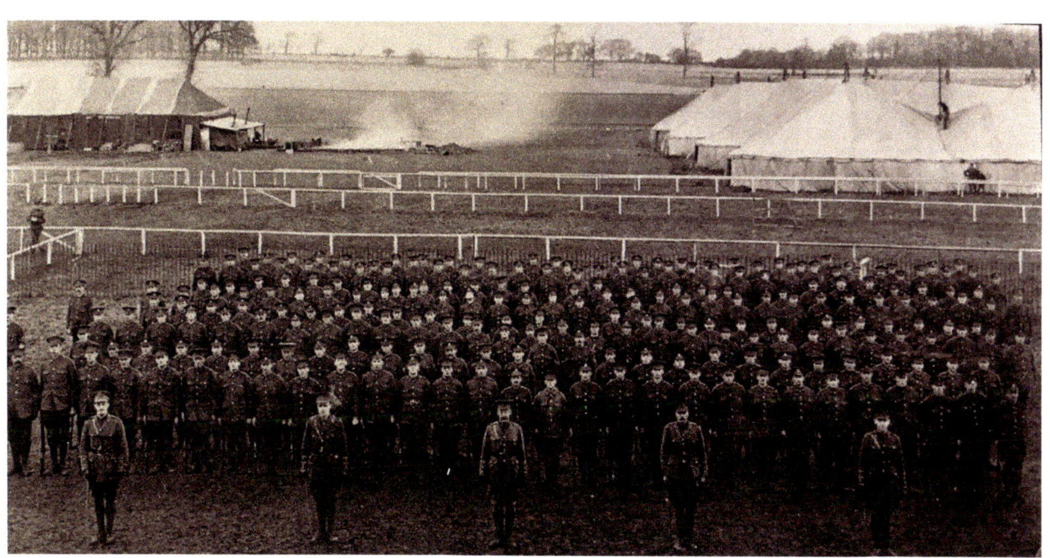

17th Battalion Liverpool Pals, Hooton Park.

Bantams – then they too were entrained and despatched to their gruelling training camps. Now renamed the 15th and 16th Battalions, Cheshire Regiment, they served in some of the most hard-fought battles of the war, including those on the Ypres Salient in Belgium and on the Somme. Two whole divisions – the 35th and 40th – had been formed from bantams battalions, but tragically were virtually annihilated during the Battle of Ypres.

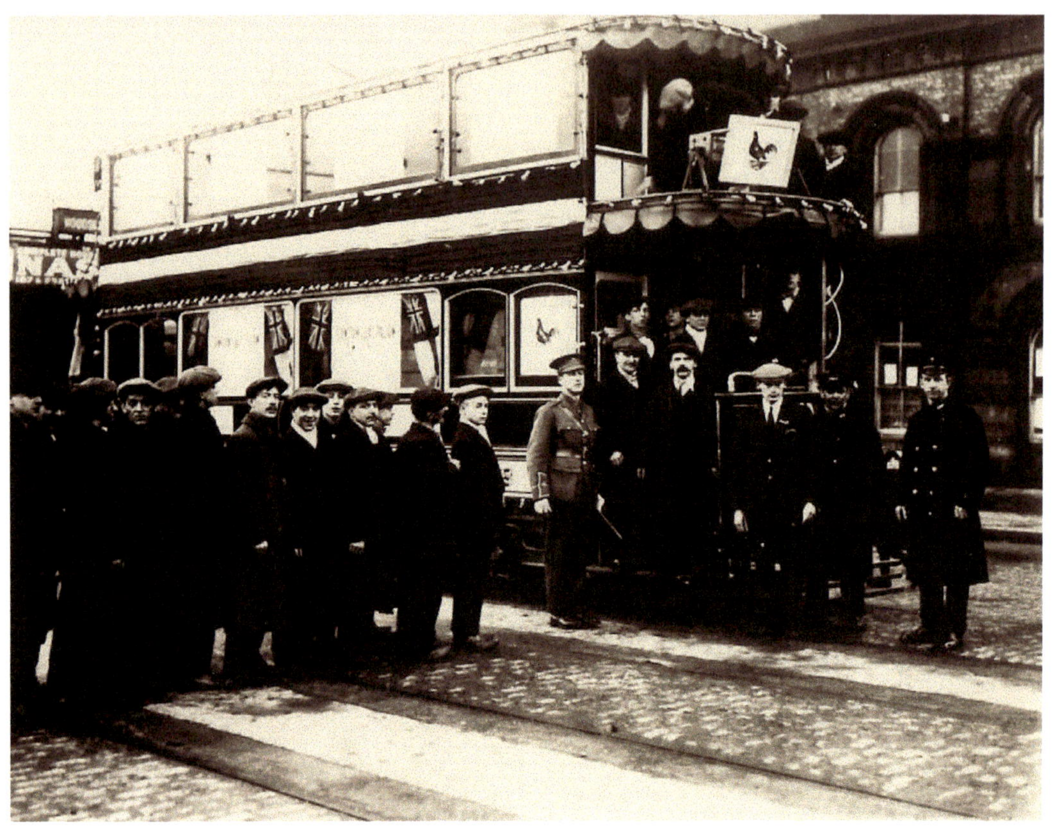

Trams were converted to use for recruitment and toured the area. The tram pictured was used for the Bantams battalion of the Cheshire Regiment – the bantam rooster insignia is displayed at the front.

Chapter 2

Home Front

Any retrospect of the year 1915 must be touched at practically every point by the effects of the war. The whole year has been tinctured with the great world conflict that is still going on. Every phase of public or private life has felt its influence. The war has crowded out a vast number of ordinary matters, temporarily in most cases, permanently in a few. Any local retrospect of the year 1915 must therefore mainly be concerned with the war, and what it has done in connection with it – what labours have been put forth, and sacrifices made, and how public life has had to be readjusted to inset its emergencies.

Birkenhead News, 8 January 1916

A soon as war was declared, the authorities realised that decisive action at home was essential. Consequently, they passed the Defence of the Realm Act (DORA) to 'secure public safety', which became law on 8 August 1914, although in its initial form it was little more than a paragraph long. However, in the second revised version it outlined a wider range of possible wartime offences against the British state. Three further revisions were passed until the government could regulate almost every aspect of the Home Front and had unprecedented powers to intervene in people's lives. Factories, workshops and resources could be taken over and utilised to contribute to the war effort. Curfews could be imposed, and censorship of newspapers and publishers was introduced. Suspects could now be imprisoned without trial, and there were now severe restrictions on movement, while discussion of military matters in public became a serious offence. Trial by courts martial, for example, was now authorised for anyone contravening regulations, which were deliberately vague 'to prevent the spread of false reports or reports likely to cause disaffection to His Majesty', and almost anyone could be arrested for 'causing alarm'. People were even forbidden to loiter near bridges and tunnels, as their actions could be deemed suspicious. Even whistling for taxis in London was banned, in case it should be mistaken for an air-raid warning. Conditions of work were strictly controlled and a blackout introduced in certain towns and cities under threat from aerial bombardment.

In Birkenhead on 10 August, a young twenty-year-old soldier was shot and killed in the confusion following a challenge by a sentry on a man behaving suspiciously late at night near ammunition trucks in a railway siding. Several soldiers had given chase, believing the man to be a German spy, but as they followed him into a wooded area shots were fired and Gunner Louis Morrice of the Royal Garrison Artillery collapsed to the ground, accidently hit by one of his comrades. He was buried in Liverpool (Ford) Roman Catholic Cemetery.

Under DORA, British summertime commenced, a measure that is still in practice today, and opening hours for pubs were cut and beer was watered down, all designed to improve the work ethic.

The day after war was declared, the government also passed the Aliens Restriction Act, aimed at controlling foreign 'enemy aliens' already settled in Britain, particularly Germans. This Act, combined with DORA, severely restricted the movement and civil liberties of non-British-born subjects (even naturalised citizens who had resided in the UK for decades). They were required to register with police, obtain permits if they intended to travel more than 5 miles, and were prohibited from entering certain areas.

IN PROHIBITED AREA
GERMANS SENT TO PRISON AT BIRKENHEAD

Four German subjects, Julius William Wohler and Theodore Wohler, Charles Engelhardt, and Michael Sessler, were sent to prison for one month by the Birkenhead magistrates, yesterday, without having a special permit issued by the registration officer, on October 3. Another German named August Hanson was sent to prison for two months for a similar offence.

The defendants lived in Liverpool, but went over to Birkenhead to work. In doing this they contravened the Order issued on September 9, prohibiting Germans from entering certain areas, of which Birkenhead was one. The men were arrested by Detective-Sergeant Hughes, who found Hansen working at a shop in Cathcart Street; the younger Wohler was employed at the National Oil Company's works; while the remainder were working at the lairages.

Detective-Inspector Eakins stated that Hansen asked for a residence permit on September 11, but this was refused by the Chief Constable. He was then told that he would have to leave the town. Defendant became very impertinent to witness. The man was slightly under the influence of drink at the time.

Mr Arthur F. Moore, who appeared for all the defendants, except Hansen, said that when the permits were first issued, the men were told that they were allowed to travel within an area of five miles, but they were not informed of the change in the order.

Sessler, replying to Superintendent Jones, admitted that he had been warned by the Liverpool Police to leave the district.

The chairman, Mr E.T. Coston, said the defendants were alone to blame. It was their duty to ascertain their position. Hansen, considering the impudence he had shown to the police, would have to go prison for two months, and the other for one month each.

Liverpool Daily Post, 7 October 1914

Each local area was expected to set aside some sort of provision for detainees. A large, disused engineering works on the banks of the Dee between Sandycroft and Queensferry, near Chester, was immediately taken over by the authorities, and within a few days around 500 German prisoners of war were interned there. Guarded by a company of the 5th Battalion Cheshire Regiment (Territorials), the prisoners comprised those formally taken in custody as prisoners of war, and others who had been resident in larger towns in Lancashire and Cheshire, and who, failing to find anyone to vouch for them under the terms of the Act, were detained.

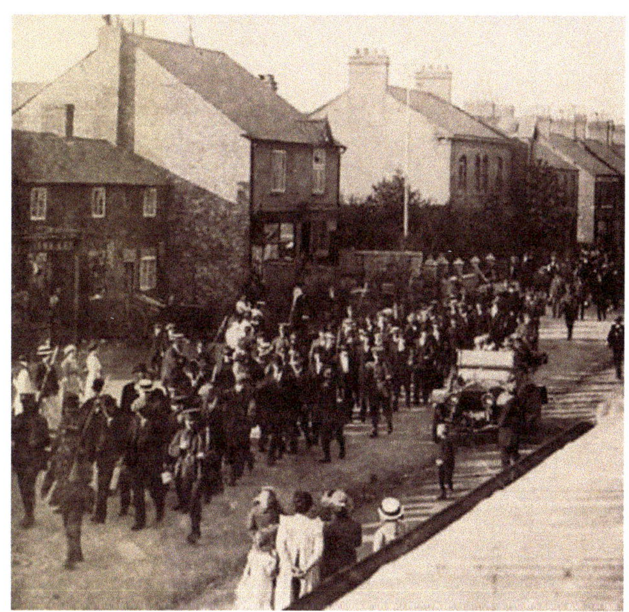

Right: German internees arriving at Queensferry, 11 August 1914.

Below: The site of the internment camp at Sandycroft on the banks of the Dee, between Queensferry and Sandycroft station.

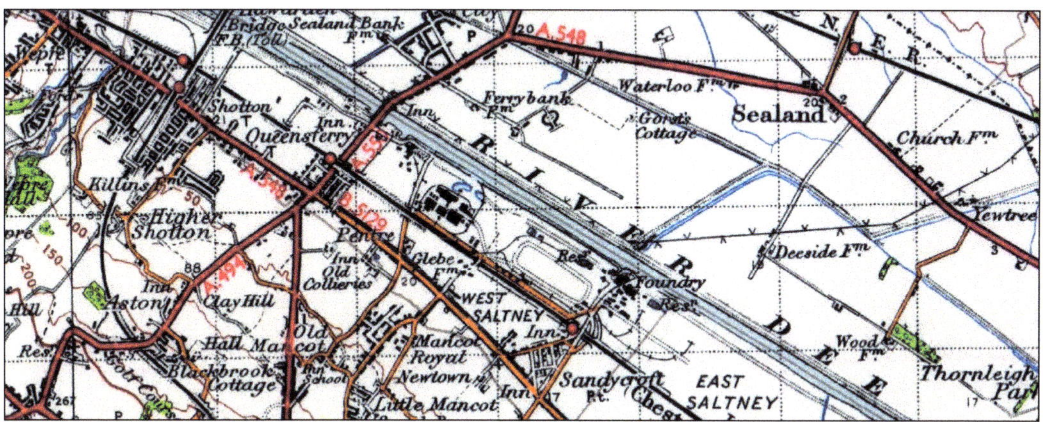

TERRITORIALS GUARD GERMANS
HUNDREDS OF PRISONERS OF WAR AT QUEENSFERRY
WORKS CONVERTED INTO A PRISON
MEN ALLOWED OPEN-AIR EXERCISE IN THE ENCLOSURE

As briefly reported in our last issue, the works between Sandycroft and Queensferry formerly occupied by Messrs. Williams & Robinson, manufactures of water tube boilers for the Admiralty, have been converted into a prison. There was great excitement in the district on Tuesday of last week, on the arrival under armed escort of 500 German prisoners of war by three special trains, which delivered them at Queensferry station. Guarded by Lancashire Fusiliers, who were armed with loaded rifles and fixed bayonets, the Germans were marched to the prison, where the custody of them was taken over by Col. Wynne Edwards and the B Company of the 5th Cheshire, under command of Captain W. A. V. Churton. The works are substantially built, and in every way admirably suited for the purpose to which they have been adapted. The prisoners take open-air exercise in an area of ground enclosed with timber posts and barbed wire.

THE DIETARY

The following scale of daily rations for prisoners of war has been approved by the military authorities: 1lb. bread or 3/4lb. biscuit, 3/4lb. fresh meat or 1lb. (nominal) preserved meat, 3oz. cheese, 5/8oz. tea, 1/4lb. jam, 3oz. sugar, 1/2oz. salt, 1/20oz. mustard, 1/36oz. pepper, 1/2lb. fresh vegetables, or in lieu 2oz. peas, beans, or dried potatoes; tobacco, 2oz. a week for smokers.

The prisoners are treated with much consideration. They sleep on straw palliasses. Among the men are a number of German naval reserve officers. Many of the prisoners are obviously seafaring men.

Flintshire Observer, 20 August 1914

The site remained a prisoner of war camp until May 1915, when the prisoners were moved to the Isle of Man. It then functioned as HM Munitions Factory Queensferry, which developed into a huge 298-acre production plant, including some former agricultural land between the Chester to Holyhead railway and the River Dee. At its peak it employed 7,000 people, many travelling from the Wirral, with women comprising the majority of the production staff. The factory specialised in the manufacture of high explosives and gun cotton (nitrocellulose, tetryl and TNT were manufactured here), which posed serious health and safety hazards for the employees. It is remarkable that only four people lost their lives, given the hazardous nature of the materials. However, serious injuries, burns and ill health were extremely common, and over 12,500 accidents were reported by the on-site hospital during 1917–18.

By November 1915, following the decision in May to intern all enemy aliens of military age, the national number of civilian internees had reached 32,440. During the early stages of the war, military and civilian prisoners in the UK were housed in the same camps, although usually separated from each other within them. As the conflict progressed, different camps evolved for the two groups. The most important

22

of these was situated on the Isle of Man. The first, and smaller, of two Manx sites utilised a former holiday camp and B&Bs on the promenade in Douglas holding a total of 2,300 prisoners. A much bigger camp was set up at Knockaloe, near Peel, on a site which had formerly acted as a base for 16,000 territorials and which would grow to hold 23,000 men, including many of those interned in the Wirral, divided between four sub-camps. Large numbers were repatriated after the war and had to fight their cases to be allowed to return to Britain.

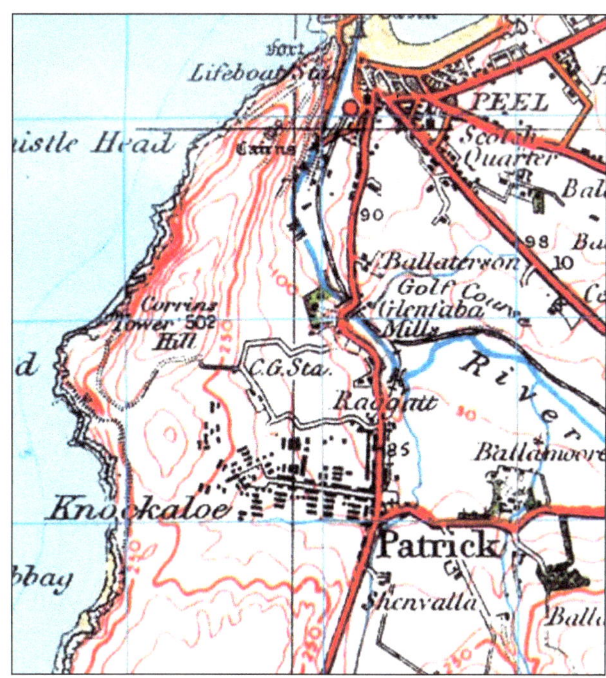

Right: The site of the internment camp at Knockaloe, just south of Peel, Isle of Man.

Below: Knockaloe civilian internment camp, Peel, Isle of Man.

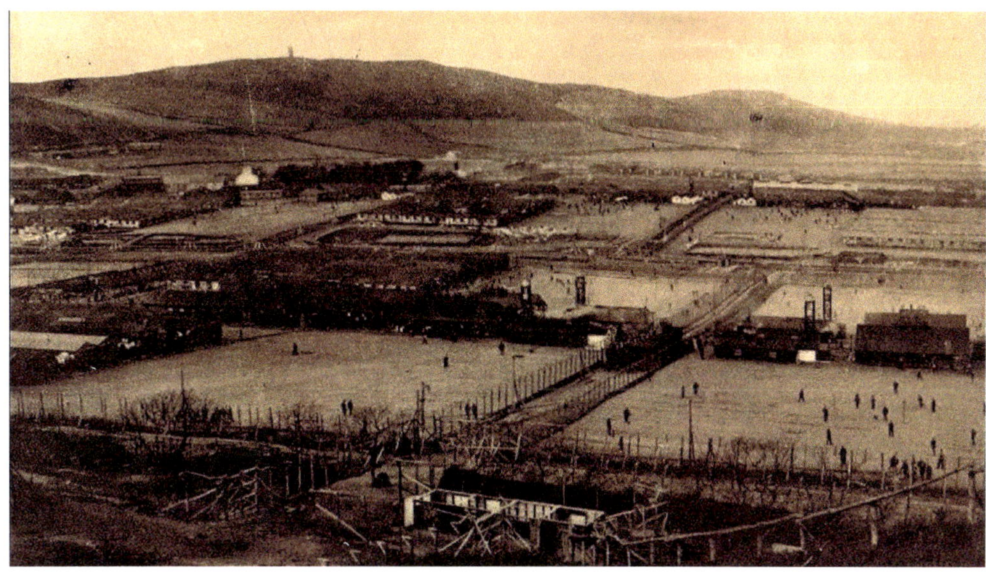

In Ellesmere Port, it took only a matter of days for rumours to spread like wildfire about there being German spies in their midst, and all centred on the local German-owned dyeworks where a number of German workers were employed (opened in 1901 by Messrs Meister, Lucius and Bruning Ltd, to manufacture indigo dyes, dyeware oils, and paints). Alarmed residents became convinced that explosives for the German war effort were being manufactured in the plant. So convincing were these rumours, and the paranoia which had swept through the town, that an explosives expert was called in to carry out a minute inspection. Nothing of a 'menacing character' was discovered, but the works were now being guarded day and night by police.

Under the terms of DORA, the government seized property and controlled labour as deemed necessary for the duration of the war (although the Act continued in existence beyond wartime). Ministers even threatened to use it against strikers. This was followed on 18 September 1914 with the 'Trading with the Enemy Act'. One of the first cases to be heard was an application from the Board of Trade to take control of the German dyeworks factory in Ellesmere Port. The Board of Trade closed the factory down to convert it for use in the war effort, and it reopened in 1916 under Levinstein and Company, who ran the factory as government agents, renaming the company 'British Dyestuffs'. It was never returned to its German owners. After the war it was acquired by I.C.I., but in the meantime, after its acquisition by the Board of Trade, production work continued on surgical orders for the government by eighty English employees and four Germans (who had lived and worked in Britain for over a decade and looked upon Ellesmere Port as their home).

Local German residents who continued, for the time being, to work at the factory were kept under constant supervision – effectively prisoners of war – and were conveyed to and from work each day by local special constables. The rest of the local German workforce, plus women and children, were interned at the workplace and were not allowed out of the works yard. All had to be indoors by 8 p.m. One exception was a German employee at the nearby cement works who was allowed to continue to work there. Also interned was Dr Dunchmann, described as the 'genial' manager of the dyeworks. The local press seemed to be speaking for most of the community stating,

...there had been much regret in the town that it had been necessary to resort to such an extreme measure as far as the Doctor was concerned. He is one of the many thousands of innocents who is having visited upon him the sins of the Kaiser. Dr Dunchmann is a thorough gentleman, well-liked by all who have met him, and he never turned a deaf ear to any appeal on behalf of local institutions. In fact, Dr Dunchmann is one of us, and hopes are expressed that circumstances may arise to enable him to enjoy that glorious freedom only known to Britishers.

Birkenhead News and Wirral General Advertiser, 22 August 1914

So although many commentators suggest that a great deal of reporting in the press was often hysterical propaganda, this article, revealing the undertones of embarrassment that a free-thinking country should treat such a man in an unjust manner, is rather heart-warming.

Reaction to foreign nationals, however, reached its nadir following the sinking of the Cunard liner RMS *Lusitania* off the tip of southern Ireland by a German submarine on 7 May 1915, killing 1,198 of the 1,959 people on board. Controversy has continued to the present day over whether the RMS *Lusitania* was a legitimate war target, the German belief being she was carrying weapons and munitions. Irrespective of this new approach to all-out war, the 'Lusie' was regarded by the Allies as a civilian vessel, and beyond the scope of the conflict. This war, which was witnessing horrors on a new level on the battlefield, by this action, together with the air raids, confirmed that the enemy no longer had to wear a uniform and carry a weapon. This realisation caused increased anti-German sentiment, and at home riots erupted in numerous cities across the country, including Liverpool, Manchester, Salford, Sheffield, Rotherham, Newcastle, South Wales, London and elsewhere. Over 200 businesses were destroyed in Liverpool alone, while in London, only two of the twenty-one Metropolitan police districts were free from riots.

Liverpool had the closest ties with the vessel – owners Cunard were based on the Pier Head. The vessel was heading for the port, and many of the crew were from both sides of the river. In the town, many of the pork butchers and shoemakers were run by German families and were generally well integrated and respected in local society. All this changed in May 1915. Riots began in the Irish north end of the city on 8 May, before spreading to the city itself and other suburbs.

Similar scenes were witnessed in Birkenhead and Seacombe. Butcher's shops were ransacked, windows smashed and belongings thrown from windows into the street.

AFTERMATH OF RIOTING
BIRKENHEAD TO PAY A HEAVY COST

The damage caused by the anti-German riots to shops and other premises in Birkenhead last night is estimated at several thousand pounds.

During this morning, a number of people visited the scenes. The damaged premises present a pitiful appearance. Every vestige of glass has disappeared from the battered window frames, while the fittings of various shops have been completely destroyed. While this destruction was being carried on, several people were injured, either by stones thrown by the crowd or by people throwing furniture from the windows. In one case a heavy clock came hurtling through the air and narrowly missed a man's head.

One or two constables were hurt and it was necessary for one to be taken to hospital, where it was found he was suffering from a huge gash in the side through being cut with a piece of glass.

The police force has now been brought up to its ordinary strength by forty of the eighty-five constables who resigned being re-enrolled. The men resumed duty at six o'clock last night, and when the rioting commenced, the whole of the effectives of this force were called out.

There was a police court sequel today to the riots, when a man named Morris was charged before Messrs T.L. Dodds and L.C. Elmslie with committing damage to the extent of £8 to a pork butcher's shop in Watson Street.

Mr T.L. Dodds, the chairman, in referring to the rioting, said that while making every allowance for the indignation felt by the populace for one of the most foul crimes committed by a nation, the magistrates could not allow them to take the law into their own hands. By such conduct, the people were simply inviting retaliation on the British in Germany.

When the end came, and Germany was called upon to account for the foul crime of sinking the Lusitania and destroying the lives of hundreds of innocent people, including children, then the rowdyism in Birkenhead and other cities would be pleaded in mitigation.

The damage committed would have to be made good by the ratepayers. The right thing for the ratepayers was to restrain their indignation and to wait for the day of reckoning.

The bench hoped there would be no repetition of the scenes witnessed last night.

Morris was remanded on his own recognisances for a week.

Liverpool Echo, 11 May 1915

AT SEACOMBE
'You would do the same if your ship was torpedoed!'

This was the remark of Frank Davies, a middle-aged man of 91 Demesne Street, Seacombe, when expostulated with by the police for taking a leading part in last night's riot in Seacombe.

He was brought before Messrs Ward Platt and Harold Coventry at Wallasey Police Court today, charged with having done wilful damage to the extent of £5 to a weighing machine, the property of Thomas Gerhard, pork butcher, 81 Poulton Road.

Chief Inspector Butler said he was with the Chief Constable at 10.30pm last night when a large crowd was assembled outside Gerhard's shop, the front of which was being wrecked. Foremost among the rioters was Davies, who was leaving the shop with a portion of the destroyed weighing-machine in his hand. On the floor close to him was the large iron chopper produced.

Owing to the hostility of the crowd, Davies was not arrested, but was persuaded to go away.

About midnight, Davies was again prominent in the crowd assembled outside a shop of a pork butcher named Gerhard of 12 Victoria Road, whose premises had been previously wrecked. After a great deal of persuasion, he went home. He told witnesses he was on the *City of Winchester*, which was torpedoed by the Germans eight months ago, and that he 'was going to have some of his own back.' Witness found that this statement in regard to the *City of Winchester* was untrue.

When arrested and charged this morning, prisoner said:- 'Did anyone see me do it? I don't remember anything about it. If it's done, it's done!'

The Chief Constable applied for a remand until tomorrow, in order that inquiries might be made, and in view of the possibility of further arrests.

Liverpool Echo, 11 May 1915

In Seacombe, a fountain pen factory also came under attack, as well as the owner's house, who was advised by police to remove all his furniture. Over the next few days, a steady stream of offenders were dealt with by the courts on both sides of the river, charges varying from criminal damage, incitement to riot and theft. In several cases it was shown that victims were not in fact German, and many had put up signs in their windows declaring they were British and had sons serving in the army. Public houses on both sides of the river were ordered to close at 6 p.m. for the rest of the week.

After a few days of disturbances, the decision was taken to use the recent legislation, and police began to round up local Germans to be interned, although in many cases it was for their own safety. What was more distressing was that many were arrested and taken away in handcuffs and even housed in the cells of the city bridewells. As they swiftly became overcrowded, they were moved to camps at Hawick in Scotland. There were numerous instances where police came knocking to arrest men they knew to be of German birth, only to be met with distain and to be informed they were away in France fighting with the British Army. Many of these new internees also ended up in the Isle of Man camps.

The strength of feeling was reflected even in the application to the Diocesan Consistory Church for a stained-glass memorial window:

LOST ON THE LUSITANIA
USE OF THE WORD 'MURDERED'

Mr T. Moore Dutton (proctor) applied for a faculty on behalf of the Ven. Archdeacon Paige Cox, Vicar, and the wardens of Hoylake to place a stained-glass window in the church of St John the Baptist, Great Meols, as a memorial of Thomas Henry Williams, formerly of

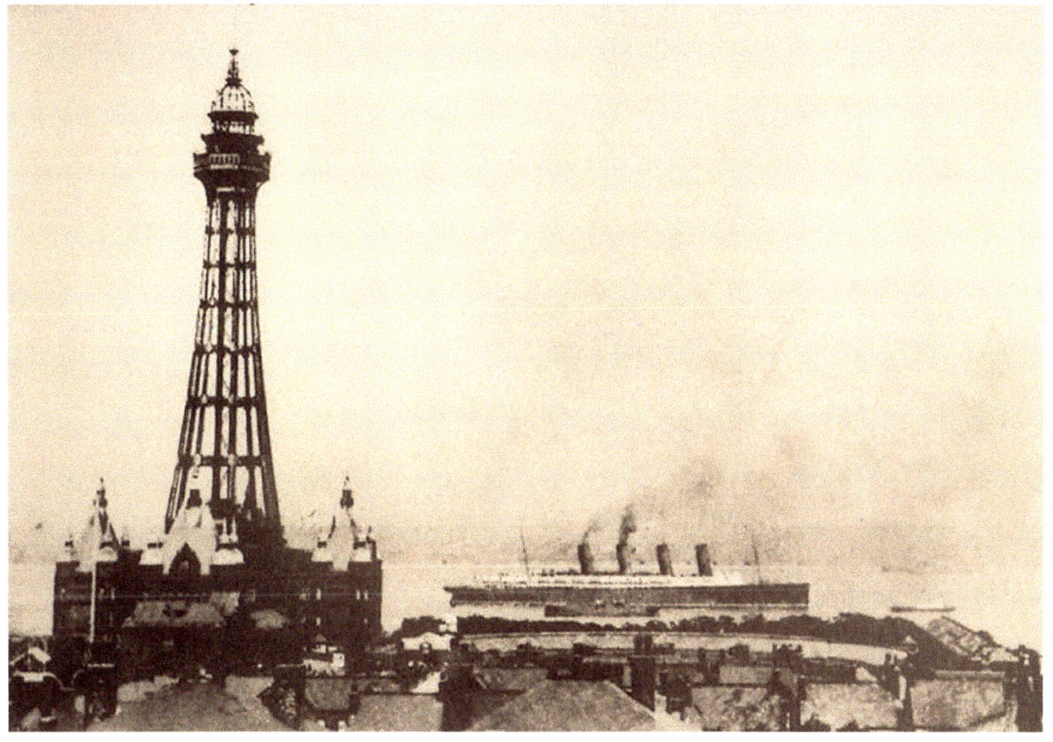

RMS *Lusitania* passing New Brighton, heading towards her berth at the Princes Landing Stage.

(b) Claims in each Police District.

Police District	Claims Lodged								Claims Paid		Claims not yet Settled		Discrimination against Claims by Alien Enemies	Remark
	By British Subjects		By Alien Enemies		By Others		Total							
	Number	Amount	Number	Amount	Number	Amount	Number	Amount	Number	Amount	Number	Amount		
		£. s. d.		£. s. d.		£. s. d		£. s. d		£. s. d				
Chester County	4	428.12.2	1	166.2.3	-	-	5	594.14.5	5	218.3.0	-	-	None	—
Birkenhead Borough	18	1160.12.3½	14	2,017.1.10	1	7.5.0	33	3,184.19.1½	29	1,687.10.0	-	-	None	—
Wallasey "	19	379.6.8	2	167.2.4	3	111.3.2	24	657.12.2	11	127.15.8	3	97.7.0	Claims by A.E. not admitted	—
Lancaster County	50	3,407.6.4	-	-	-	-	50	2,407.6.4	43	1,545.14.10	-	-	—	—
Bootle Borough	45	3,243.6.7½	3	643.18.4	1	7.19.9	49	3,961.4.8½	49	2,719.9.7	-	-	None	—
Liverpool "	543	26,476.9.7	63	21,760.4.8½	19	562.9.4	625	48,799.3.7½	450	22,280.6.1	46	6,322.14.18	[illegible]	—
Manchester "	99	1,970.2.10	20	941.4.8	1	32.4.3	120	2,943.11.9	51	904.11	3	214.4.3	[illegible]	[illegible]
Salford "	58	2,351.120½	4	363.4.9	4	66.3.1	66	2,780.19.10½	51	1,521.6.10	-	-	Claims not admitted	—

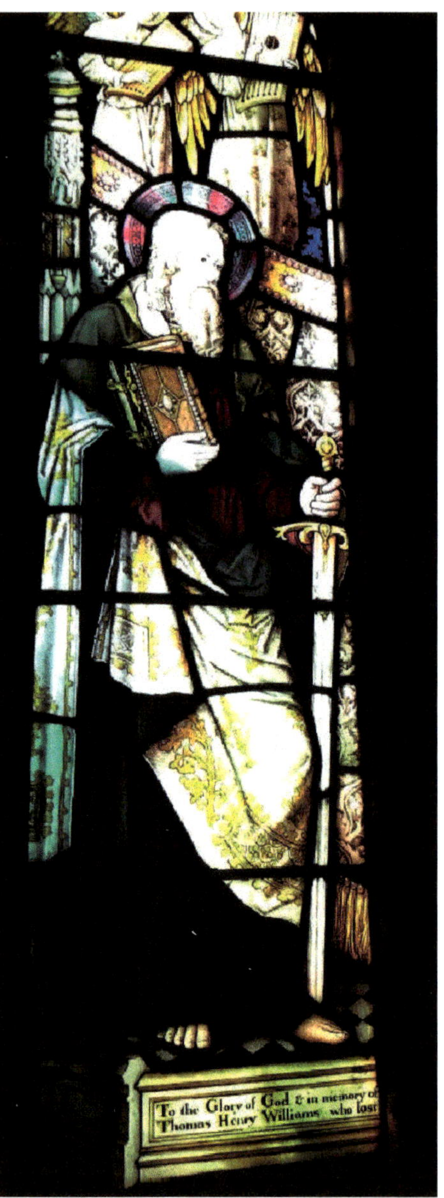

Above: 'Abstract of Claims made under the Riot (Damages) Act during the war in each Police District'. Documents contained in the Whitehall papers regarding the anti-German riots.

Left: Stained-glass window, St John the Baptist, Great Meols, dedicated to Thomas Henry Williams who lost his life on the *Lusitania*.

'Cartref', Great Meols, who was lost with the steamship Lusitania. The cost of the memorial being defrayed by his father, Thomas Williams.

Mr T. Moore Dutton said the originally proposed inscription stated that deceased was murdered on the Lusitania by Germans, but the vestry, while not refusing to sanction the inscription, though the substitution of the word 'drowned' would be preferable.

The Chancellor said he agreed with the vestry. It might be perfectly true to say those that were lost on the Lusitania were murdered by Germans, and that was what the jury found, but while that may be appropriate for a newspaper article, he did not think the wall of a church was an appropriate place for anything to show perpetuation of hatred. It had been suggested that the word 'drowned' should be substituted. He should prefer himself 'In memory of Thomas Henry Williams, who was drowned on the passenger ship Lusitania' or 'who lost his life when the liner was torpedoed by Germans.'

Mr Moore Dutton: Will your Worship decree the faculty, subject to the question of the inscription being reconsidered and submitted to you?

The Chancellor said he thought 'lost with the steamship Lusitania' was in very good form. Certainly, the word 'murder' must come out. He thought, on the whole, he should omit the reference to the Germans. He would grant a faculty, subject to the inscription being in terms he approved of.

Chester Chronicle, 23 October 1915

The final inscription chosen was one that still referenced the German role:

To the glory of God and in memory of Thomas Henry Williams, who lost his life when the S.S. Lusitania was torpedoed by a German submarine 7th May 1915.

Tom Williams was a cotton merchant and was travelling home first class to get married after spending several months abroad on business. Regarded as a fine cello player, he was one of many from the Wirral who went down with the vessel.

Chapter 3

The Experience of War

Over 3,000,000 men had volunteered in the first stages of the war, but such were the immense losses that the supply of recruits was not enough. When the war started, the British Army had a strength of around 710,000 men, including reserves, out of which there were approximately 80,000 regulars ready for action. By January 1915, a million men had enlisted from a total of 5.5 million of military age (with around half a million more reaching the required age each year). By the end of September 1915, the enlisted figure had risen to 2.25 million, while 1.5 million were officially in reserved occupations.

Those in charge of recruitment were dismayed to find that almost 40 per cent of the volunteers were entirely unsuitable for military service on health grounds. After the disaster of the Gallipoli campaign, enlistment dropped to around 70,000 a month and it was clear that government intervention was necessary, although initially they stopped short of conscription. The National Registration Act (1915) was introduced on 15 July 1915, requiring each person to register. On Sunday 15 August 1915, forms were completed by those between the ages of fifteen and sixty-five who were not already in the military, giving details of their employment. Recruitment would then be focused on them, and they were targeted in a number of ways, such as poster campaigns, public meetings, stories of wicked German atrocities, and even the threat of shame within their local communities.

But as 1915 was coming to a close, it was clear that the numbers of volunteers were not enough. Consequently, the government decided to introduce conscription in January 1916. By the terms of the Military Service Act, single men between the ages of eighteen and forty-one were liable to be called up for military service, although they could be exempted if they were widowed with children, or ministers of religion. Conscription started on 2 March 1916. The Act was extended to married men on 25 May 1916. The law went through several changes before the war's end, with the age limit eventually being raised to fifty-one. By the end of the war almost a quarter of the male population of Britain and Ireland had joined up, a total of over five million men. Of these, 2.67 million were volunteers and 2.77 million were conscripts.

BIRKENHEAD SOLDIER'S EXPERIENCE
'Writing on My Upturned Boot'
HALF AN INCH OF CANDLE

The following letter has been received from Private Tom Nevin by his father, who resides at 4 Ridley Street, Birkenhead: -

'Dear Dad, I have just got an opportunity to write after being in action. The nervous strain I can hardly explain; to tell you the truth it is awful, I think we all suffered from the effects. At the time of writing, we are all enjoying a well-earned rest. Just imagine marching for eight miles carrying 90lbs weight. Well, that's what everybody had to do. Talk about suffering for your sins! It's not in it, and to make thing's worse, the ground and roads are most awful, sinking up to our knees, making going ten times harder.

'Everybody I have met are absolutely fed up and praying for the day when peace is declared. I have just received the newspaper and card, and the newspaper was most welcome, also the singlet. I thank you very much for them. When I put the latter on, I did a fling. Washing under-clothes is impossible; the only thing to do is to throw them away, as we cannot carry them about.

I shall be thankful for some cigarettes and a few candles, a thing most necessary. I am still in the best of health, and growing. To see the rush for letters when the mail arrives is a sight; it reminds them of home, the place they miss. Even in the trenches we get our letters and parcels. The transport arrangements of the British Army, by what I have seen and heard, are most wonderful; they work to perfection. It's a peculiar sight to see about 50 motor wagons pass one on the road with Jacob's Biscuits, Bent's Brewery, furniture removers names, and so on, printed on their sides. I have not seen any of the Birkenhead Brewery wagons yet. I have not had my clothes or boots off for five days – a thing I am used to by now. Anyway, it's for a good cause. To tell you about our boys in action would take some time, but it's an experience that will remain in one's memory a lifetime; the shell fire being awful. The shrapnel one gets used to, but the Coal Boxes are terrible, tearing up holes in the ground, big enough to bury a horse and cart. Several of these have burst within 100 yards of me, quite close enough for me, thank you!

'Up to now,' the letter continues, 'we have given no complaints as regards food, because what we have received has been both plentiful and nourishing…. The candle is just burning to a finish, and I shall have to close.'

Private Nevin then adds, 'I am writing this in a barn on my upturned boot, by the light of a half-inch candle, and while our company holds 200 men.'

Birkenhead News, 26 December 1914

Private Tom Nevin was the son of an Irishman with whom he worked as a painter and decorator, together with two of his brothers. He was an early volunteer when war broke out, signing on with the King's Liverpool Regiment. Later promoted to Sergeant, he transferred to the Labour Corps, with whom he served out the war.

He returned safely to the family home in 4 Ridley Street, where they had first moved into in 1892, their family home for half a century, and continued his trade. Thomas passed away in St Catherine's Hospital, Birkenhead, on 14 June 1953.

From the government perspective the war effort clearly had to be made to work, yet support from across the political spectrum was not guaranteed, and many political parties and organisations such as the Independent Labour Party and the Women's International League opposed the war. Following the Conscription Act of 1916, many individuals applied to be exempted, and Wirral tribunals dealt with a myriad of appeals from locals seeking not to serve. Conscription caused real hardships for the British people, and the pages of the local press frequently reveal the poverty, resignation, anger and despair in many homes, most especially after breadwinners had been called up. Farm workers were frequently granted exemption, their work understandably considered to be of national importance, as were munitions workers, and certain dock workers.

WIRRAL TRIBUNAL

There were forty applications for exemption on personal or business grounds. A dental surgeon, who is doing work for the Government, was granted conditional exemption.

A farmer and teamsman who applied for exemption, considered he would be of better use to the country growing foodstuff than as a soldier. His brother, who was a joint tenant of the farm, was seventy years of age. Absolute exemption was granted in this case.

A baker, who stated that his business had increased to the extent of an output of 400 loaves a week, was put back for three months.

Concerning the application made for exemption of a farm hand aged nineteen, who was considered indispensable: Mr T. Davies [member of the Tribunal panel] said he refused to be dictated to by the War Office, as to what should be done with regard to farm labourers. Young men, he said, were wanted on the land. A member said if a young man of nineteen was indispensable to the farm it should be shut up. Exemption granted.

A farmer, explaining his difficulties to the tribunal, said he knew of three farms in his district without workmen to do the necessary labour.

Liverpool Daily Post, 7 March 1916

Nationally, a small percentage (around 2 per cent) of the men appearing before Military Service Tribunals appealed against conscription as conscientious objectors, totalling around 16,500 men who refused to fight. Tribunals dealt with a regular stream of such men appealing for exemption of the grounds of conscience. The prisoner was likely to have been fined at the court hearing 40 shillings, technically the army fine for being absent without leave, and now being in the hands of the military, he would be taken to attest. There he would usually refuse to sign up, or refuse to obey an officer. Despatched to the cells, he would then appear before a court martial and be sentenced to 112 days with hard labour, the maximum sentence at the time. This would be served in a military prison as the men were considered to be soldiers. However, this was amended by an Army order in mid-1916, largely after intense lobbying by the anti-conscription movement, and those sentenced following a court martial were now sent to civilian prisons. The sentence would begin with a month on bread and water in solitary confinement, while carrying out boring repetitive jobs, like hand-sewing mailbags, picking oakum to recycle rope and stone breaking.

There were regular appeals heard on religious grounds. A clause was added in 1916 allowing those whose 'conscience' did not allow them to bear arms to be freed from military service – for example, religious objectors who believed it was against their faith, such as Quakers, or pacifists who were against war in general. This was the first time the legal right to refuse to fight was recognised in British law.

CHESHIRE APPEAL TRIBUNAL
WIRRAL QUAKER'S APPEAL ALLOWED

At a sitting of the West Cheshire Appeal Tribunal at Birkenhead on Tuesday, Mr J.F.T. Royds presiding; a lifelong member of the Society of Friends, living at Willaston (Wirral) appealed against the decisions of the Local Tribunal exempting him from combatant service.

The appellant's father, who appeared, said his son had already served at the front for eight months with the Friends' Ambulance Unit,* and had broken down in health as a result. A medical certificate was produced showing that the young man was suffering from acute neurasthenia. He was willing to rejoin the Friends' Unit when fit.

The Chairman asked Captain Rigby, the military representative, if he was satisfied that the man was a life-long member of the Society of Friends, and Captain Rigby said he was quite satisfied.

The appeal was allowed, and conditional exemption granted, the condition attached being that the appellant joined the Friends' Ambulance Unit when medically fit.

Chester Chronicle, 8 April 1916

[*The Friends' Ambulance Unit was a civilian volunteer ambulance service, founded by individual members of the British Religious Society of Friends (Quakers), in line with their Peace Testimony. It was independent of the Quakers' organisation and chiefly staffed by registered conscientious objectors, both Quaker and non-Quaker. The unit provided an alternative for many of those objectors who refused to fight, but were prepared to help the injured from the battlefield.]

Walter Bone was a young bookbinder who lived with his family at 37 Woodchurch Road in Birkenhead. As a thirty-eight-year-old married man, Walter was not called up until early 1917, but his appeal for exemption was turned down. However, as a Quaker and conscientious objector, he was passed as exempt from combatant service only, and was given the chance to serve as non-combatant, a form of alternative military service granted to those unwilling to bear arms due to religious reasons. Walter Bone, however, was an Absolutist, and as a member of the Fellowship of Reconciliation, not only was he refusing to bear arms, he was also unwilling to make any contribution to the war effort whatsoever, as it would violate his pacifist beliefs.

By the time he was compelled to appear for the enlistment process in June 1917, all avenues within the appeal process were exhausted, and on 27 July 1917 he found himself in the Guard Detention Room at the Cheshire Regiment headquarters in Birkenhead, awaiting trial after refusing to sign the enlistment papers. Escorted to Chester Castle, he was court martialled on 7 August 1917 and convicted of 'When on active service disobeying a lawful command given by his superior officer'. He was given the maximum sentence of 112 days with hard labour and was also fined 40 shillings for his 'absence'.

He was enlisted as Private 4336 Walter Bone of the Non-Combatant Corps (or the 'No Courage Corps' as they soon became known), a unit providing logistical support behind the lines. He was issued with a uniform, albeit without belts and a rifle; as far as the Army was concerned, he was a soldier and would be treated as such, including being punished for any non-compliance.

At the end of his sentence, which he had served in Wormwood Scrubs, he was brought before a tribunal panel on 11 October 1917, which was tasked with implementing the Home Office Scheme. Also known as the Brace Scheme after the committee chairman, William Brace, this was introduced in July 1916 by the Central Tribunal (the ultimate conscription exemption appeal court), whereby work was offered to those whom they deemed had a genuine case. Under the scheme, COs were released from prison to work camps where they were expected to carry out work of national importance. For Walter, this was clearly too much of a compromise for his principles and he turned the offer down, knowing full well the difficulties he would soon face. Returned to his army unit, he was sent back to No. 1 Company Non-Combatant Corps, Aldershot, on 9 November 1917.

Despite his experience thus far, Walter was determined to maintain his stance and resist all military orders. Consequently, on 13 November he was back in the Guard Detention Room, charged with again refusing to obey orders. Again court martialled, this time he was jailed for twelve months on 20 November 1917, again with hard labour. Three days later he was despatched to HM Prison Winchester (he would now serve his sentence in a civilian prison, following the amendment to Army law).

Serving out his sentence, he was returned to duty at Aldershot on 21 September 1918, but days later on the 26th, Walter was in familiar territory, in a Guard Detention Room awaiting a court martial, which took place on 7 October. Inevitably, the charge was as before, again a guilty verdict, with a sentence of one year's imprisonment with hard labour. He was returned to Winchester prison on 9 October 1918.

There may have been an Armistice just weeks later on 11 November 1918, but it made little difference to the COs in HM Prison Winchester. The government was understandably more concerned about demobilising disgruntled soldiers than it was in looking after the concerns of COs. It was not until April 1919 before orders were given to process the release documentation.

Yet all this was too late for Walter. While in the midst of the harsh winter of 1918/19, and still in the miserable cold, damp conditions in Winchester, deprived of decent food and exercise, he was struck down with influenza. Walter was no doubt a victim of the Spanish flu pandemic, and succumbed to pneumonia on 23 February 1919. His body was returned home to his wife, and he was buried in Flaybrick Cemetery. His grave was afforded an NCC war grave headstone, but Mary was denied a pension, and no doubt had to carry the stigma for years to come. This was the final indignity imposed by the Army. As he had died in Winchester, a civilian prison, the military escaped liability, despite his incarceration resulting from their inflexible legal procedure. Documents show that Mary was originally granted a paltry nine shillings (40p, the equivalent of £18 today) on 2 August 1919, in compensation for the loss of her husband, but realising their error, administrators swiftly struck through the award and scrawled 'not admissible'.

Walter is remembered today on the Conscientious Objector Memorial Plaque (Peace Pledge Union Peaceworks, 1 Peace Passage, London) with the other COs who died during the war, under the inscription 'It is by the faith of the idealist that the ideal comes true.' Tragic casualties were not confined to the battlefield.

In 1917, the National Eisteddfod was held in Birkenhead Park, where on 6 September the ceremony of Chairing the Bard took place. The entry under the pseudonym *Fleur de Lys* was declared the winner by the adjudicators, and after a trumpet volley the audience awaited the author to identify themselves and come forward. After the summons had been made three times, there was a pause, before it was announced that the winner had been killed in action just six weeks previously. A black sheet was then draped over the empty chair. The poet was Ellis H. Evans, who had won his first chair (*Cadair y Bardd*) in Bala in 1907, following which he was given the bardic name *Hedd Wyn* ('blessed peace') in 1910 (a reference to the sun's rays penetrating the mists in the valleys of Meirionydd).

While serving with the 15th Battalion, Royal Welch Fusiliers in the Third Battle of Ypres, Private Ellis Evans fell during the Battle of Pilckem Ridge, during the opening attack in what became known as the Battle of Passchendaele. He had been hit by shrapnel from an exploding shell and died shortly afterwards from his wounds. He was buried in Artillery Wood Cemetery, near Boezinge, where his headstone was later amended to add the words *Y Prifardd Hedd Wyn* ('The Chief Bard, Hedd Wyn').

Extract from Walter Bone's attestation form which he refused to sign.

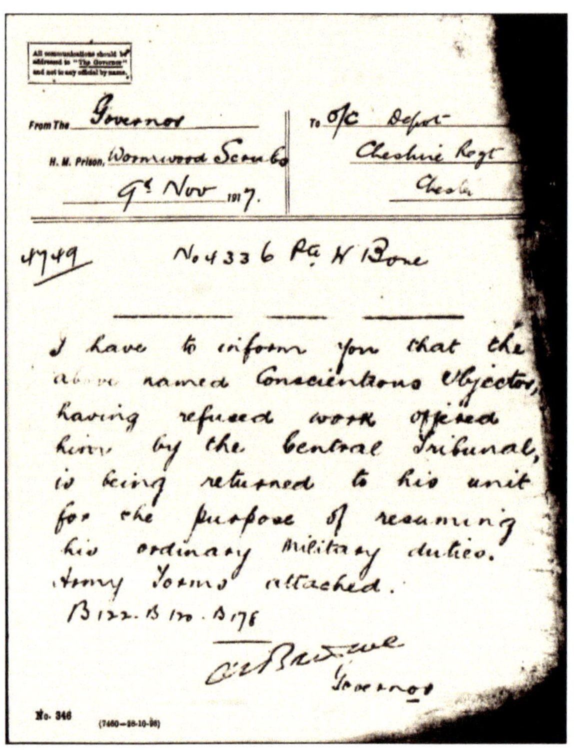

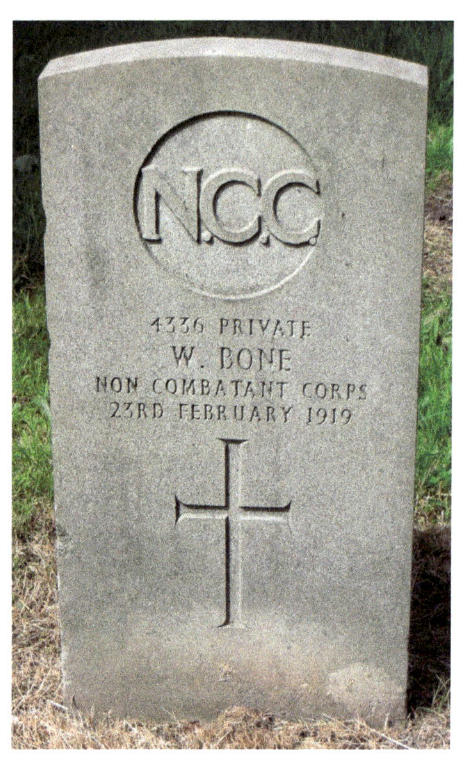

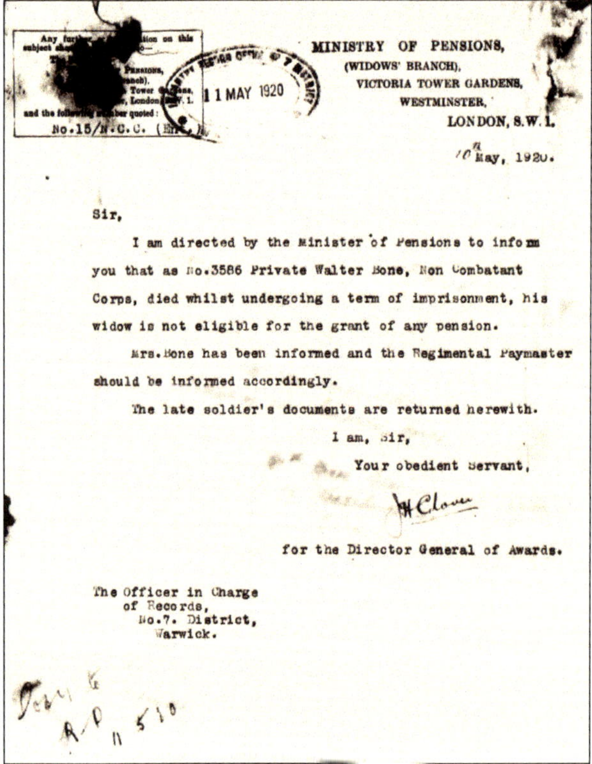

Above left: Tribunal correspondence confirming Walter Bone's rejection of the Brace work scheme offer.

Above right: Commonwealth war grave of Walter Bone of the Non-Combatant Corps, Flaybrick Cemetery, Wirral.

Left: Army correspondence confirming pension denial to Mary Bone.

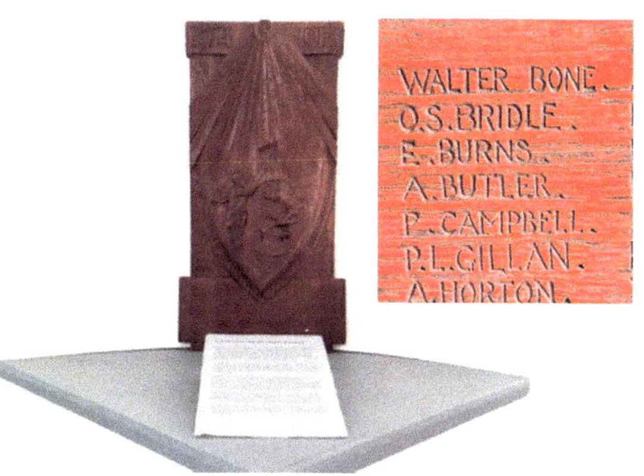

Walter Bone is recorded on the Conscientious Objector memorial plaque at the Peace Pledge Union, London. The idea for the plaque was originated by several COs in Liverpool in 1923.

In September 2017, to mark the centenary of the poet's death, a memorial to Hedd Wyn was unveiled in Birkenhead Park, the site of the 1917 National Eisteddfod, still known as the *Eisteddfod y Gadair Ddu* (the Eisteddfod of the Black Chair), while a Bardic chair was presented to the Welsh government in celebration of his life.

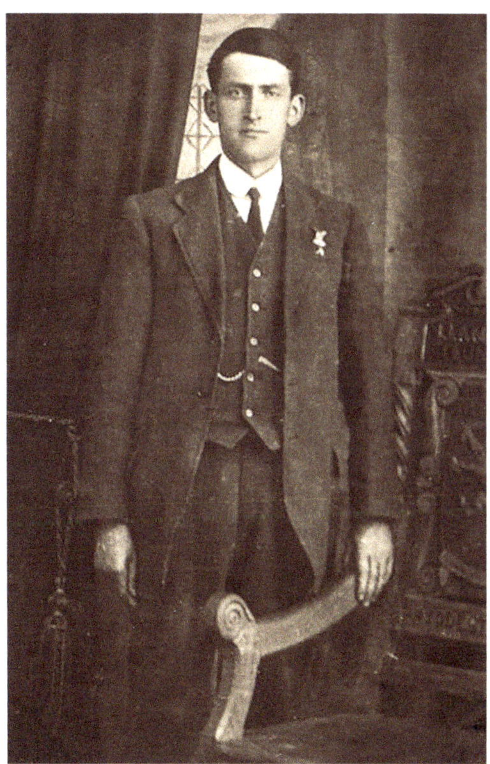

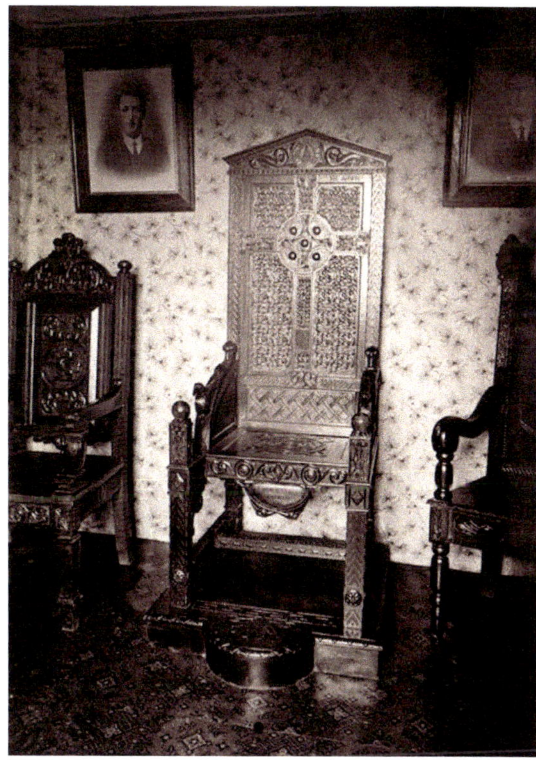

Above left: Hedd Wyn.

Above right: Hedd Wyn's Bardic Chair in the family home, Trawsfynydd (carved by Flemish craftsman, Eugeen Vanfleteren, who had fled to England from Belgium on the outbreak of war and had settled in Birkenhead). It was presented to Evans' parents, still with the draped cloth. It is on permanent display at his family's hill farm near Trawsfynydd.

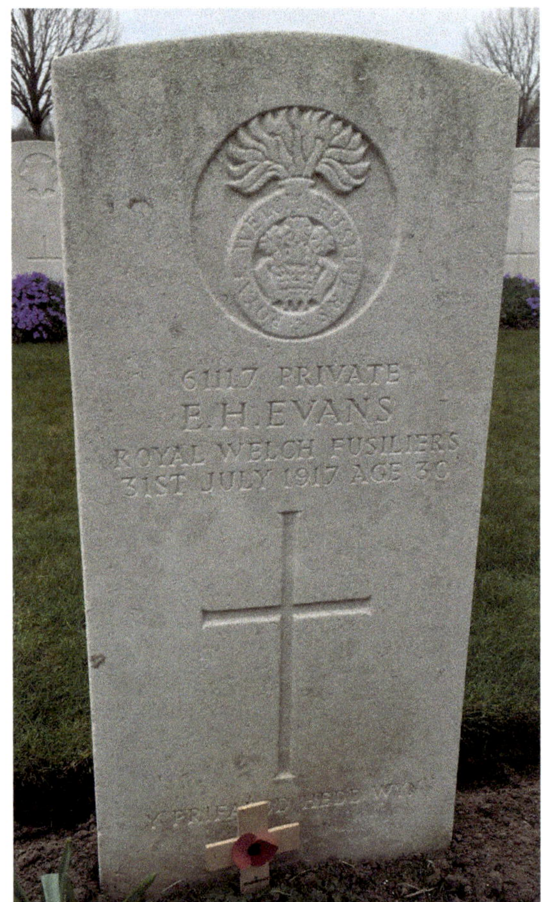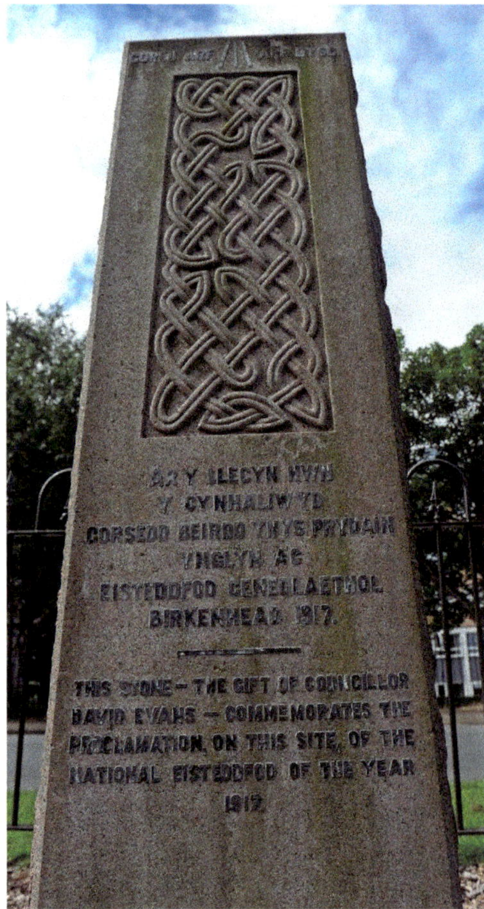

Above left: The grave of Private Ellis H. Evans, Royal Welch Fusiliers, Artillery Wood Cemetery, near Boezinge, who was killed in action on 31 July 1917, at the age of thirty.

Above right: Hedd Wyn memorial, Birkenhead Park.

Wilfred Edward Salter Owen was born in Oswestry on 18 March 1893, the son of Tom and Susan Owen. The family lodged for a short time in Birkenhead in early 1897, due to Tom Owen's temporarily posting as a railway employee. In April 1897, Tom was transferred to Shrewsbury, where they lodged with his parents until a promotion to Stationmaster at Woodside Station saw them return to Birkenhead in early 1898, moving firstly to 7 Elm Grove, Higher Tranmere, then later to nearby 14 Wilmer Road, and 51 Milton Road. Wilfred was educated at the Birkenhead Institute, first attending at the age of seven on 15 January 1901, while holidays were often spent with his uncle, Edward Quayle, at his home in Meols.

However, in 1907, Wilfred's time in Birkenhead came to an end at the age of thirteen, due to his father's relocation to a post with the railway in Oswestry. By the time of the outbreak of war, Wilfred was already in France, having moved there in 1913 to work as a tutor at the Berlitz School in Bordeaux, then with family as their private tutor. It was

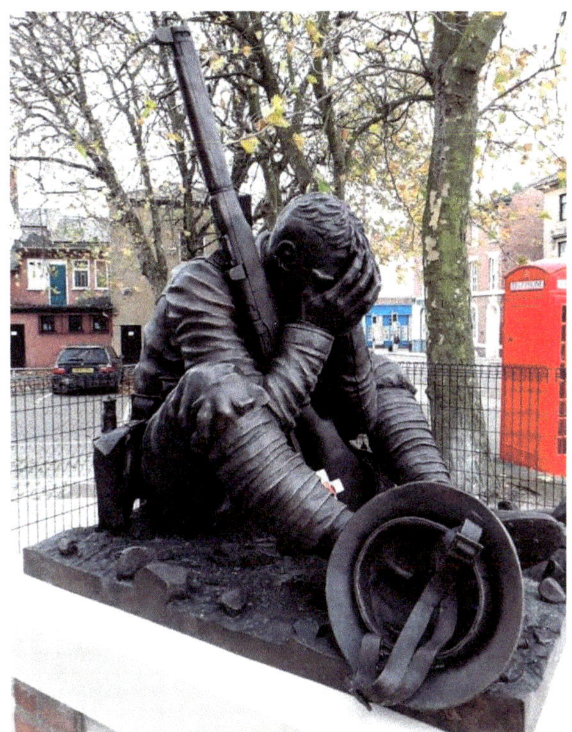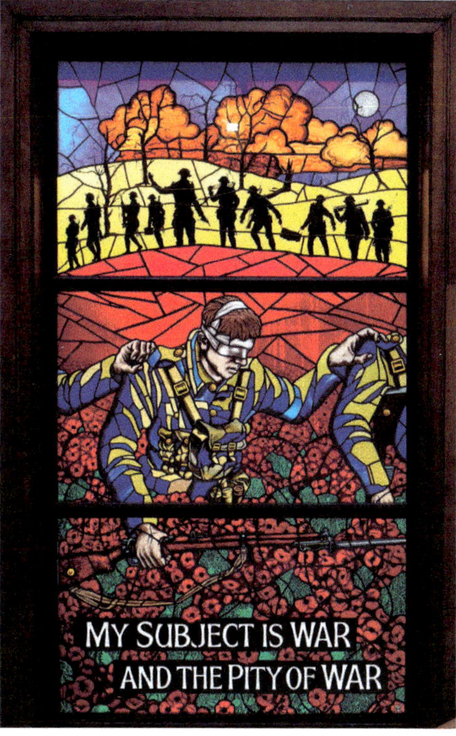

Above left: Wilfred Owen (1893–1918) memorial, Hamilton Square, Birkenhead.

Above right: Wilfred Owen stained-glass window memorial, Birkenhead Central Library.

not until September 1915 before he returned to England to enlist, joining the Artists Rifles Officers' Training Corps on 21 October 1915, before receiving a commission into the Manchester Regiment on 4 June 1916. After suffering shell shock in August 1917, he was transferred to Craiglockhart War Hospital in Edinburgh for treatment, where his meeting with fellow poet Siegfried Sassoon would have a profound effect on his short life. By the end of August 1918, he was back on the front line in France, where he showed conspicuous gallantry on 1/2 October (earning a posthumous award of the Military Cross). A month later he was killed in action on 4 November 1918 on the Sambre-Oise Canal bank, just days before the end of the war. He is buried in the churchyard at Ors. Wilfred Owen is remembered in several sites and memorials in Birkenhead, including the stained-glass window in the Central Library, and the bronze statue located in Hamilton Square (both by artist Jim Whelan).

A FAMILY AT WAR

A number of Wirral members of the Royden family served in or experienced contrasting roles during the war. Several men served in the armed forces and Home Guard, while a number of women worked as volunteers in the various Wirral aid groups. One was a fighter pilot, while his cousin was a pacifist of national and later international fame. Another played a key role assisting the government in the movement of troops, represented the Foreign Office in Washington, and was also present at the Versailles peace talks. For many others it was a case of keeping family and home together in the midst of hardship like the majority of Wirral families.

RIFLEMAN 86590 ALFRED ROYDEN

1/6th Battalion, The King's Liverpool Regiment (Liverpool Rifles)
Alfred was born in Storeton, Wirral, in 1898, where his father George was working as a labourer on a local farm. Alfred's grandfather, Thomas, had first settled there after moving from Caldy where the family had farmed for generations (some of the land later occupied by the shipbuilding family at Frankby Hall and Royden Park). By 1901, George, now a blacksmith at Storeton Quarry, had moved his family close by to 20 School Lane, Higher Bebington. Meanwhile, son Alfred had found work after leaving school in Price's Candle Factory in Bromborough Pool. As soon as he was old enough in 1917, he attested for the 1/6th Battalion, King's Liverpool Regiment (Liverpool Rifles). After training he was despatched to the Front, arriving in France on 17 April 1918 before being moved to the line in the defence of Givenchy. Within a month he had to be treated by the Wessex Field Ambulance after receiving a gunshot wound to the chin on 18 May. It wasn't serious enough to see him brought home however, and within six days he had returned to his unit. Young Alfred had little time to fully recover, as on 9 June he was in the thick of a gas attack, which was serious enough this time to see him hospitalised in 20 General

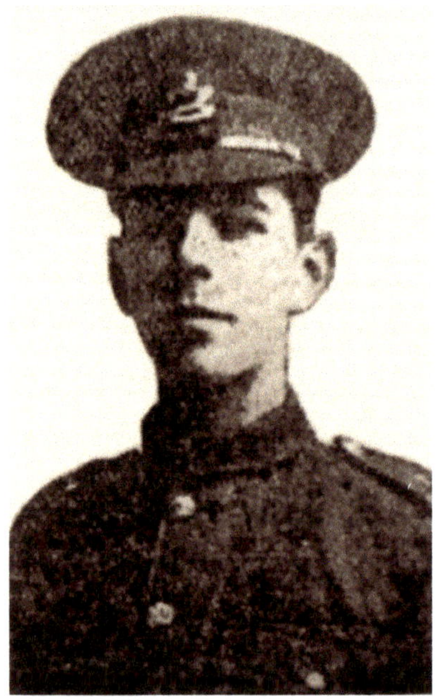

Rifleman 86590 Alfred Royden.

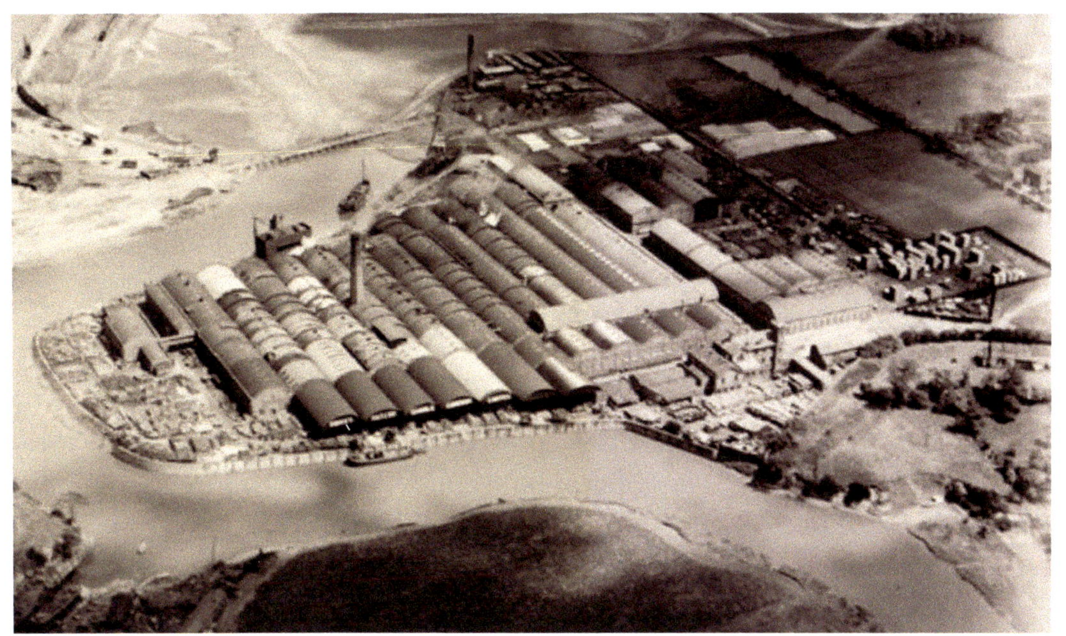

Candle Works, Bromborough, 1928.

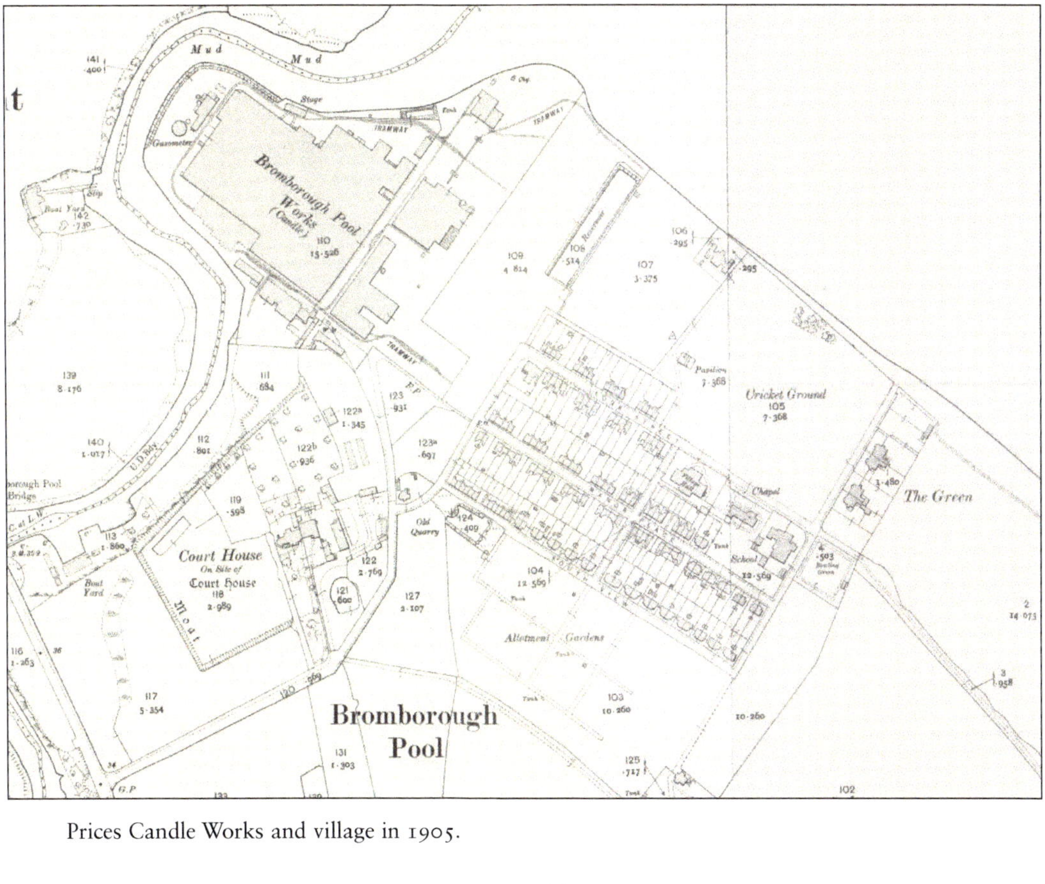

Prices Candle Works and village in 1905.

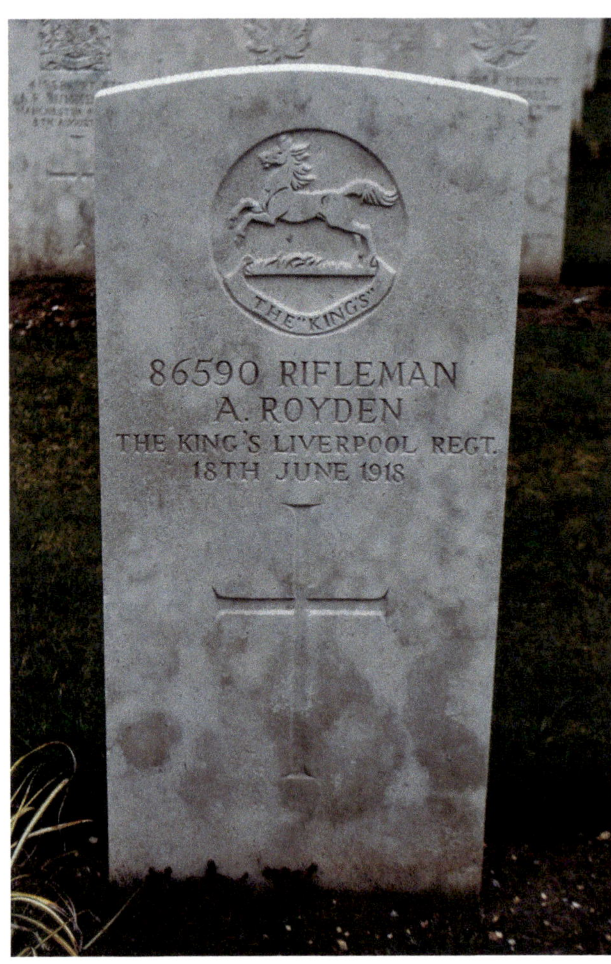

Left: Alfred Royden's Commonwealth war grave in Etaples Military Cemetery.

Below: Etaples Military Cemetery

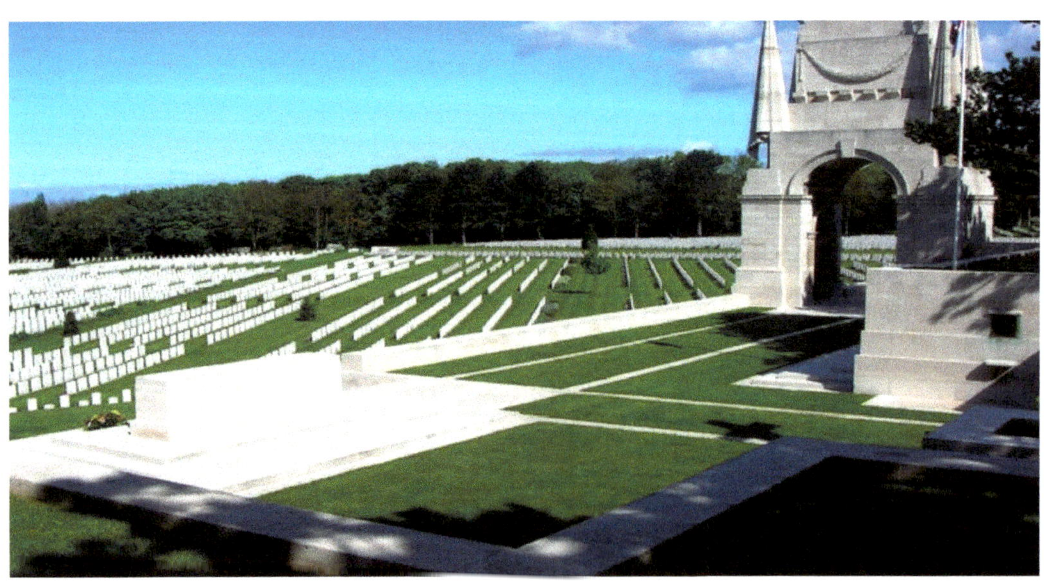

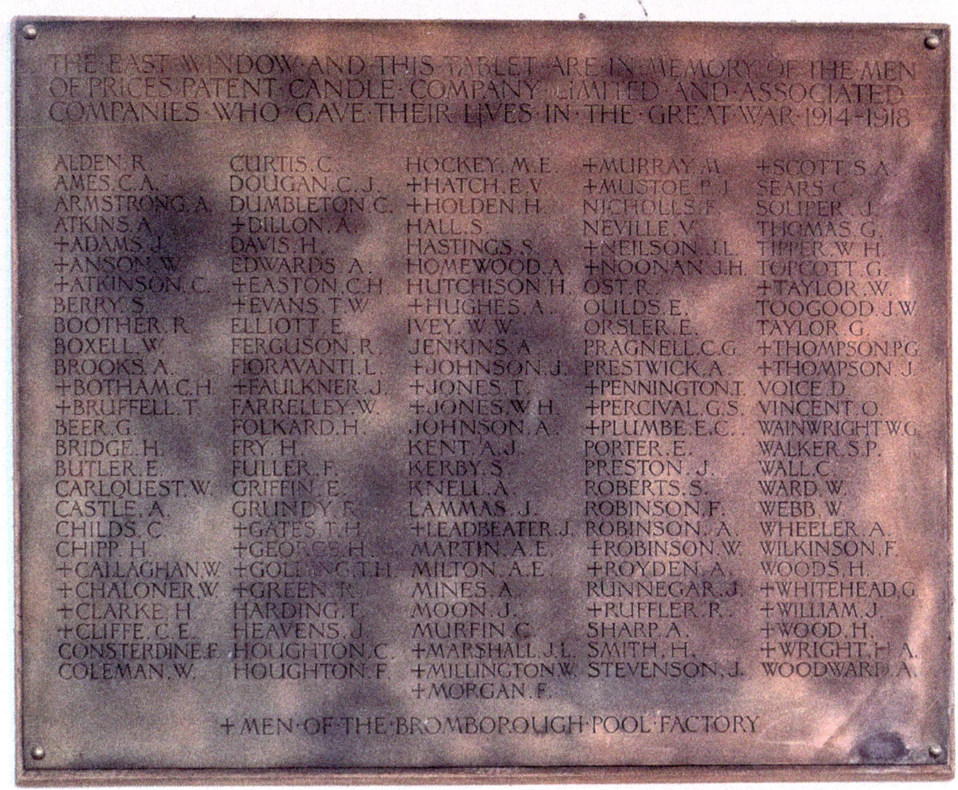

Prices Patent Candle Company Ltd Employees Memorial Plaque, St Matthew's Church, Park Road, Bromborough Pool Village.

Hospital, Camiers, near Etaples. His family were notified, and his father George rushed to France to be at his bedside, arriving shortly before his death on 18 June. He was just eighteen. His two brothers, who also served, survived the war. Their sons would serve in the Second World War. (*See Chapter 9*)

SECOND LIEUTENANT THOMAS UTTING ROYDEN

17th Battalion, King's Liverpool Regiment/19th & 1st Battalion,
King's Royal Rifle Corps

Thomas Utting Royden was born on 26 September 1896 in Birkenhead, Wirral, the son of Thomas Royden, a wine merchant, and Louisa Priscilla Utting. Thomas senior was the son of Joseph Royden, a farmer of Prenton, and like Alfred Royden, they were part of the Royden family which had farmed the West Kirby/Caldy area since coming to the Wirral from Chester in the early 1720s. Louisa, who had attended Kensington House School, a private girls' boarding school at Nos 59–63 Bidston Road, Oxton, Birkenhead, was the daughter of Liverpool surgeon John Utting of

Anfield Road. [Professor Sir John Utting was the first Professor of Anaesthetics at Liverpool University, Liverpool's chief medical officer, and was also Liverpool Football Club's first club doctor. He was elected Mayor of Liverpool in 1917. He died at his Anfield home at St Anne's Hill on the 27 February 1927. The nearby Utting Avenue is named after him].

Thomas and Louise moved into 67 Willowbank Road in Birkenhead, while young Thomas was packed off to boarding school at Lucton Kingsland, Herefordshire. On the day war was declared in August 1914, Thomas had been working as a clerk in the office of a local cotton importer. He immediately heeded Lord Derby's call for volunteers in his new Pal's Battalion, and attested in Liverpool on 1 September 1914. Underage, he declared himself to be nineteen years and six days old, although in reality he was still only seventeen, and still almost a month off his eighteenth birthday. Dark-haired and 6 feet tall, he cut a dashing figure in the queue of volunteers, and was able to pass off as older than his years. He was enlisted in the 1st City Battalion, King's Liverpool Regiment (later renamed the 17th (Service) Battalion) and reported at the old Watch Factory in Prescot where the 17ths were to complete their initial training. On 30 April 1915 they left for further training at Belton Park in Grantham, Lincolnshire, and by 7 November all four Pals battalions had left for France.

However, Thomas was not with them. He had been re-enlisted into the Inns of Court OTC (Officer Training Corps) and on 30 July, Thomas found himself on the train to Berkhamsted to train as an officer. He was commissioned in the spring of 1916, and posted to his new unit, the 2nd Battalion, The King's Royal Rifles, on 25 April, which was in the throes of moving their training base in Banbury to their new camp on Wimbledon Common, before his despatch to the Front on

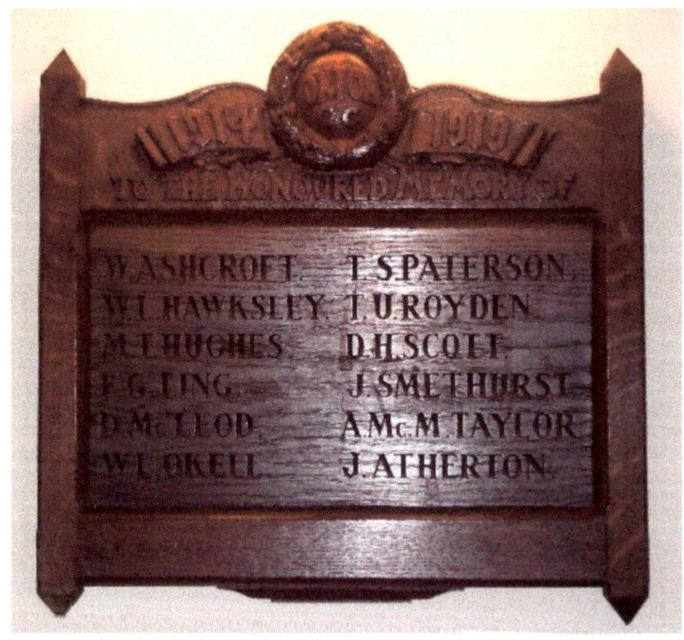

Second Lieutenant Thomas Utting Royden recorded on Upton Cricket Club war memorial plaque.

3 July 1916. He arrived on 15 July, right into the action on the Battle of the Somme. He survived the intensity and carnage of the Battle of Delville Wood, but was still a raw nineteen-year-old officer and leader of a battle-hardened unit. By October the battalion had moved to the Ancre Valley, and were soon engaged in the Battle of the Ancre (13–18 November), and it was here that young Thomas lost his life on 16 November while standing up directing the fire of his men. He was twenty years of age. His body was never recovered, lost in the sea of mud and carnage of no man's land. He is remembered on the Thiepval Memorial to the Missing on the Somme, plus several memorials at home, including Birkenhead War Memorial and Upton Cricket Club memorial, where he was a former player.

This wasn't the end of his story however, as his eighteen-year-old girlfriend, who he met during his time with the OTC in Berkhamsted, was pregnant with his child, who he would never live to see. (His full story can be found at www.roydenhistory. co.uk/mrlhp/articles/ww1/ww1.htm)

SIR THOMAS ROYDEN CH, 2ND BARONET (FRANKBY HALL, WIRRAL)

Thomas Royden was the son of the head of the Royden shipbuilding and ship-owning branch of the family. At the outbreak of war, Thomas' experienced roll as Deputy Chairman of Cunard Line, and his extensive knowledge of shipping, enabled him to render distinguished service to his country. In 1913, he shared in the preparation of a confidential plan for the transport of British troops and munitions across the Channel, a plan which was brought into operation on the outbreak of war in August 1914. Thomas was asked by the British government to report on the

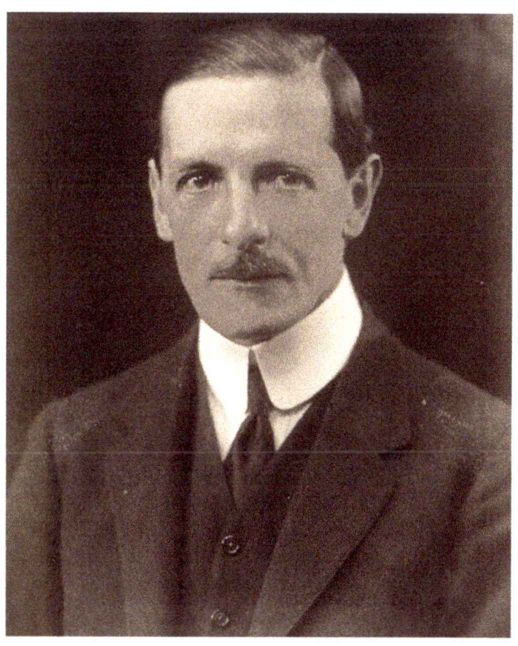

Sir Thomas Royden CH, 2nd Baronet.

facilities available to transport an expeditionary force to France, and it was largely down to his advice and recommendations that so much was so swiftly achieved in coordinating the passage of the BEF to France and Flanders and to maintain the supply route.

According to Frederick Edwin Smith (1st Earl of Birkenhead, Lord Chancellor) in *Contemporary Personalities* (1924),

> When Lord Haldane became Lord Chancellor, Major-General John Seely was made Secretary of State for War in 1912. Seely invited four of the ablest shipowners in the world to advise him in his dilemma. They were, Sir Thomas Royden, of the Cunard Line; Sir Lionel Fletcher, of the White Star Line; Sir Richard Holt, of the Blue Funnel Line; and Mr Owen Phillips, of the Royal Mail Line. Sir Thomas Royden and Sir Lionel Fletcher took up the task, and, in order fully to discharge it, gave up all their private work for many months. It is hardly too much to say that the labours of Sir Thomas Royden, and his colleagues, saved the situation in France in the first two critical months. Probably Paris would have fallen if the shipping arrangements had been less intelligently conceived and prepared.

His wide experience of shipping affairs was invaluable. Thomas was frequently entrusted with foreign missions requiring the greatest tact and ability. Early in the war he went to Mudros in order to organise the transport arrangements in connexion with the Gallipoli campaign, and in 1917 he was in Washington discussing the international shipping problems that arose when the United States joined the Allies. A telegram from J. P. Maclay, Minister of Shipping, sent to the Prime Minister on 31 Aug 1917 gives an insight into his worth, in which the Minister writes how keen he was for 'Royden to remain at his post if possible, notwithstanding the death of his father ... Royden's work with regard to ship confiscation is invaluable, hope I may retain him permanently'. Thomas did stay of course, and he organised the shipment of American and Colonial troops and war materials to the various theatres of war.

Edward N. Hurley, part of the US Federal Trade Commission from 1915 to 1917, and appointed Chairman of the US Shipping Board by President Woodrow Wilson, met with Thomas Royden several times:

> I had many consultations with British shipping representatives. Taken as a whole I found them patriotic, broadminded men who fully appreciated the vital importance of shipping from the point of view of the United States and who were willing to forego private advantages as soon as our military situation was explained to them. There was Sir Thomas Royden, for instance, now Chairman of the Board of Directors of the Cunard Steamship Company, Ltd., who represented Great Britain in the negotiations affecting the War Sword and other ships built in our yards under contracts with British subjects. He was a fine type of business man, very keen in looking after the interests of his country and in urging the adoption of a policy which would have committed us to turning over to the British, after the war, those ships which they had ordered or acquired in this country.
>
> Edward N. Hurley, *The Bridge to France* (1920)

In April 1919, Sir Thomas Royden, 2nd Baronet, MP, as he was by then*, was selected to represent the Shipping Controller as Assistant Secretary of the Ministry of Shipping at the Paris Peace Conference at Versailles. Shortly afterwards he was invested as a Companion of Honour, and following Versailles, Sir Thomas was also honoured by the French, Italians, Maltese and Afghans. He continued in his role of Chairman of Cunard Line throughout the 1920s, and put the plans and funding into place for the construction of the RMS *Queen Mary* and RMS *Queen Elizabeth* before his retirement in 1932.

[*His father, shipbuilder Sir Thomas Bland Royden, had died in 1917, and in 1918 Sir Thomas was elected MP for Bootle.]

ETHEL MARTHA ROYDEN OBE

Ethel Martha Royden, a sister of Sir Thomas Royden, became prominent in the Girl Guide Movement for ten years as Director of the World Association of Girl Guides. She travelled extensively on behalf of the Girl Guide Movement, attending conferences in such places as Warsaw, the Scandinavian capitals and Switzerland. But it was through her lifelong friend Dame Katherine Furse, first Director of the 'Wrens', that she became involved in the WRNS during the First World War. She was effectively an ADC to Dame Katherine, carrying the rank of Deputy Assistant Director WRNS overseeing Drafting and Demobilisation. She was appointed Officer, Order of the British Empire in 1919.

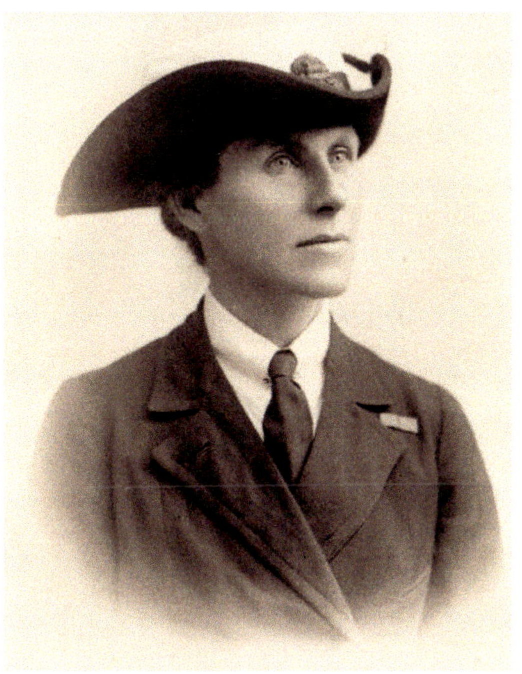

Ethel Martha Royden OBE.

In the first half of the twentieth century, Agnes Maude Royden became internationally famous as a preacher, lecturer, author and suffragist. She campaigned tirelessly throughout her life, on issues of women's political, social, and religious rights; social justice for the poor and disenfranchised; and world peace. She was equally at home working in the slums of Liverpool, as in the company of world leaders, who frequently welcomed her to their countries when she visited on her lecture tours.

Maude was the sister of Ethel and Sir Thomas above (and Ernest of Bidston Court/Hill Bark), the youngest of eight. Although born in Mossley Hill, Liverpool, Frankby Hall, built by her grandfather, became the family home following his death and her father's retirement. After her education at Lady Margaret Hall, Oxford University, where she gained a degree in History in 1897, she and her university friends threw themselves into the suffrage cause, joining the National Union of Women's Suffrage Societies, which would dominate her time until the start of the First World War. A regular speaker for the NUWSS, she was appointed to its executive committee in 1911, and became editor of its newspaper, *The Common Cause*, and in 1915 she was elected vice-president of the National Union of Women's Suffrage Societies. However, as a committed Christian and pacifist, she found she could no longer reconcile her views with those of the NUWSS over its support for the war effort and she resigned from the movement. She then helped form the 'Fellowship of Reconciliation' with other Christian pacifists, and became its travelling secretary in 1915.

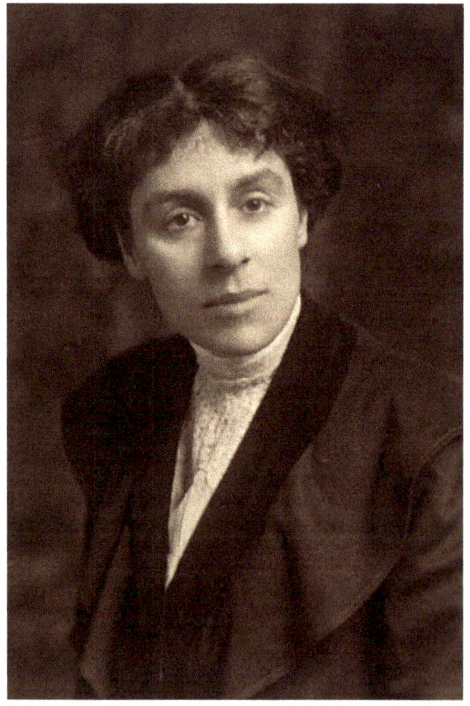

Dr Maude Royden CH DD LLD.

As her fame as a suffragist spread, Maude became even more well known as a speaker on social and religious issues and for her attempt to become a preacher. Already attacked and vilified for her suffragist views and pacifism, here was yet another campaign where she would endure ceaseless opposition. On 18 May 1917, she was controversially invited to preach in the City Temple in London, which began a confrontational relationship with church authorities, a body which tried to block her attempts to speak from the pulpit throughout the next decade. Maude forged on regardless, and with an appointment at the Guildhall in London, she regularly addressed full attendances.

After the war, in 1926, Maude was the first woman to preach at Liverpool Cathedral, and in 1928 embarked on a world lecture tour covering the USA, New Zealand and Australia, followed by Japan, China and India. Her energy was

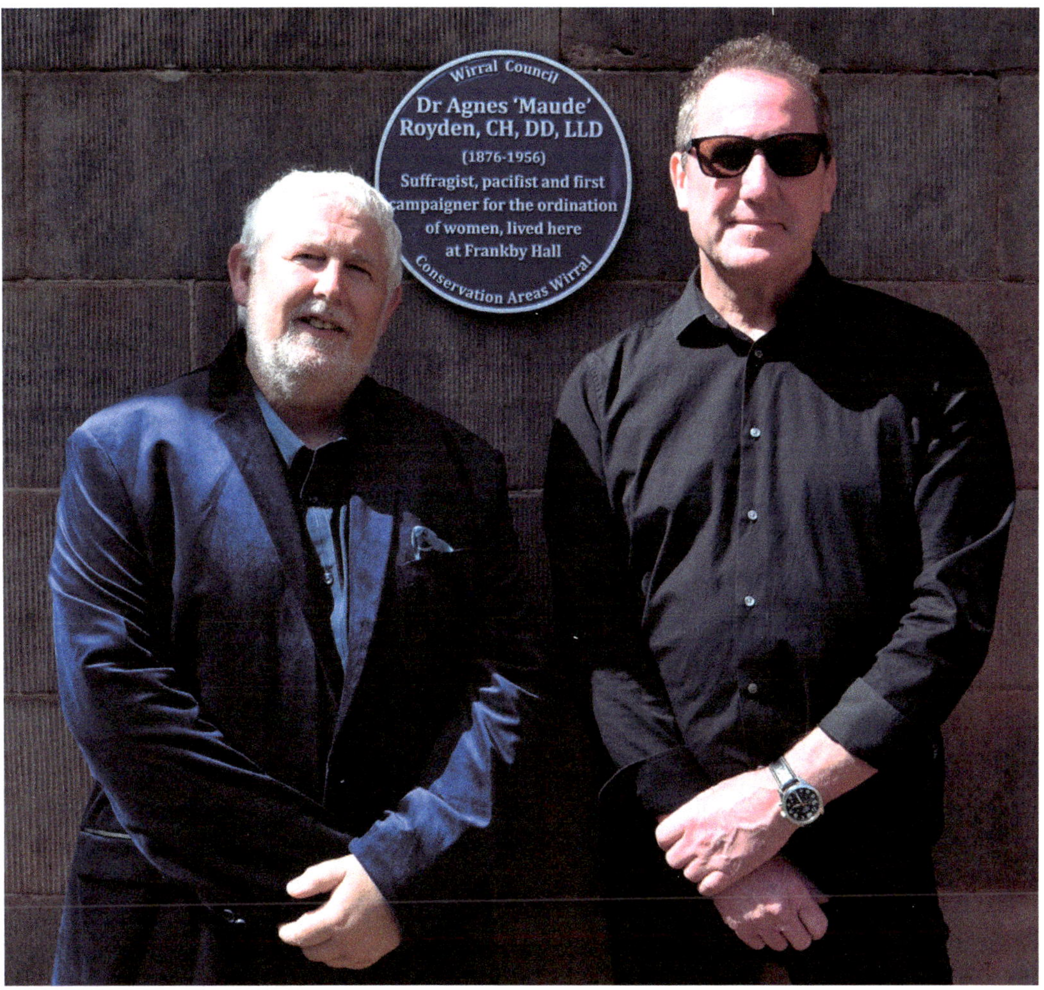

The author with Andy McCluskey, well-known frontman of Wirral rock band Orchestral Manoeuvres in the Dark, at the unveiling of the blue plaque for Maude Royden at Frankby Hall. Andy lives in the former home of one of Maude's sisters and is a keen supporter of the history and conservation of the village.

boundless, and considering she had been born with dislocated hips, for which she never had effective treatment, it made her accomplishments all the more remarkable.

In 1930, she joined her brother, Sir Thomas Royden, as a recipient of the Companion of Honour, the only time two siblings have held the award. A year later, Glasgow University made her Britain's first female Doctor of Divinity, and in 1935 she was awarded an honorary Doctor of Laws by the University of Liverpool. On 24 April 2018, a statue to Millicent Fawcett, suffragist leader and social campaigner, was unveiled in London. On the statue plinth are the names and tiled images of fifty-five women and four men who supported women's suffrage. Among them is the image of Agnes Maude Royden. Meanwhile in the Wirral, in June 2019, a blue plaque honouring Maude was unveiled on her former family home at Frankby Hall.

ERNEST ROYDEN

Ernest was the younger brother of Sir Thomas. Due to contracting polio as a child, he could not serve in any physical capacity, but gave his Woodhey home in Spital, Bromborough, for the use as a small military hospital for the duration of the war.

ROOPER BROTHERS: JOHN ROYDEN ROOPER, TREVOR ROOPER AND RALPH ROOPER

The brothers were sons of Daisy Royden (the eldest sister of Sir Thomas, Ethel and Maude Royden above) and her husband, Percy Rooper. On the outbreak of war, John signed up for the Denbighshire Hussar Yeomanry based in Wrexham. His brother Trevor served under him as a motorcycle rider for five months, before being commissioned as a second lieutenant on 23 December 1914. In September 1916, Trevor was seconded to the Royal Flying Corps, where he became an accomplished pilot. He was posted to No. 1 Squadron RFC in April 1917, where he flew fighters

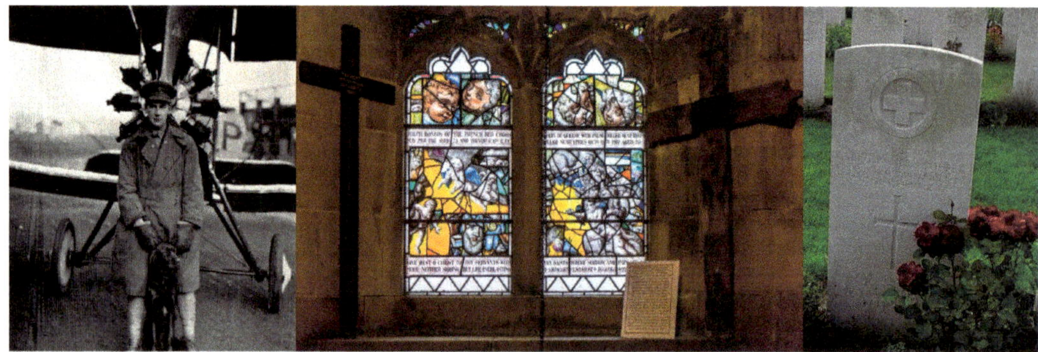

Left to right: Captain Trevor Rooper RFC; Rooper memorial window and grave markers, Gresford Church; Commonwealth war grave of Chauffeur/Conducteur (Driver) Ralph Rooper, French Red Cross, Marfaux British Cemetery, France.

over the Flanders front. Promoted to lieutenant on 1 July, he gained his first victory on 28 July, with two further victories in early August. Later that month he was appointed a flight commander with the acting rank of captain on the 24th. Three more victories followed in September, and two more in early October to take his final tally to eight. On 9 October 1917, he was shot down by over Polygon Wood, Ypres, and crashed near the British front lines, receiving fatal injuries. He is buried at the Communal Cemetery Extension in Bailleul, Nord, France.

Ralph was determined to serve overseas, although he had already confided in Maude his struggle with pacifism. Despite being rejected by the army due to his heart condition, he left for France in April 1915 and joined the Friends Ambulance Unit serving as a Motor Ambulance Driver attached to the French Army. However, he was wounded near Ypres and returned home to recover, but left for the Front again in May 1917, serving with the Scottish Branch of the Croix Rouge Francaise in Poperinghe, Ypres, Soissons, and Rheims. Into 1918, he had become increasingly disillusioned with the war, and his conversations with Maude led her to worry that he may return home and become a conscientious objector. While acting as a Conducteur SSA, he was killed in action at Gueux near Rheims, France, on 29 May 1918 during the final German advance. He was awarded the Croix de Guerre with Palm. He is buried in Marfeux British Cemetery, near Rheims.

Captain John Royden Rooper continued to serve in the Denbighshire Hussars until ill health forced him to relinquish his commission on 9 June 1916, after which he resumed his shipping career and later became Chairman of Port Line and a director of Cunard Line. He would experience family tragedy again during the Second World War when he and his wife lost two sons in the conflict.

A stained-glass window dedicated to the brothers, together with their original wooden cross grave markers, hang in their family church in Gresford near Chester, where they are also recorded together on the war memorial.

Chapter 4
The Experience at Home

From the earliest days of the war, many local men who were unable to volunteer for the armed forces for whatever reason were still keen to serve in a civilian militia for home defence. Those pioneer Wirral groups were rather ad hoc and poorly equipped, and usually led by veterans of the Boer War or retired reservists. Neston were quick to form their 'home guard', announcing the formation of three companies at the end of August:

NESTON & PARKGATE
LOCAL PATRIOTISM
THREE COMPANIES OF VOLUNTEERS

The large drill scheme is being splendidly supported, and a fine, unselfish spirit is moving the district. Already, 114 names have been enrolled and have seen service. Two companies will be formed, and a further company will later be enrolled of those unfamiliar with any drill, use of arms, etc. Major Grundy and Lieut. Mansfield will be with one company, and Major F.W. Jones and Lieut. F.H. Bacon with the other. Capt. Coventry of the Boys' Brigade has accepted the responsibility of being adjutant. Sergeant Birch will be orderly sergeant, and Mr T. Bairds and Mr D. Wharam drill instructors. Colour Sergeant Swift, Sergeant Basnett, Sergeant Fleming and Sergeant T.P Swift will be section commanders. Drill commences this Friday night, and during the initial stages will be in the Drill Hall and the Town Hall. It is calculated that from the various homes in the neighbourhood, some 50 persons are now with the various forces, and it is highly pleasing to note that some twenty boys, who during the past six or seven years have passed through Captain Coventry's hands in the Boys' Brigade, are now serving their country as members of the Regular Army, Territorial Force and New Army. Two choristers from St Michael's Mission Church have been keenly missed, but write regularly to Captain Scholey and Miss Jackson.

Chester Observer, 29 August 1914

As time went by, equipment and training improved and the various associations across the Wirral began to merge into a 'Volunteer Training Corps'. The Central Association of Volunteer Training Corps (VTC) gradually became recognised as the body to which individual corps could affiliate, and was responsible for drawing up the rules and regulations on a national basis.

VOLUNTEERING IN WIRRAL
AN AID TO RECRUITING

The Volunteer Training Corps in Birkenhead and district are attracting a number of men who will prove extremely useful in case of emergency. Recruiting for the corps has been very brisk, and the battalion, which comprises detachments from Birkenhead, Rock Ferry, and Port Sunlight, has earned the praise of the Commandant, Lieutenant-Colonel M. Ellis V.D., an old Territorial officer. The new recruiting scheme (*for the front-line army*) will deplete the ranks of the Volunteer Training Corps considerably, and those who previously considered themselves too old for the Army will now have no excuse.

The Wirral Battalion is fast reaching its required strength, viz., 10,000. The district of Neston, Heswall, Parkgate, Hoylake, and West Kirby are included. The response to the appeal of Colonel Alan Sykes MP, for men is a very creditable. The number for the West Kirby district, viz., 250, was almost obtained in one night.

The Commandant is Mr Charles McIver JP., of Heswall, than whom there is none better qualified to take charge of the men of Wirral.

Chester Chronicle, 22 May 1915

THE THREAT FROM ABOVE

This war was the first time that Britain came under threat from air attack. This was initially by the shelling of towns on the east coast by German warships, which was followed by bombing attacks by Zeppelin airships, then later Gotha aeroplane bombers. The worst of the naval attacks took place on 16 December 1914, when the towns of Scarborough, Whitby and Hartlepool were hit by an eighteen-strong battle-cruiser squadron, resulting in 137 deaths and 592 injured, the vast majority civilians. The attacks were effectively used and exploited by the British government to increase emotional feeling against the enemy. The rallying cry of 'Remember Scarborough' and 'Baby-Killers' became common, and the raid was used as propaganda to encourage enlistment, with numerous posters appearing across the country.

Liverpool, as one of the largest ports in Europe, was an early target, but the Zeppelins failed in their campaign to hit or even reach the city. Nevertheless, the German propaganda machine went into overdrive, when it was publicly announced that their 'raids' on Liverpool were an unqualified success, claiming they hit the city on the night of 31 January 1916. Two Zeppelins were involved, with the captain of L21 reporting at 8.50 p.m. that he was over the west coast of England. In fact, they were nowhere near Liverpool, both reports being seriously inaccurate. The L21 was actually attacking west Birmingham, while the L15 was over Burton-on-Trent.

53

In fact, the closest the Zeppelins got to Merseyside was when L61 flew over the Mersey on 12 April 1918 near Widnes, and dropped two bombs on Bold near St Helens, carrying on to Wigan where it dropped a further seventeen bombs, killing seven people. Again, their navigation was way off, the commander thinking he was over Sheffield.

PRISONER OF WAR

Sapper Tommy Lewis has been moved to a fresh camp three times in one month, and is now in Frankfurt. He asks how things are in Ellesmere Port, and says he heard we had some 'surprise visitors' near there. The writer has evidently heard about the Liverpool docks being destroyed by Zeppelins. He asks the secretary to convey his sincere thanks to all who are interested in his welfare, especially the ladies, who must be doing great deal of hard work. He says he is quite well, and, as usual, signs himself 'Nil Desperandum'.

Chester Chronicle, 8 April 1916

DAYLIGHT AIR RAIDS
WARNING TO BIRKENHEAD PUBLIC

Arrangements have been made to issue a public warning (by day only) on the approach of hostile air craft. The warning will come into operation at once, and the method adopted will be the firing off of two maroons [rockets], 20 seconds between each, at all police stations and fire station. The maroons will be fired from a tube and will give a loud detonation at a height of from 750 to 1,000 feet. The warning will be given for the purpose of enabling the public to take cover, and experience has shown that the risk of serious casualties is greatly diminished if persons take cover, even such cover as is afforded by ordinary dwelling houses. The warning will be operative between half hour before sunrise to half hour after sunset.

It should be noted that the system of warning to the public by reducing the electric lighting gradually for ten minutes and then shutting it off entirely, and the reducing of gas lighting to a minimum will remain operative for the rest of the 24 hours. When local danger is past, the public will be informed by police officers on bicycles, blowing their whistle and carrying cards bearing the words, 'All Clear'.

Birkenhead Advertiser & Wallasey Guardian, 9 March 1918

In Wirral, the British War Department had requisitioned the Hooton Park estate in August 1914, which was swiftly put to use as an army training ground for the 18th Battalion, King's Liverpool Regiment (Liverpool Pals), with barracks constructed in the grounds. The hall, meanwhile, became a headquarters, hospital, and officers' mess. Following their departure to France, Hooton Park was converted into an airfield for the storage of imported American aircraft and for the training of US and Canadian pilots. Construction began on one single and three double aircraft hangars, which were completed in 1917. Now known as No. 4 Training Depot Station, the Royal Flying Corps moved in to Hooton Park to train the fighter squadrons under great demand in France, using Avro 504s, Sopwith Scouts and Dolphins. By the end of the war, the aircraft at Hooton were moved to nearby RAF Sealand and RAF Hooton Park was closed. The airfield was returned to farmland, the hangars left empty and the hall was eventually demolished in 1932.

AEROPLANES

We are getting quite accustomed to visits, almost daily, of these instruments of war, the manufactory of which is not a hundred miles away. On Saturday last, one descended in a meadow belonging to Mr R Scott of Little Neston, and there being no school on Saturdays, it was amusing to watch the little ones rushing to the meadow to see the unusual sight of an aeroplane resting like a bird on mother earth. Others, of the older craft, were there, and to the delight of everyone, the time was spent by the occupants of the machine in explaining the mechanical workings etc, of the monster, and, after a short rest, the aeroplane rose, amidst applause and clapping of hands from the crowd, and sailed away towards home.

Chester Chronicle, 8 December 1917

Worried that national and personal debt would get out of control, the government introduced a new scheme to reduce borrowing and to raise funds for the war effort. The National Savings Movement was established in 1916 with the public being encouraged to 'save and prosper'. Meanwhile, a battered tank from the Western Front was set up in prominent public places, such as town squares, where it was used to promote National War Bonds and War Savings Certificates to raise money for the war effort. As well as the tank visiting Wallasey, in Birkenhead a tram was dressed up to look like a tank, with appropriate adverts to publicise the campaign.

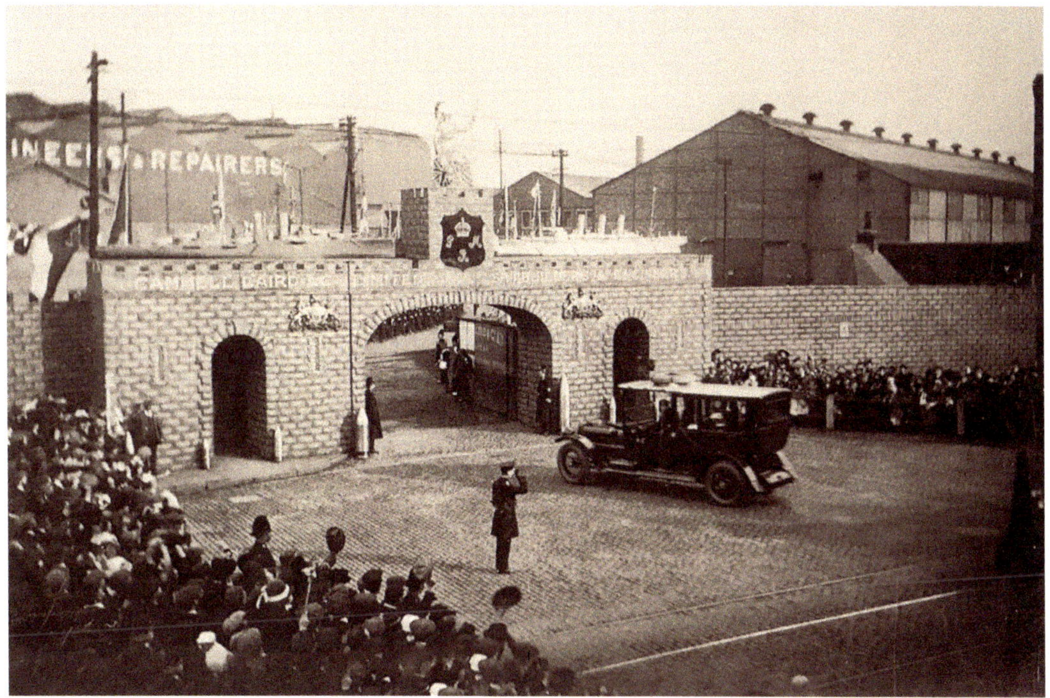

Arrival of the King and Queen to Cammell Lairds, 25 March 1914, passing through a specially constructed gate for their visit.

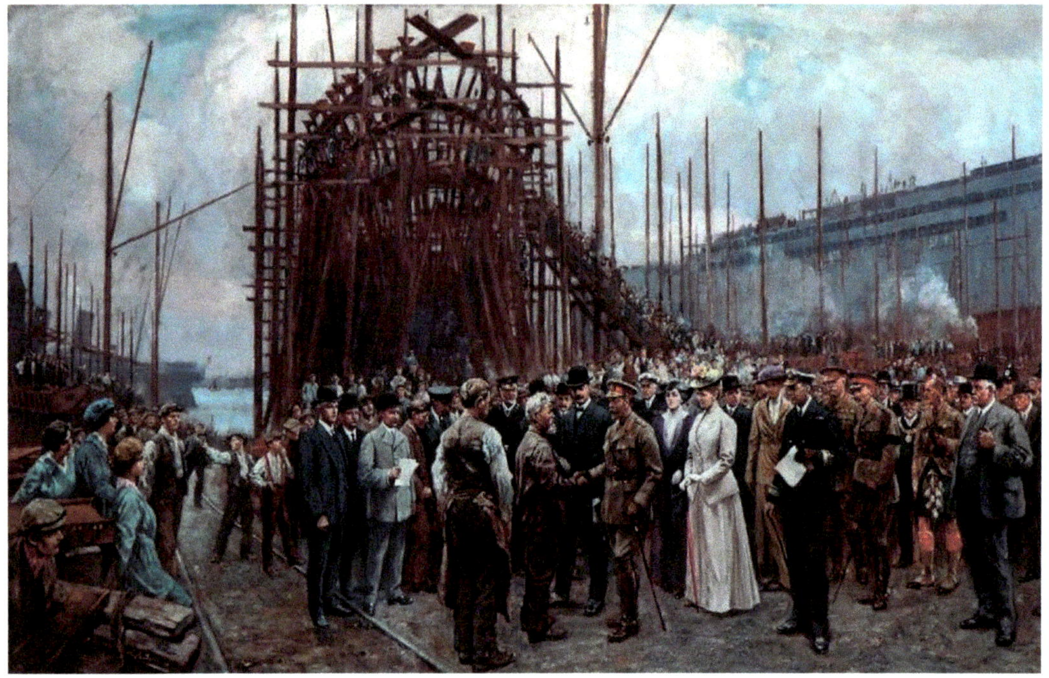

Painting of the second royal visit of the King and Queen to Cammell Lairds, on 14 May 1917, who had again come to thank staff for their phenomenal efforts. (*Arthur James Wetherall Burgess (1879–1957) and Edward Frederick Skinner (1865–1924) – Williamson Art Gallery*)

Towns and villages across Wirral began to set up Comforts Funds to help alleviate the strains the fighting men abroad were living under, by providing foodstuffs, clothing and other necessities. Funds were raised in a variety of ways, ranging from regular door-to-door collections, to benefit concerts and whist drives. Invitations to concerts were frequently extended to local soldiers who were home on leave, or parties of men from the local military hospital, usually accompanied by the sister in charge and her staff.

The economy was also seriously affected by the U-boat threat on shipping, and as food and essential supplies diminished, hoarding and panic buying became common. Agriculture was also hit by the loss of both men and horse power to the Front, and by January 1918 the government had no alternative but to introduce rationing. Potatoes were often in short supply and sugar was often difficult to get hold of. Consequently, sugar was the first to be rationed, and this was later followed by butcher's meat. The local press constantly pushed the message of thrift and frugality, frequently devoting extensive column inches to advice in parsimony, alternative recipes when certain ingredients were in short supply, and the best use of coal.

It was not long before the distressing scenes of the wounded arriving at local stations began to be witnessed. In Tranmere, the workhouse institution was converted to the Tranmere Military Infirmary and two blocks were set aside by the Board of Guardians to cope just with receptions. Even the newly opened

Wallasey Town Hall was brought into use, deployed as an extension ward to No. 1 Western General Hospital at Fazakerley in Liverpool, while nearby Guinea Gap Swimming Baths was utilised for hydrotherapy and recuperative exercise for the injured. More than 400 hospital beds were installed in the Town Hall, with estimates of those treated there ranging between 3,500 and 6,500 casualties. It would not be until November 1920 before the building could be returned for civic use. Birkenhead Borough Hospital and Annexe, Palm Grove Hospital, Arrowe Hall, Bromborough, Heswall, Parkgate and Hooton all provided capacity on a smaller scale. Even local schools such as Temple Road and Hemingford Street Council Schools in Birkenhead (the former of which was for many months occupied by the military) were fitted out as makeshift hospitals for the duration. Whenever a trainload of wounded arrived, the limited number of ambulances (many being at the Front) were deployed for the stretcher cases, while local people freely lent their motor cars to convey the walking wounded. The Voluntary Aid Detachment, Red Cross nurses, ambulance crews all worked tirelessly to alleviate the situation. The men arriving at the hospital were not necessarily from the same area; they would be despatched to whatever accommodation could be found at a time when resources were extremely stretched. Nevertheless, there was much support from the local communities in the form of gifts and entertainment. Red Cross had also secured their own buildings, equipment and staff, and the organisation was able to set up temporary hospitals as soon as wounded men began to arrive, which included the following: Manor Hill, Birkenhead (transferred from 19 Pal Grove), and annexe; Priory Ward, Upton Road, Birkenhead; Abbotsford, Rock Ferry; Penkett Road, Wallasey; The Cenacle, New Brighton; Vernon Institute, Great Saughall; The Châlet, Hoylake (and annexe, New Bunnee, Hoylake); Parkgate Hospital (Parade); Red Cross Hospital, Bromborough; Neston Institute, Neston: Heathfield, Whitby Heath (later renamed the Cottage Hospital); and Thornton Manor, Thornton Hough. An officer's hospital also opened at Dawpool.

WOUNDED ARRIVE AT BIRKENHEAD

One hundred and sixty soldiers, of whom sixty were stretcher cases, arrived at Woodside Station, Birkenhead, by hospital train last evening. The men were received by the men's detachment of the V.A.D., which was in the charge of Mr A. Lennie, commandant, the work being supervised by Mr Roland Jackson, transport officer. Motor-cars and motor ambulances were used in transferring the wounded to the various hospitals; the dispositions being as follows;- Tranmere Military Hospital 59; Borough Hospital 33; Parkgate 9; Royden's Hospital*, Bromborough 7; Golf Club Bromborough 4; Heswall 10; Arrowe Hall 20; and Liscard Central Hospital, 18.

Liverpool Echo, 25 June 1915

[*Royden's hospital was Woodhey in Spital, Bromborough, the home of Ernest Royden.]

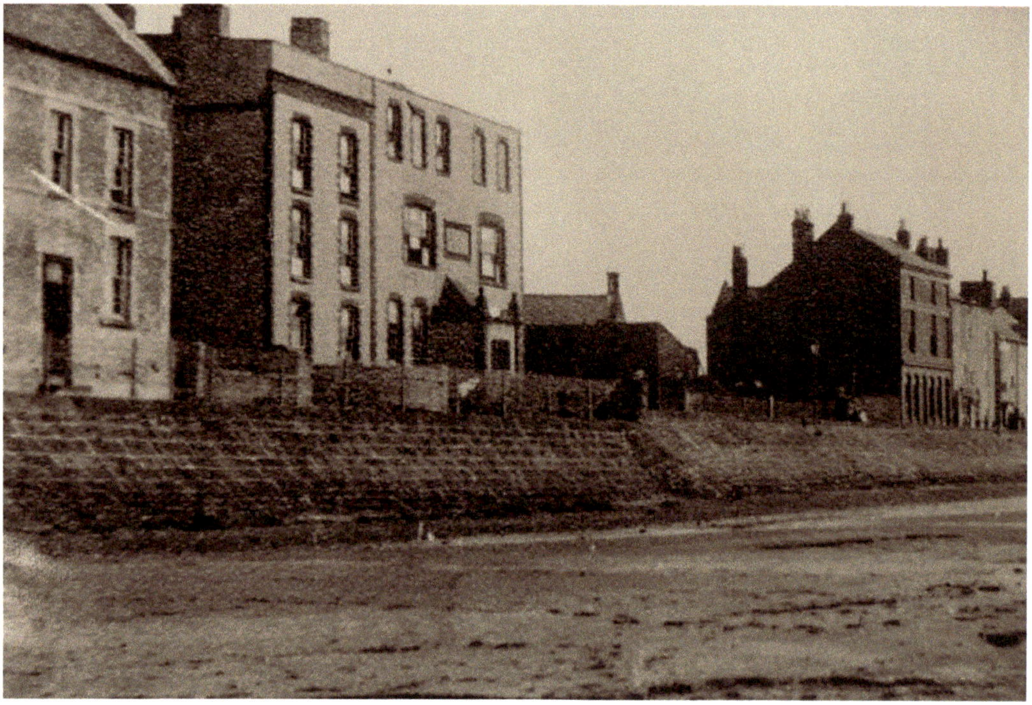

The Parkgate Hospital on the Parade opened in October 1914 with thirty beds. In November 1915, ten more were added and over 200 patients were treated there.

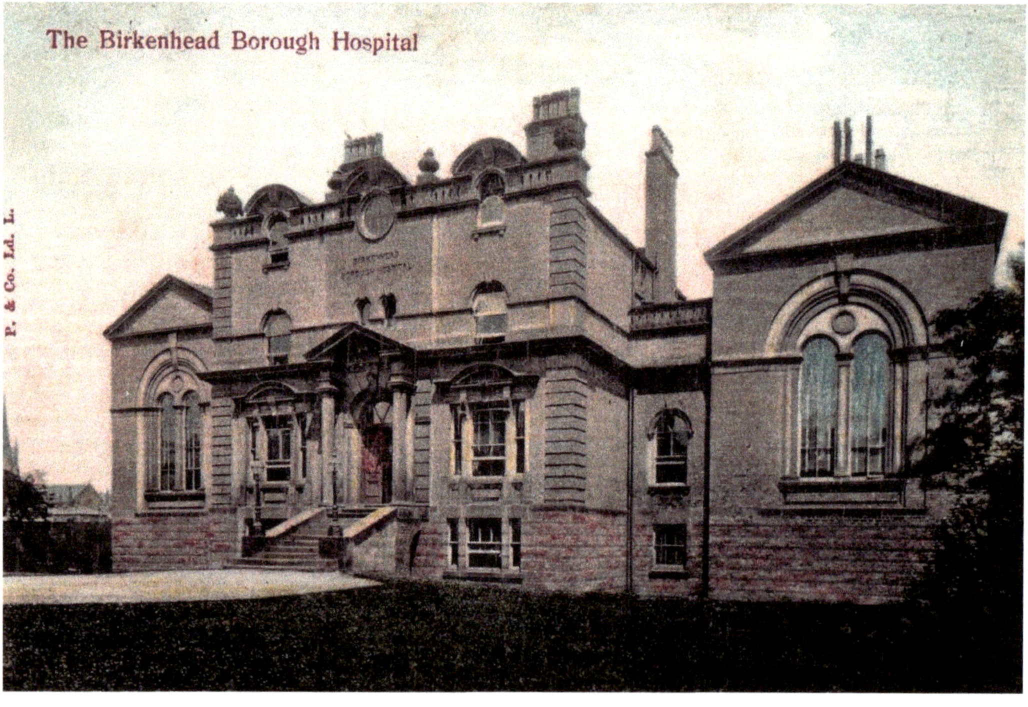

Birkenhead Borough Hospital.

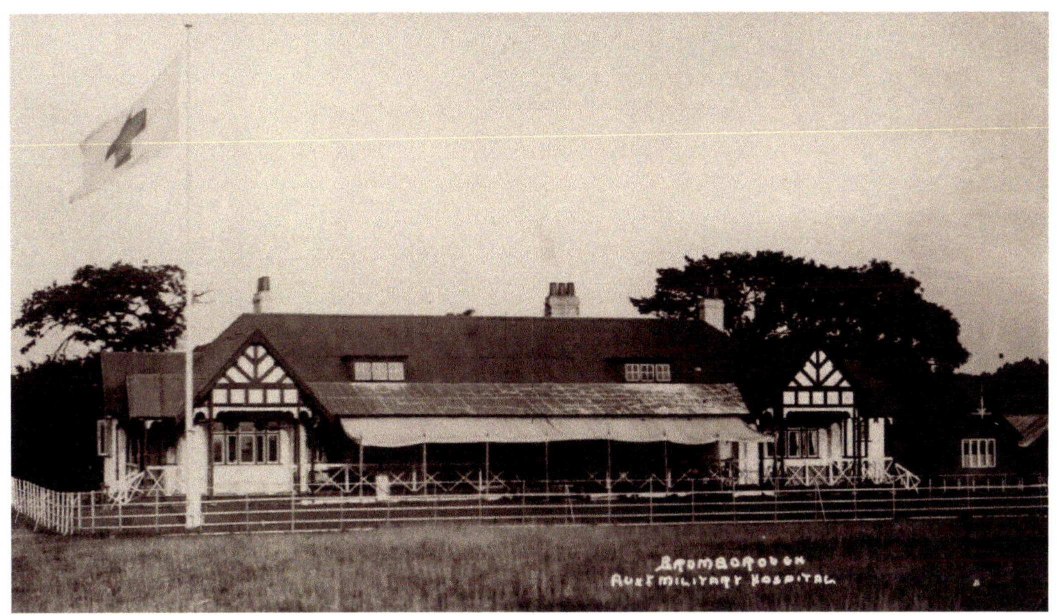

Bromborough Golf Clubhouse, which had temporarily closed for the duration in 1914 and lying idle, was opened on 22 May 1915 as Red Cross Auxiliary Home Hospital, Bromborough. An operating theatre was installed, and was initially staffed by two professional nurses, a number of volunteers, a masseuse and doctors Garson, Guthrie and Knott.

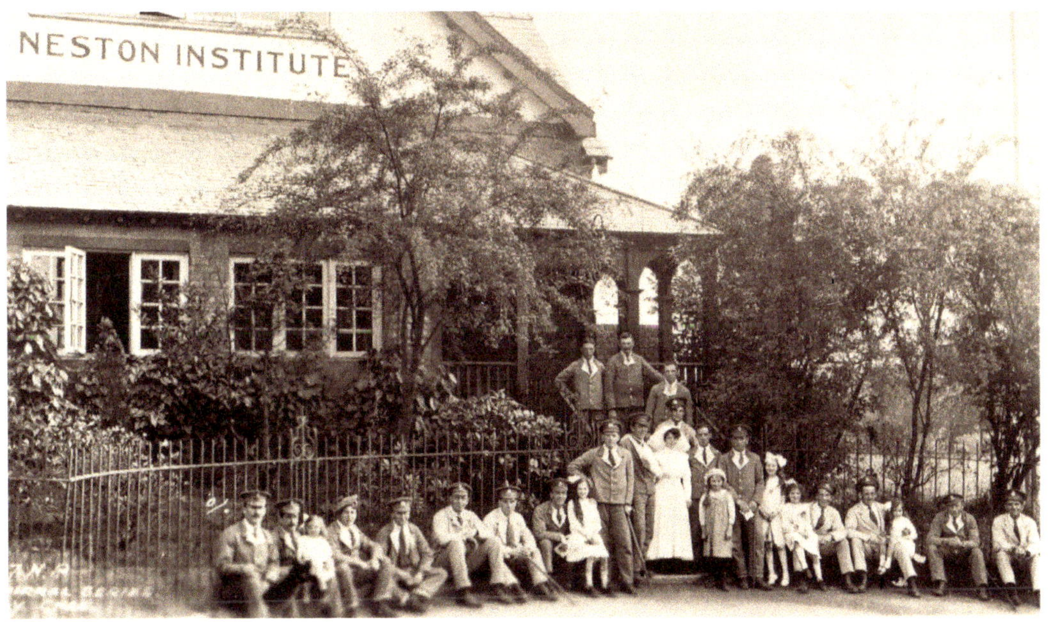

Red Cross Hospital, Neston. In Neston, the Swiss chalet-style institute (originally built by William Lever as a Liberal Club) was opened in early February 1916 as an Auxiliary Red Cross Hospital with a thirty-five-bed main ward and an observation ward with a further five beds. The hospital was staffed with a number of Voluntary Red Cross nurses, two trained staff nurses, and the professional services of Dr Grant and Dr Gunn.

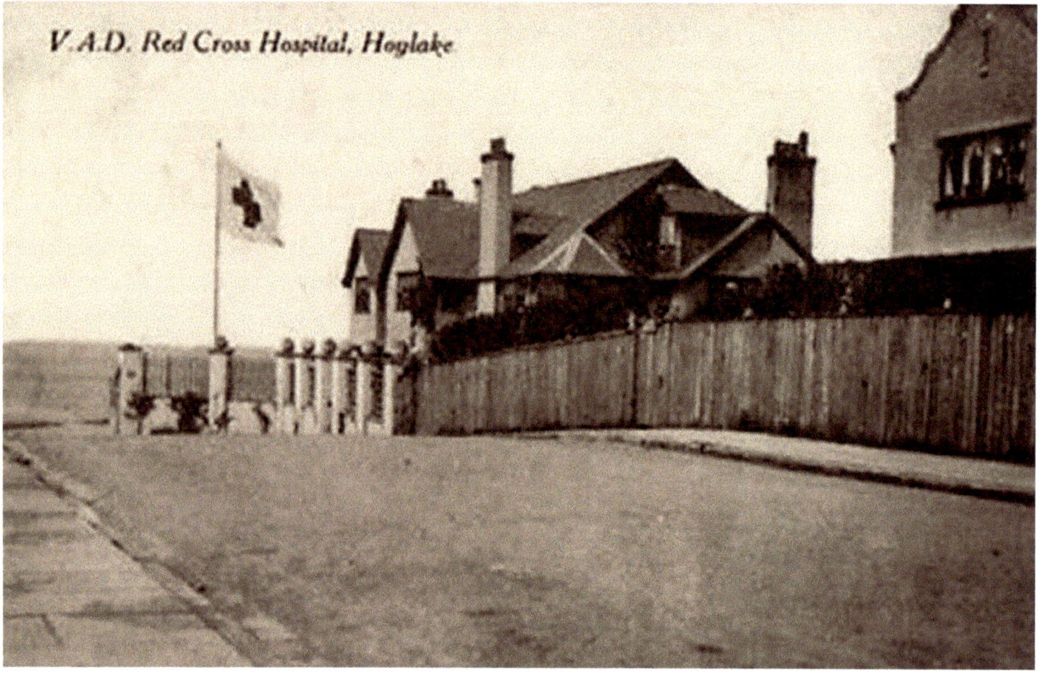

Hoylake Red Cross Hospital.

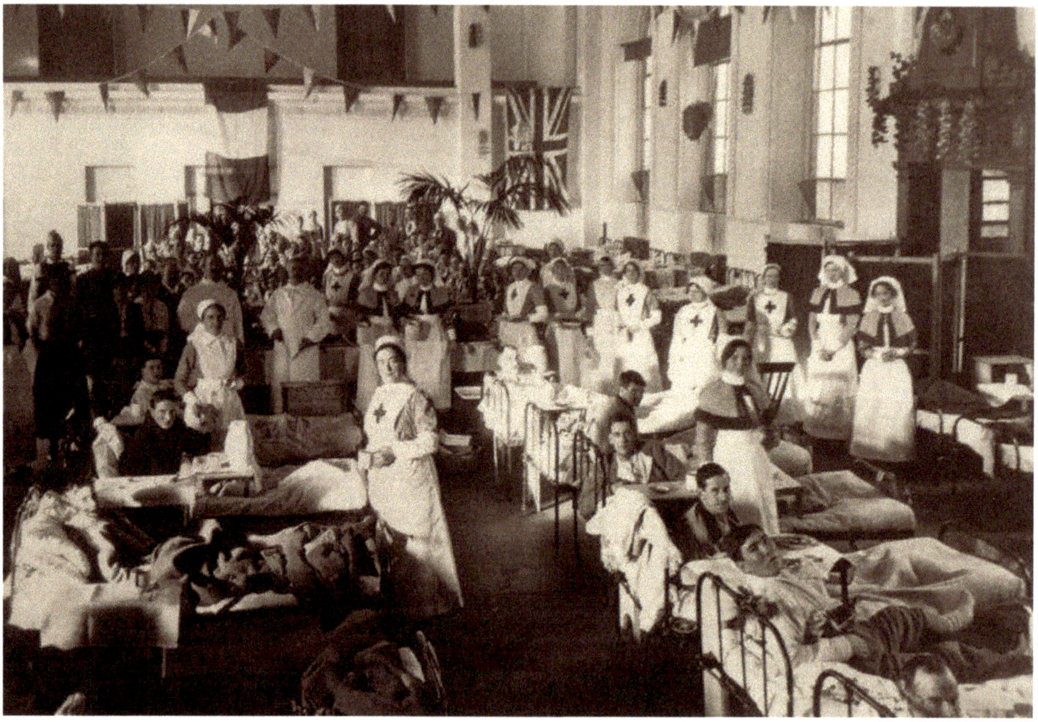

Wallasey Town Hall military hospital.

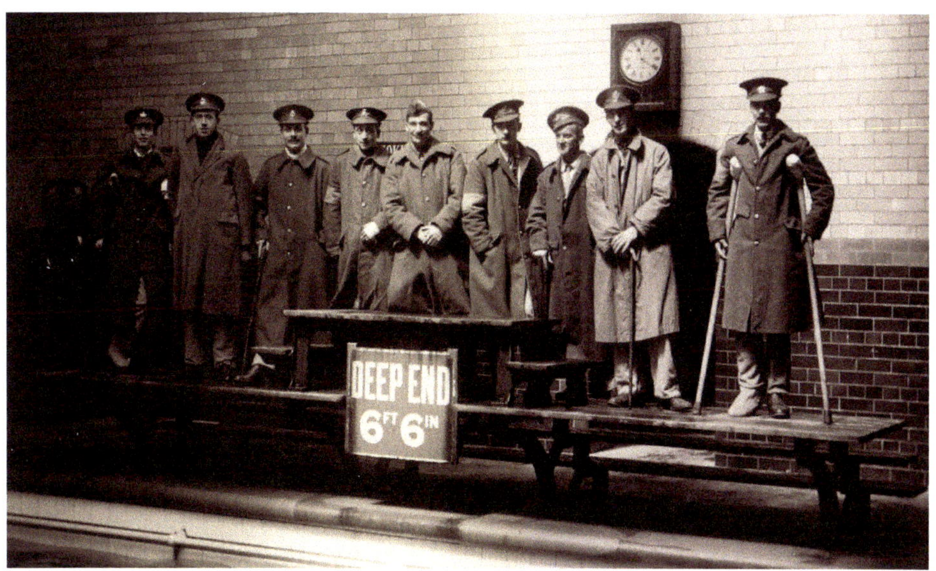

Soldier patients arriving to use hydrotherapy facilities at Guinea Gap Baths.

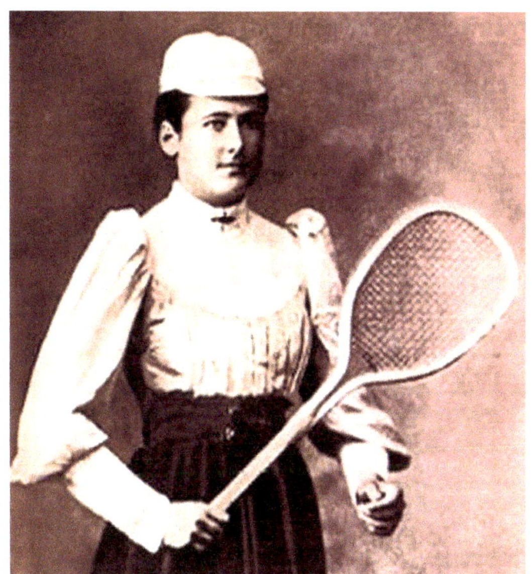

Born on 24 September 1871 in Bebington, Wirral, Charlotte 'Lottie' Dod won the Wimbledon Ladies' Singles Tennis Championship five times. She joined Rock Ferry Tennis Club at the age of eleven, and within four years she was Wimbledon Champion in 1887. At the age of just fifteen, this is still the record for the youngest ladies' singles champion. She successfully competed in so many other sports (including a silver medal at the 1908 Summer Olympics in archery) that the *Guinness Book of Records* has named her as the most versatile female athlete of all time. Her brother Willy also won the Olympic gold medal in archery at the 1908 games. She worked for the British Red Cross during wartime from November 1916 at Chelsea VAD Hospital, and in a military hospital in Speen, Berkshire. She was awarded the Red Cross Service Medal for serving more than 1,000 hours during the conflict. After the war, she continued to attend Wimbledon every year into her late eighties. She passed away in 1960 at the age of eighty-eight in Sway, Hampshire.

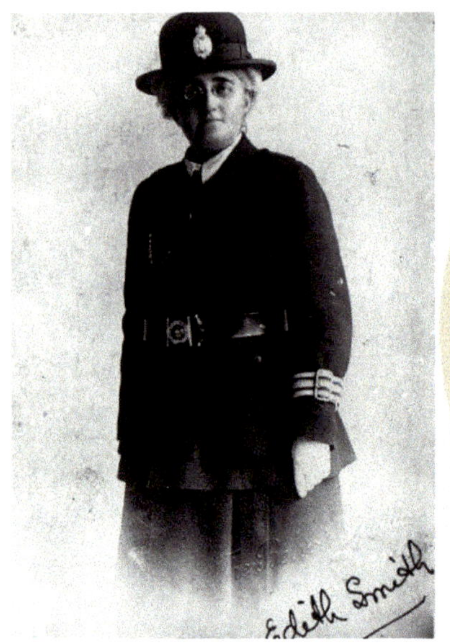

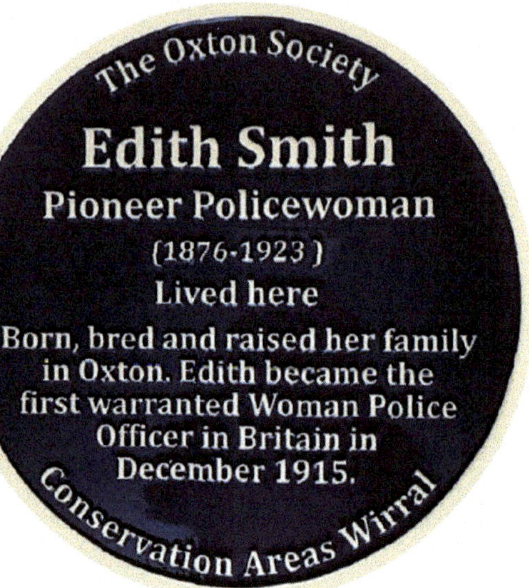

Edith Smith became the first warranted female police officer in the United Kingdom in December 1915 with full power of arrest. She was born on 21 November 1876, in Oxton, Birkenhead, where she lived until moving to London to work as a midwife. She volunteered with the Women's Police during the First World War, and later moved to Runcorn to work for a nursing association where she died on 26 June 1923. On 16 June 2018 the Oxton Society placed a plaque at No. 18 Palm Hill, Oxton village, where Edith Smith grew up.

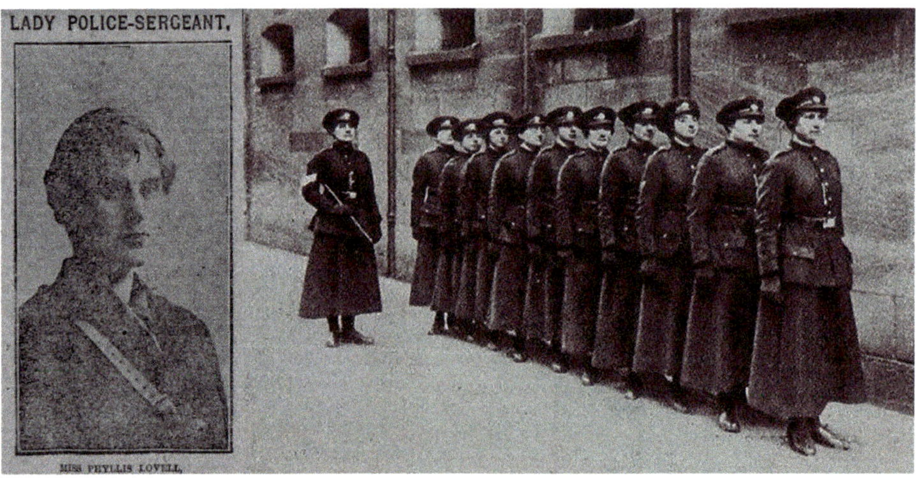

'A War-Time Innovation in Birkenhead: Women-Police. Smart, well set-up, and obviously in earnest, this squad of women-police is seen starting duty, having been enrolled for the work of ordinary constables. It may be hoped that the "enterprising burglar" will "cease from burgling" in the districts which these patriotic young women will patrol.'

Suffragette Phyllis Lovell founded the Liverpool Women's Home Service Corps in 1915, which recruited 2,000 women members and worked closely with local police services. She was instrumental in the formation of the Birkenhead Police Aid Detachment in January 1917 and was appointed Sergeant-in-Charge. The first ten police women were also enrolled, and were employed on normal patrols, but without the power of arrest.

Chapter 5

Armistice and Home Again

As the war moved into the autumn of 1918 and approached the day of Armistice, the battlefront at home was becoming increasingly entrenched as hardships were taking their toll. Increased rationing, unemployment, and the devastating effect of losing family members to the conflict were becoming the norm to most, to which there was now added a ravaging illness spreading across the country. There was increasing concern in government, both local and national, as treatment for the disease seemed ineffectual, and it was beginning to reach epidemic proportions. In north Wirral it was reported,

> Unfortunately, there does not appear to be any appreciable check to the ravages of influenza in Birkenhead, and the undertakers in the town are still unable to fully cope with the large numbers of fatal cases. It is a grim experience to witness the despatch of coffins on their tragic journeys in the dark hours of the night, and it brings vividly to the imagination the serious nature of the epidemic. So far, Birkenhead has not followed the latest regulations observed in Liverpool with regard to the earlier start of theatrical performances. Had there really been any need to take similar precautions they would have been taken, but the theatres and cinemas generally in Birkenhead have always been models of good ventilation.
>
> *Birkenhead News*, November 1918

Initially, doctors had called it the 'three-day fever', as in many cases recovery had been swift, but it was soon apparent that this was no ordinary outbreak, and would soon result in the highest mortality rate for any epidemic since the outbreak of cholera in 1849. Its affects could be devastatingly swift. Those fit and well in the morning could be dead by the evening. Pneumonia or septicaemia developed in around a fifth of cases, which often progressed to heliotrope cyanosis, a lavender hue of the skin that signalled shortage of oxygen and imminent death.

It starts with what appears to be an ordinary attack of *la grippe* [so called by soldiers in France]. When brought to the hospital, patients very rapidly develop the most vicious type of pneumonia that has ever been seen. Two hours after admission, they have mahogany spots over the cheekbones, and a few hours later you can begin to see the cyanosis [blueness due to lack of oxygen] extending from their ears and spreading all over the face. It is only a matter of a few hours then until death comes, and it is simply a struggle for air until they suffocate. It is horrible.

Professor Roy Grist, Glasgow physician, 29 September 1918

As the influenza epidemic spread across the country during the last months of the war, the death toll escalated, with final figures estimated at around 228,000. As we have witnessed from 2020 onwards with Covid-19, this became a pandemic of epic proportions and is one aspect of the First World War that the world today has arguably the greatest empathy. The First World War outbreak was, in fact, a strain of the H1N1 influenza virus (the second pandemic of this strain was in 2009) and infected a staggering 500 million people worldwide between January 1919 and December 1920, even reaching remote Pacific islands and the Arctic. Statistics vary a great deal, and it has been estimated that it killed between 3 and 5 per cent of the world's population, death rates varying between 50 to 100 million, one of the deadliest natural disasters in human history. Reportage on Britain was supressed to an extent under DORA, so as to maintain wartime morale, but in Spain, news was less restricted, and due to this selective reporting at home, it was widely believed that Spain was uniquely hit hard, resulting in the nickname 'Spanish flu' for the pandemic.

Of course, the nature of warfare on the Western Front – the tight-knit units, and huge troop movement – undoubtedly increased the transmission of the virus, and may have even made it more lethal. The fact that soldiers' personal defences and immune systems were at a very low ebb due to malnourishment, injuries, chemical attacks and battle fatigue all increased their chances of infection. Extensive studies have also looked at the source of the outbreak but without any firm conclusions. A British team led by virologist John Oxford of St Bartholomew's Hospital and the Royal London Hospital have pointed the finger at the major troop staging and hospital camp in Étaples, France, as almost certainly being the centre of the pandemic. There is also the suggestion that an early form of the virus was harboured in birds and mutated to the pigs that were kept near to the Front.

The authorities were ill-equipped to cope with the epidemic, especially given the state of the nation's infrastructure after four years of war. Hospitals and staff were overwhelmed, treatments were largely ineffective, and there were no antibiotics against secondary problems such as pneumonia. The public health authorities took up fundamental measures to control epidemics that dated back to the medieval times of the bubonic plague. They aimed to reduce the transmission by preventing contact. Good ventilation and the avoidance of contact were the way forward, which, declared the British Medical Journal on 19 October 1918, 'the best of all general measures for prevention, and this implies the avoidance of crowded meetings'. Public gatherings were discouraged, and town councils closed theatres, dance halls, churches and cinemas. Streets were sprayed with chemicals and people wore anti-germ masks. Some factories even relaxed smoking bans and allowed workers to smoke on-site, believing that cigarettes would help prevent infection. Many schools began to close in early November. Meanwhile, on 3 November 1918, the *News of the World* suggested several anti-flu precautions:

> Wash inside the nose with soap and water each night and morning; force yourself to sneeze night and morning, then breathe deeply; do not wear a muffler; take sharp walks regularly and walk home from work; eat plenty of porridge.

But despite all these valiant attempts, treatments devised to cope with this new strain of influenza were proving to be completely futile, while at the same time, newspapers were carrying reports of Germany and Austria wanting peace talks. This too would be futile, as still the war continued, the Allies pressing for outright victory. Finally, this came on 11 November 1918; the Armistice was signed, and the war was over. A few days later the Birkenhead News reported,

THE FIRST WEEK OF THE PEACE
A NEW BIRKENHEAD AND A HAPPIER ONE

After 1,559 days of war, peace came to the world on Monday. The special services of thanksgiving with which it was hailed in Birkenhead were fully described in our Wednesday's issue, but some aspects of the week's doings are worthy of placing on record for the benefit of the local historian of the future.

There were not wanting those who made much of the coincidence that the terms of the Armistice between the Entente Allies and Germany came into force at 11.00am on the eleventh day of the eleventh month of the year, at which time such a pandemonium was let loose locally that many people's heads, as well as the welkin, fairly rang. The notes of sirens and buzzer, mingled with the discharge of guns, and wherever two or three people were gathered together, there was hearty cheering for the British Army. Flags and every kind of bunting sprang into being on all hands as if by magic, and most wonderful of all, considering how repressive has been the hand of 'DORA' upon the small boy, fireworks were in evidence everywhere. 'This makes up for what we missed on November 5th', said one youngster as he touched off a 'French cannon', and to many of the boys November 11th was a glorified Guy Fawkes – with the Kaiser as the guy.

Work people 'downed tools' with one accord, and at one large works practically the whole of the week was taken as a holiday. This would have been a serious matter a few days ago when munitions were still urgently needed, but now, well 'it is not every day we celebrate peace' as one of the munitions girls said. The prevailing epidemic of holiday-making affected even the tram service on Monday, but the ferries' employees 'stuck to the ship' and garnered a rich harvest for the Corporation. Large crowds of people carrying flags crowded the streets, and bands discoursed national airs, even the

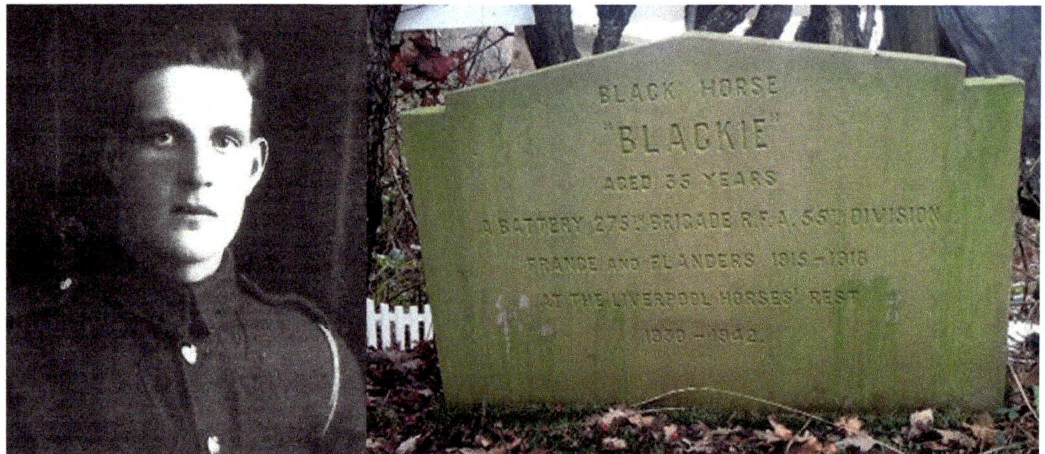

Second Lieutenant Leonard Comer Wall RFA and Blackie the war horse. Second Lieutenant Leonard Comer Wall of West Kirby served with the RFA and was Mentioned in Despatches. He was killed in action during the Battle of Messines on 9 June 1917, at the age of twenty. He made special provision in his will for his war horse, Blackie, who had gone with him from Liverpool to France, to be cared for in the event of his death. When Blackie died at the 'Horse's Rest' in Halewood in 1942, he was buried there with his former master's war medals. The grave was given Grade II listed status in December 2017, the first of its kind in the country. (The full story of 2nd Lt Wall and Blackie can be found here: www.roydenhistory.co.uk/mrlhp/articles/ww1/ww1.htm)

Salvation Army musicians bursting into the 'Marseillaise' and what a time a number of soldiers and girls had energetically dancing a two-step. For the first time in many weary months the Town Hall clock chimed the hours, and sweet music were the joy bells, of which alas! Only two full peals exist in Birkenhead.

As the evening wore on, illuminations, which were as novel as they were beautiful, were to be seen on every hand, and even the street lamps were allowed to shine with unaccustomed brightness. Bonfires were lit, and the 'specials' who had been called out to augment the regular police force turned a blind eye to many defiances of those lighting regulations which should now become a thing of the past. Places of amusement were crowded to their utmost capacity, and for the nonce [*ie. this particular moment*] almost everyone seemed to be given over to merry-making. The pessimist who had been predicting another winter campaign was forgotten, and the only other fly in the ointment was the strictly limited supply of beer and other intoxicants. It may have been partly due to this, but it was also owing to the good sense of the people, that the sad manner in which the war has come home to many, that the rejoicings were much of a more sober character than was the case in the days of the Boer War, and the police state that the townspeople were wonderfully orderly for such an auspicious occasion. Those who had only known the gloomy Birkenhead of the war, were surprised and delighted at the new condition of things, and happiest people of all were the school children who by a coincidence, which was happy for them at least, were enjoying an extra week's holiday on account of the influenza epidemic. Thus, peace came to Birkenhead and the Wirral – a district which has nobly done its share in the war.

Birkenhead and Cheshire Advertiser and Wallasey Guardian, 16 November 1918

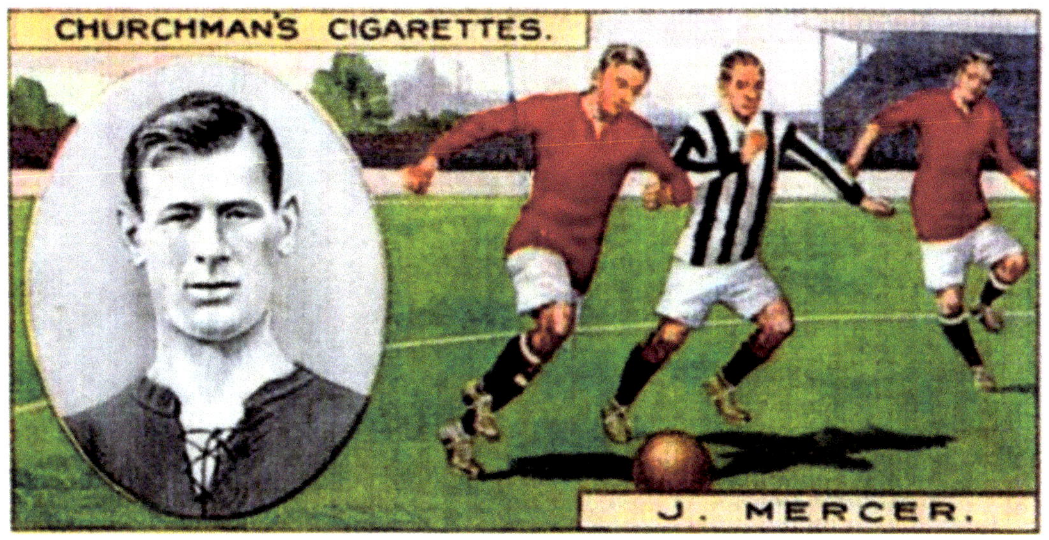

Joe Mercer (Nottingham Forest).

SERGEANT JOSEPH MERCER, 17TH SERVICE (FOOTBALL) BATTALION, MIDDLESEX REGIMENT

As the military began its demobilisation, the end of the war also saw the return home of thousands of prisoners of war. One such soldier from the Wirral was Joe Mercer, originally from Higher Bebington, who at the outbreak of war had been playing as a centre-half for Nottingham Forest, then in the top flight. In December 1914 he had enlisted in the 17th Service (Football) Battalion of the Middlesex Regiment, the recently formed 'Football Pals' unit. Mercer served in the Battle of the Somme where he was wounded before being taken prisoner. After the war he resumed his career at Nottingham Forest, before returning to the Wirral in 1921 to play for Tranmere Rovers.

Considering he had taken a bullet to the shoulder, shrapnel in the head, wounds to the leg, then resumed a physically demanding career, it is surprising that his death in 1927 was caused by health problems resulting from a gas attack in the trenches ten years earlier. To have coped with such handicaps in his post-war career is remarkable. Something to consider next time the latest player dives like a swan and rolls over half a dozen times, after a passing defender happens to cause a heavy draft of air turbulence. When Mercer went down, he really had been shot.

PRIVATE 3612 TOM MCNAUGHT, 1/10TH BATTALION (SCOTTISH), THE KING'S (LIVERPOOL REGIMENT)

Tom McNaught was born in 1892 in Renfrew, Scotland, but grew up in Birkenhead, where his father, George, was an Inspector of Ships' Provisions. After his education

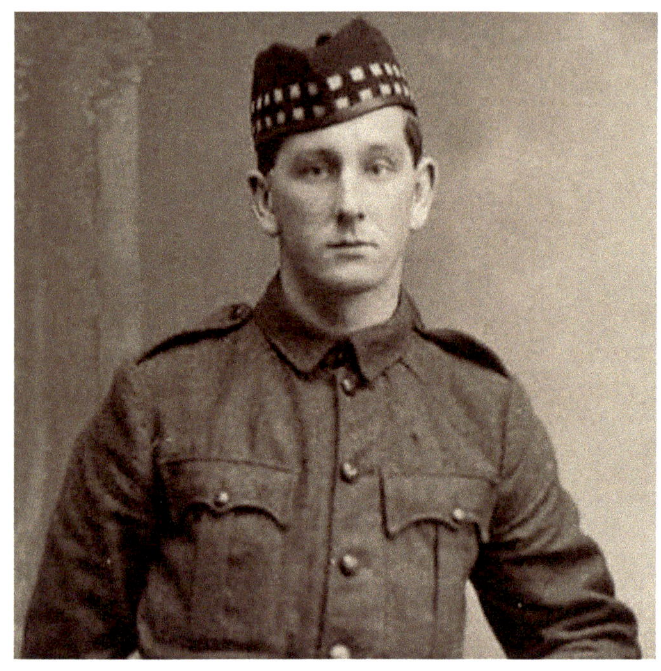

Private 3612 Tom McNaught,
1/10th Battalion (Scottish), The
King's (Liverpool Regiment).

at Birkenhead Institute, he trained as a teacher at Borough Road College in London, but had returned to teach in Rock Ferry Council School while also turning out for Tranmere Rovers FC reserves, and as centre-forward for Hoylake FC, at the time war broke out. He joined the 1st/10th Battalion Liverpool Scottish (The King's Liverpool Regiment) on 12 September 1914, but just three weeks after arriving in France on 23 January, he was killed in action on 12 March 1915 whilst running in the trenches with bandages to help other wounded comrades. Although buried in Lillebeck, Belgium, with fallen comrades, his body was never recovered following the later carnage, and he is remembered on the Menin Gate Memorial to the Missing in Ypres, Belgium, as well as on the Birkenhead War Memorial in Hamilton Square.

The strength of character that had seen many men through the war was to be tested even further on their return. The brave new world they had fought for was not as it had been promised. It soon became obvious that prospects for the returning soldiers were not good. Despite the lauded political rhetoric of 'land and homes fit for heroes', there would be inadequate support regarding housing, pensions and welfare, and unemployment was rising.

The local factories and industry began reverting to its pre-war patterns of long hours, hard work and poor pay. And if you were not prepared to comply, there were plenty more who would take your place. Some local men were more fortunate. The Wirral Battalion raised at Port Sunlight had been promised their jobs on their return by Lord Leverhulme at the works recruitment meeting back in 1914. Following the Armistice, families at home were now expecting their menfolk to turn up within days, but the reality was very different.

Of those soldiers who were regulars and still serving in their normal period, they would remain in the army until their term was completed, but those who were volunteers or conscripted for the duration of the war understandably hoped to return home at once. However, this was not feasible, as it was physically impossible to cope with processing so many men so quickly. Furthermore, the British Army was still on operations, even though the firing may have stopped. A continued military presence was required as the Army moved into Germany, and other regiments, including the 17th Battalion, King's Liverpool Regiment (Liverpool Pals) were despatched to Russia in the unrest following the revolution. Their Russian campaign lasted several months into 1919, before gradual withdrawal, with the remnants of the battalion finally leaving for home on the SS *Kildonan* on 2 September. The 18th Battalion, King's Liverpool Regiment – one of the Liverpool Pals battalions which had trained at Hooton – found themselves marching to the Rhine with the British occupation force until orders were changed. Instead they went to Huy in Belgium, then to Assesse and Natoye, before arriving at Antwerp on 19 May 1919, returning for England on the SS *Sicilian* five days later.

Men who fitted certain criteria were released early; for example, those with industrial skills now scarce at home, such as miners. Men who volunteered in the early stages of the war were also given priority, generally leaving the conscripts, especially those who were aged eighteen in 1918, to the last. Most men were home by the end of 1919, but for them the war seemed to be dragging on and on.

But for many others the 1920s remained a struggle, and for those who had secured work, many found themselves on the scrapheap once more after the crash of 1929. As the depression years moved towards September 1939, for those men who had fought and endured so much in this so-called war to end all wars, how dejected and disheartened they must have felt as they saw the country edge to war with the same enemy once more. This time the Home Front would face hostilities and hardship on an even greater scale, and witness destruction and loss of life much closer to hand as large areas of our cities would be laid waste.

PART 2
THE SECOND WORLD WAR

HMS *THETIS*

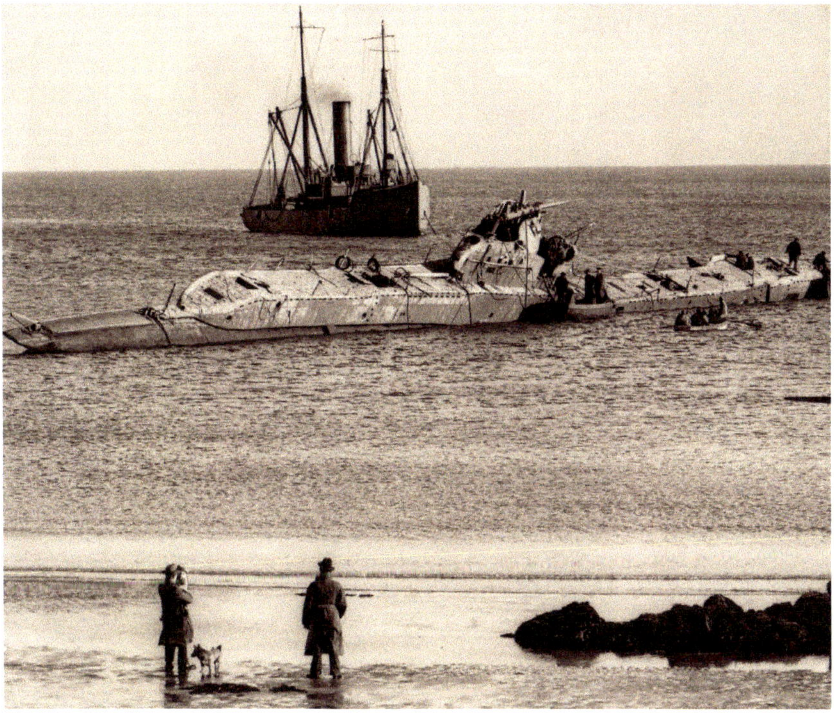

At the start of the war, people of Wirral were still dealing with the HMS *Thetis* tragedy. Built at Cammell Lairds and launched on 29 June 1938, the Royal Navy T-class submarine sank just a few miles off the Great Orme in Llandudno, while undergoing sea trials on 1 June 1939. The sinking was due to complications with an outer hatch being open at the same time as a torpedo tube. Only four men survived out of the 103 on board, and a diver also died in the attempted rescue. The photo shows her during salvage work on 8 November 1939, after her intentional grounding at Traeth Bychan, Anglesey, on Sunday 3 September, the day that war was declared. The casualties that had not been recovered by the salvage team were now brought out to a naval funeral, with full honours. After her salvage, she was repaired, and recommissioned as HMS *Thunderbolt* in 1940. She was lost during war service with all hands in the Mediterranean on 14 March 1943.

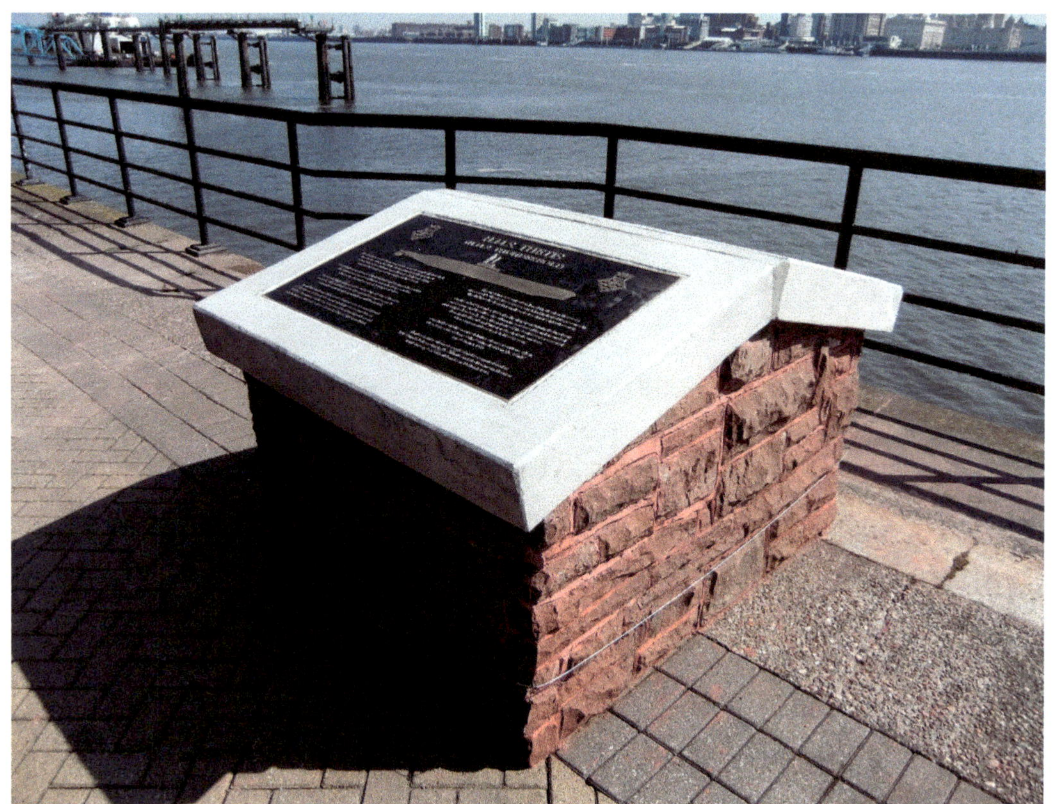

A memorial to those lost on the HMS *Thetis* stands at Woodside, Birkenhead.

Chapter 6

The Phoney War

When the dreaded news of war came through yesterday, members of the public in the streets looked perhaps a little more thoughtful, but carried on with whatever they were about.

It was a beautiful day. The sun has hardly been hotter this summer and at times there was a pleasant breeze. Usually on a Sunday morning there are numbers of people moving around, principally making their way across the water or to the trains. After the Prime Minister made his dramatic announcement over the wireless, people who had heard it went onto the streets and simply said, 'War!' to all whom they met, strangers included.

Receivers of the news uttered, 'I thought so', and went on their way.

Liverpool Daily Post, Monday 4 September 1939

Chamberlain's announcement was certainly no surprise. On a local level, preparations were already well underway, and this was just the expected confirmation, reflected in the calm on the streets. Local authorities had already been putting plans for defence and local safety in place for some time. A structure of command was introduced from the outset in compliance with Home Office directives, all reporting to the government's Regional Commissioner for Civil Defence. The Birkenhead 'Controller' was the Town Clerk, while in Wallasey, it was the Chief Constable; in Bebington and other rural areas it was the Chief Constable of Cheshire. Liverpool Town Clerk acted as Group Controller, and to whom the Emergency Committee, which comprised representatives from all the Civil Defence and technical services, would report directly.

At the time of the broadcast, hundreds of schoolchildren were being evacuated from Birkenhead stations, an operation that was already well established. The Government Evacuation Scheme was developed as early as the summer of 1938. The zones to be evacuated were published in the local press on 10 January 1939, while Public Information Leaflet No. 3 was circulated to parents, schools, churches and other authorities, which explained all aspects of the scheme, under which the at-risk areas of Birkenhead and Wallasey were included. Parents were instructed to take their children to school at the prescribed time, with their food for the day, plus basic luggage, and not forgetting their gas masks.

Around 9,000 children left their schools shortly before nine o'clock on the morning of 1 September and caught trains for reception areas distributed over a wide area, mainly in North Wales, Cheshire and Shropshire. During the day, fifteen trains left Birkenhead, six from Woodside Station, six from Park Station, and another three from direct from Rock Ferry. According to those in charge, the evacuation scheme worked with exceptional smoothness, while trains left the stations on time.

BIRKENHEAD

FIRST CHILDREN LEAVE FOR NORTH WALES

The children regarded the whole affair as an interesting experience, and while waiting to go to the station sang songs heartily. Outside, mothers stood to watch the youngsters leave and gave them a cheering send off.

The children regarded the whole affair as a huge holiday. They had assembled in their classrooms, and were greatly delighted at the idea of going away, and sang songs, such as 'John Brown's Body', and 'The Lambeth Walk'. To carry their spare clothing, the children had been provided with a variety of containers from pillowcases to rucksacks and haversacks.

Officials from the Education department, the staff of which, under the direction of Mr G.B. Dempsey, the Director of Education, has been responsible for working out the details of the evacuation scheme, were at the stations with guides and helpers to supervise the despatching of the scholars. The teachers accompanied the children to the different areas and will assist in their education.

Today, tomorrow and on Monday, other children will be evacuated from the town, fifteen trains being due to leave each day, until the whole of the 16,000 to 17,000 children from the town's priority classes will have been evacuated. After the children have been evacuated, all the schools in the town will be closed. The evacuation does not apply to areas like Prenton, Upton and Thingwall.

WALLASEY

Removal from their homes of Wallasey schoolchildren in the Seacombe and Poulton areas, accompanied by teachers and helpers, and numbering in all about 3,700, was carried out in perfect order.

The first train left Poulton Station at nine o'clock, followed by two other trains from that station and four from Seacombe at intervals up to two o'clock. The destination of the evacuees was in the Deeside area, and in no one case did the train journey exceed half an hour.

Adults with children under five and expectant mothers, numbering in all nearly 3,000 are to be evacuated by train today, while the blind and crippled evacuees will be conveyed by bus from the arranged collecting centres.

The first evacuees to arrive in Flintshire were chosen from five Wallasey schools. There was a large crowd at the station to watch them disembark, and the children looked happy and quite at ease as they marched to the reception centre.

74

A Wallasey schoolmaster said, 'The arrangements have gone through without a hitch. The children will be kept in school groups, which will be billeted together.

Liverpool Echo, 1 September 1939

Time went on, and we never listened or wanted to know about all the ugly talk of impending war. War? - who cared? - we were young - nothing could touch us, life was a big adventure and war could never happen. Ah, but it did! I do so remember getting ready to go out on a lovely autumn afternoon, and we had the radio on. The announcement came, and to me it didn't mean so much - but the faces of the older people - my mother and father, and granny – were shocked and tense.

The next thing we knew was that the younger children had to be evacuated. The two younger boys, Jack and Jim had to go. I remember going to see them off at Woodside Station. They had their gas masks in boxes and a string for them to slip over their shoulder, and big labels pinned to their coats giving their names and destination. Our boys were going to a place called Weston Rhyn, which was in Shropshire, and they were so very unhappy. Jack was in tears and poor little Jim looked so lost and bewildered. My sister Nell and I were in tears, and I know that mother was very close to tears, but she tried so hard not to alarm the children, and finally they boarded the train and off they went. In silence we walked home. Over a cup of tea, we told Granny about it and then started to reason with each other, finding comfort as we could, in saying it was all for the best, it was the law now anyway. We were at war, and they dropped bombs during a war didn't they? - people got killed. No, the boys were better off in the country.

Nora Gauterin, Unpublished Memoir, November 2016

Worried parents were reassured that there was plenty of bedding, and children on arrival would be taken to various chapels and churches for a meal. They would then be personally conducted to their new homes. Furthermore, the allocations had been made with great care and there would be no overcrowding. Organisers assured that a warm welcome would be waiting for the children who were heading for rural

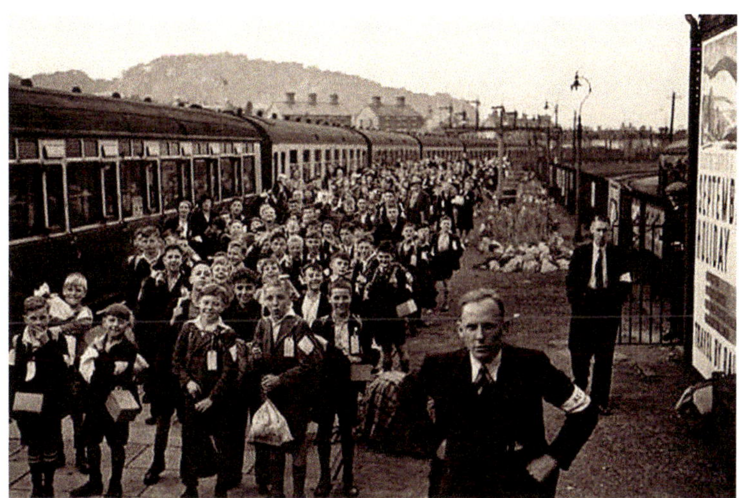

Birkenhead children arriving in Oswestry.

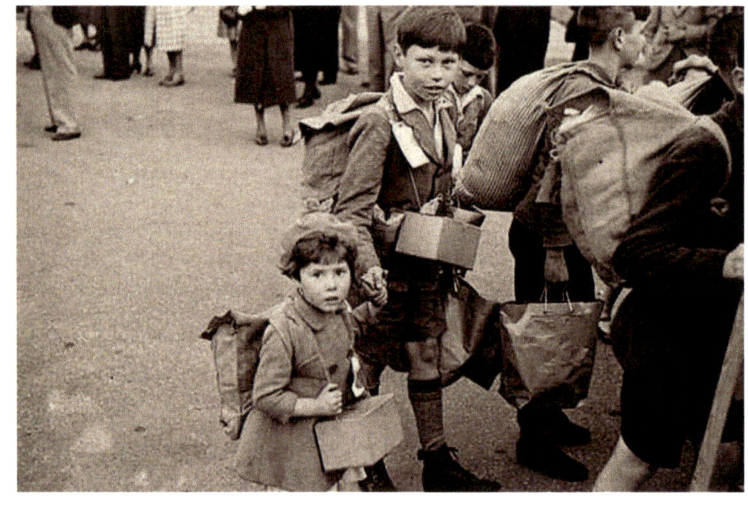

Birkenhead children arriving in Oswestry.

Cheshire and Shropshire. Arrangements for their reception had been in place for a few months, and after refreshments, a fleet of buses would be laid on to take them to their new homes in the villages. But despite the reassuring official reports in the press that all was going well, it was certainly not the case for everyone,

> We were herded like cattle around the streets of Oswestry, officials knocking on the doors of those who had put their names down as wanting an evacuee. That person come out of his house and chose whom they like the look of. It was total chaos. Some children were still being walked around the streets at midnight.
>
> Margaret Corlett, *Our Evacuee*, Oswestry Heritage Centre

[Margaret and her brother, Harold, were evacuated from Birkenhead. Margaret remembers that she 'was billeted by 9pm', so she was lucky compared to some other children. She stayed with Mr and Mrs Cyril Brayne and their son, John, who was aged seven when she arrived. Margaret went back home to Birkenhead in 1942.]

Institutions and schools were kept together as far as possible, often evacuated en bloc. The Royal School for the Blind in Liverpool was evacuated to Rhyl, boys from the Birkenhead Institute were sent to Oswestry High School, while the children from the Royal Liverpool Seamen's Orphan Institution, based in Newsham Park, were evacuated to the Hill Bark estate in Frankby on the Wirral. The house and grounds were owned by shipowner Ernest Royden, who was a member of the institution's Executive Committee (due to the active interest the Royden family had taken in the safety of ships at sea, and care for its seamen for over a century). The extensive grounds of Hill Bark were ideal for what the RLSOI required. The evacuation took place on 11 September 1939, and wooden huts were built for sleeping, schooling and playing, with separate accommodation for girls and boys. A separate hut was built near the stables to be used as the dining room, while part of the stables became the bathing area. Toilets were built in front of the stables, although they often froze up

76

during very cold weather. The children were assigned tasks to keep the camp running, and at the age of fourteen they had to leave and find employment and accommodation elsewhere. The orphanage stayed at Hill Bark for nine years, returning to Liverpool in July 1948. Phyllis Gallimore was five when she went to live at Newsham, and like many other children who were evacuated, life improved during the war. She recalled,

The war was one of the best things that ever happened for us children. It was an absolute relief. All the old harsh masters and mistresses left, and we got a whole era of new teachers who cared for us. We got the countryside, and a fantastic place to live. It was heaven for us kids. Everything was so much easier. I was nine by the time we went to live in Frankby. When we arrived on the estate, they'd built a lot of huts to house the younger children, but us older ones had a dormitory up in the big house. There were secret rooms up there, great panelled rooms and recessed windows. I was a real bookworm as a kid, but had been deprived of them at the orphanage. I used to love climbing up into these big windows with a book, drawing the curtains round so no one could see, and hiding away for hours. Any spare time I had, that's where I'd spend it. There was no domestic staff, so because I was one of the older ones I used to help look after the youngies. I used to do everything for those children – bath them, darn their socks, clean their shoes, see they were at school every morning... that was my job. I used to love knitting, but during the War you couldn't get knitting needles. I remember we used to knit scarves on nine-inch nails! I even made a pair of slippers on them! Overall, I saw it as a positive experience. The orphanage was cruel, but Frankby was a fantastic place to live. I learnt how to look after myself – and others – when I was very young, and grew up very independent. I brought my children up to be very independent too. I always say to them – 'If you want anything, there's the world, now go out and get it'.
Life in the orphanage, BBC *Your Memories* website, 3 November 2008

Edna Robertson also recalled her time there:

Mr Royden was such a kind man, if ever we met him on our walks around the grounds, he'd always find time to have a chat to us. I remember going to his wife's funeral too in 1947. I just think it is so sad that Mr Royden is gone and forgotten – but not by me. I don't think anyone today would share their beautiful home with a crowd of young boys and girls, the senior girls had a dormitory in the house and we also had a sanatorium in there. At Christmas and prize-giving days, he let us use the Great Hall to receive our awards. I loved Frankby, and living on the Royden estate was a privilege and the happiest memories I have. When my children were young, I went over there and took them on all the lovely walks I went on as a child, and my eldest son takes his children over there now.

Of course, not all experiences were as happy as at Hill Bark. One of the most traumatic evacuations took place on Guernsey prior to the Nazi occupation. Around 5,000 children were brought to the mainland before being put onto trains and taken with their school teachers to many parts of England and Scotland, where they were to remain for the next five years. (The IoM Steam Packet vessel SS *Viking*, crewed by men from the Isle of Man and Merseyside, evacuated almost

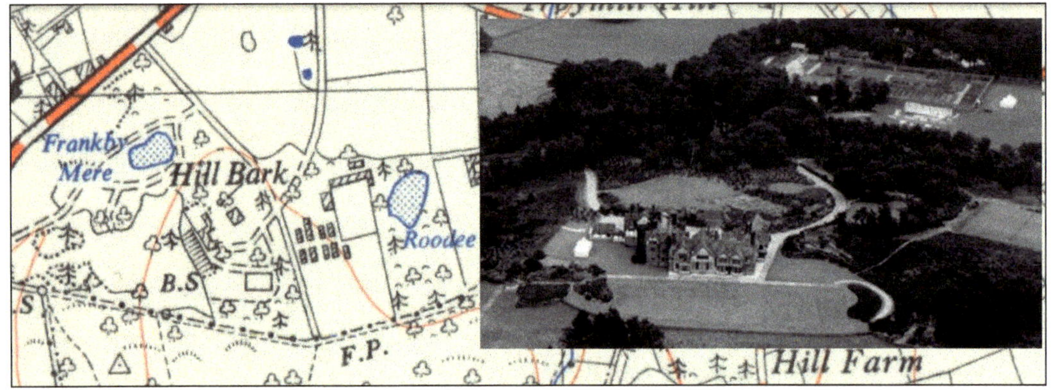

Map of Hill Bark showing the evacuation camp between the house and Roodee Mere. *Right:* Aerial view of Hill Bark at the start of the war. The evacuation camp can be seen at the top of the photograph.

the entire child population of the island, running the gauntlet of air attacks while steaming from St Peter Port to Weymouth*.) Some of the children were brought to Birkenhead, where they were allocated homes:

Financial gain sometimes played its part in the fostering of evacuees, and Rosemary Hall and her brother suffered in a Birkenhead billet: My brother and I stood in a church hall for ages, people wanted me but not my brother. A woman said, 'I will have the little girl' but she was told 'They don't want to be separated.' The woman said 'I don't want two of them.' The Salvation Army said, 'If you take them both you will get nearly 20 shillings a week to keep them.' The woman quickly changed her mind and we spent a horrendous four months sleeping on camp beds in her hallway behind the front door. We weren't allowed in any other part of the house except the hall and the lavatory in the backyard, we were constantly hungry. She clearly took us in to get the regular twenty shillings. After four months, our mum tracked us down. She knocked on the door of the house, saw the state of us, and removed us immediately from the premises without waiting for the woman to come back from the shops. She took us into a little flat that she had found in Bury. We were much happier there.'

Gillian Mawsom, *Guernsey Evacuees:*
The Forgotten Evacuees of the Second World War (2012)

[*For the roll played by the SS Viking, see Mike Royden, *Ferries to the Rescue* www. roydenhistory.co.uk/mrlhp/articles/ww2/ww2.htm pp.41-44]

A happier time was experienced by Guernsey evacuees in Irby:

St Andrew's school from Guernsey was evacuated to Irby, together with teachers Mabel le Pelley, Winifred Woodgate, Peter Cherry and the Headmaster, Lester Robilliard, who were given Irby Village Hall to set up school, while the children were taken in by local families. Don Broster was a little lad at the time, and his mother took in two boys to their home at Caves Farm. Eventually, Mr and Mrs Broster took in seven lads. Caves Farm was quite a large working farm, the young refugees loved living there and were a great help. Mr and Mrs Broster also took in bombed-out children from Wallasey. After the war, Mrs Broster and Don were invited over to Guernsey for a reunion, and to stay with the family of Charlie Pinchemain, one of the seven lads they had taken in. They were made very welcome by the Pinchemain family, who worked on farms and market gardens. In the summer of 2017 Don Broster's daughter Shelley went over to Guernsey for a holiday and visited Charlie Pinchemain who is now 87, and the last of the seven Guernsey lads who spent the war years with the Brosters at Caves Farm.

Greg Dawson, 'Why the Guernsey Children came to Irby in the Second World War',
Heswall & District Magazine, August 2017

Preparations for the blackout had commenced in July 1939, and air-raid regulations came into force on 1 September. Civilian ARP wardens were responsible for enforcement, ensuring that no building allowed the slightest chink or glow of light. Offenders were liable to stringent legal penalties, which were regularly imposed in the local courts. Wardens had to report the extent of bomb damage to the control centre, and assess the local need for help from the emergency and rescue services. Volunteers had also been signing on for various roles in the emergency services, including fire-watchers, who would monitor enemy movements in the night sky, usually from rooftops, ready to report attacks and damage. Many were stationed at their workplace on a rota basis while still being expected in to work the next day.

After this front-line, a second line was also put into place consisting of the Women's Voluntary Service, which would help care for survivors and those made homeless by manning rest centres in community halls and churches. Support came from the Public Assistance Committee and the British War Relief Society, which provided clothes and bedding and small sums of money. There were also teams of drivers and volunteers manning mobile canteens serving tea, sandwiches and soup to emergency and rescue workers grateful for a moment's respite.

The government provided protection in homes in the form of Anderson shelters for those with gardens, while Morrison shelters could be used indoors, designed as cages to fit under the kitchen table, with just enough space for a small family to squeeze into. Communal shelters were constructed across the region to provide cover for those in terrace housing, flats and tenements, or those on the move around the city when the air-raid siren sounded. Gas masks were issued to everyone by the government, and came in three sizes, while Public Gas Cleaning Centres were set up for immediate treatment in the event of a gas attack.

In Birkenhead and Tranmere, there was the particular problem of how to protect large factory workforces and dock workers. It was essential for the war effort that all were working to maximum efficiency, especially the crucial work being carried out by Cammell Laird. Consequently, the Town Council laid down plans to construct two large civilian air-raid shelters in Tranmere and Bidston for the protection of Cammell Laird employees and their families. It was a vast undertaking and took over two years to build, stretching over 6,500 feet underground, and when complete was designed to hold bunks and seats for over 6,000 people. The result was one of the country's largest wartime bunkers. Facilities included dormitories, kitchens, a canteen, medical

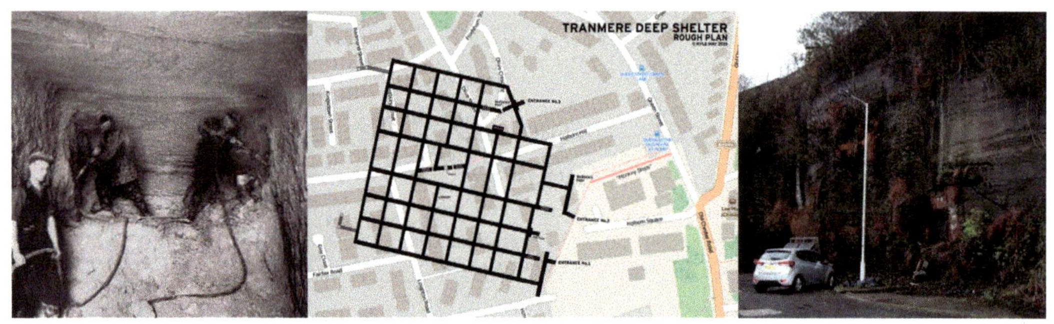

Workmen beneath Bidston Hill creating the Second World War tunnels, started in 1941 and completed by 1943; Map of Tranmere tunnels (Kyle May, 2015); Tranmere Tunnels entrance, Holborn Square.

wing, washrooms and toilets, stables, and even a library, built with extra heating to keep the books in good condition. All three entrances to the bunker were secured by double gas-proof doors to provide a tight seal against a gas attack. But by the time the tunnels were completed at a final cost of £131,000, the need for them had passed and the danger of air attack or invasion was over. Another tunnel was constructed under Bidston Hill's rhododendron garden, which had 2,213 bunks and 793 seats.

[Although the local council have ensured the entrances are now sealed for health and safety reasons, they have been the subject of fascinating investigation by urban explorers – see www.28dayslater.co.uk]

The Cammell Laird yard had already produced the first British purpose-built aircraft carrier, HMS *Ark Royal*, launched on 13 April 1937, when some 30,000 people gathered to watch the event as one of Britain's most famous warships glided onto the Mersey. She was followed down the slipway a year later on 28 July 1938 by RMS *Mauretania*, the largest merchant ship ever built at an English yard. Launched on 28 July 1938, her pre-war commercial operation was brief, before being requisitioned and refitted. She was painted in battle grey and armed with two 6-inch (152-mm) guns and some smaller weapons. Deployed as a troop carrier, she transported 335,000 troops and covered more than 500,000 miles. This integral role played by the yard and its workforce continued throughout the war, just as it had during the First World War, building 106 warships, including the submarines *Ulysses* and *Undaunted*, while also repairing 2,000 merchant ships, nine battleships, eleven aircraft carriers and 100 other warships.

On 3 September 1939, all men aged between eighteen and forty became legally liable for call-up under the new National Service (Armed Forces) Act, with the upper age limit being extended to fifty-one at the end of 1941. This was followed by legislation passed on 18 December 1941 which made all single women between the ages of nineteen and thirty-one potentially liable for service in the Woman's Royal Naval Service, the Auxiliary Territorial Service, the Women's Auxiliary Air Force or Civil Defence (while also making provision that no woman could be required to use a lethal weapon unless she consented in writing to do so). Married women and women with dependent children under fourteen were excluded. In practice, those aged between twenty and twenty-four were targeted for call-up, and those already performing 'socially useful' work, such as nursing or teaching, would be exempted.

Meanwhile, into mid-1940, the period of the 'Phoney War' was drawing to a close, as military activity began to be stepped up, and local defences to protect the port and local population were constructed to an extent never seen before on the peninsular.

Their Majesties In The Wirral

Pictures of their Majesties' visit to the bombed areas and people of Birkenhead and Wallasey. 1. Their Majesties acknowledge their warm welcome. 2. Mrs. McCabe, of Birkenhead, chatting with the Queen. 3. The children cheerily join the greeting.

King George VI and Queen Elizabeth Visit Birkenhead and Wallasey on 6 November 1940.

King George VI and Queen Elizabeth spent much time walking through the bomb-damaged streets of Birkenhead and Wallasey chatting to many locals who had lost family members in the raids or had been bombed out of their homes. Some stood in front of their destroyed houses to give the royals a first-hand account of their hardships.

It was also an opportunity for the King and Queen to meet those in the front line of home defence and the army of volunteers.

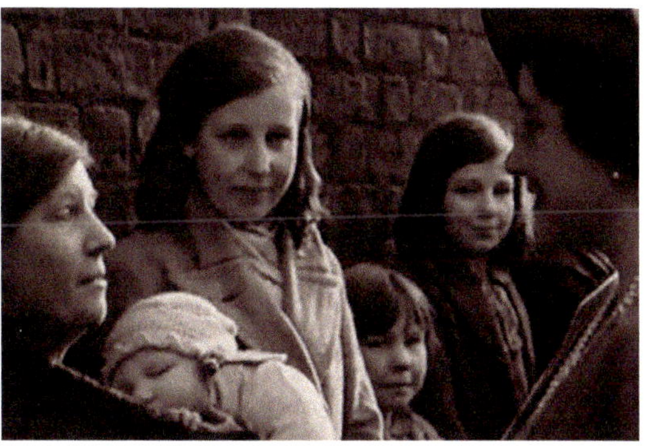

Chapter 7

Wirral Defences

Dock estates on the shores of the Mersey were thought certain to be a prime target, and although the enemy failed to reach the area in the First World War, the technology had moved on way beyond airships and bi-plane bombers. Either side of the river, shore batteries were supported by a network of defences, including coastal obstacles to hamper invasion, pillboxes and gun emplacements, barrage balloon launch sites, sandbags stacked high around building entrances and ARP warden posts, AA gun sites and searchlights. On a larger scale Hooton Airfield was again put on a war footing, while another RAF base was constructed near West Kirby, and air-raid decoys located on the Dee side of the Wirral.

Naval vessels became an increasingly common sight on the river, while merchant traffic began to increase once Western Approaches Command was relocated to Liverpool and supply convoys were stepped up. At the channel approaches to the port, two 6-inch guns and four searchlights were positioned at Fort Perch Rock in New Brighton, with similar defences on the opposite shore at Crosby. An electronically controlled minefield was laid across the narrow entrance to the river between New Brighton and Gladstone Dock. A new 93rd Anti-Aircraft Regiment had been formed just before the war, with their HQ in Birkenhead and included 267 (Wirral) AA Battery. Anti-Aircraft guns were installed mainly on the outer edge of urban zones, as the blast alone from the guns could shatter windows and cause structural damage, while smaller Bofors guns were located in public parks. The site of an anti-aircraft battery can still be seen at Green Lane, Leasowe.

Barrage balloons soon became a familiar sight on both sides of the river. Two balloon squadrons controlled them from their headquarters at No. 8 Balloon Centre RAF Fazakerley (Lime Tree Farm), aiming to have nine balloons per mile in the target zone. No. 919 Squadron, still under RAF Fazakerley, covered Birkenhead, manned with fifty-two balloons (plus twelve waterborne) while No. 923 covered both Birkenhead and Runcorn and were based for a time at Rake Lane in Wallasey.

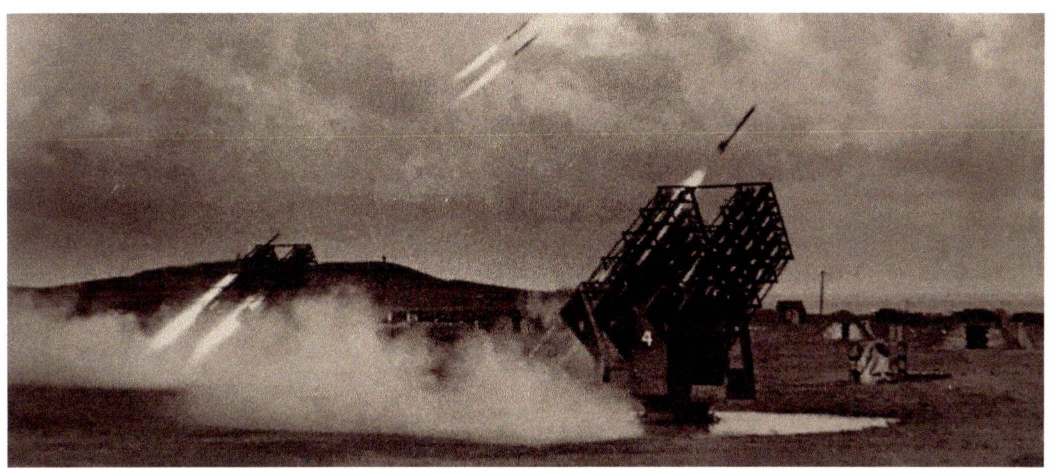

Leasowe gun battery was located with associated barbed-wire obstructions, trackways, anti-aircraft obstacles and a small military camp. It was armed with four 4.5-inch guns with GL Mark II radar in 1942, and manned by the Home Guard.

Many of the sites were operated by WAAFs, who would keep them at a level of 500 feet when not in action, raising them to 5,000 feet when an attack was imminent. They also had parachutes attached, which would open if the balloon was hit by an aircraft. The impact would release the tether, and the drag created by the chutes would inflict fatal damage to enemy aircraft. They also worked in cooperation with the army to man the local anti-aircraft guns sites.

In the park I recall the raising of a barrage balloon which was tethered to large vehicle and the wire gradually unwound until the silver fabric covered balloon was high in the air. From the school roof playground, the dock areas could clearly be seen, and barrage balloons seemed to be everywhere. A search light battery and an anti-aircraft gun emplacement was set up in the park at the corner of the cricket field, and we passed it going to our allotment. Lots of sandbags were placed around the school at ground level especially around the windows of the classrooms. Wasps and bees colonised them and many children were stung. On occasion we were sent home from school carrying our gas masks to see how quickly we could get there. I ran as quickly as possible, holding my breath thinking that I would not breathe any gas until I arrived home. I can recall the air raid sirens going off one afternoon at school, and all the classes occupied the corridors away from the possibility of flying glass if a bomb exploded nearby. Usually the air raids were at night, but there was double British Summer Time in operation which meant that night time was later and people could work longer daylight hours. After an air raid it was common practice to collect pieces of shrapnel, incendiary bomb fins and shell cases to swop with other children.

David Millar, *BBC WW2 People's War*, 14 November 2003

I remember the Ack-Ack guns on Shorefields [New Ferry]. They were manned by Poles, who lived in the barracks which had been quickly erected next to the guns. The guns were to shoot down enemy bombers flying over the estuary trying to drop bombs on the docks.

Barrage balloons were kept in the sky above the field. The Luftwaffe bombers stopped coming after January 1942, and later that year the soldiers and the guns went away. After that, the barracks were used as a small internment camp for German prisoners of war (1945-7), and subsequently as temporary homes for people who had been bombed out in Birkenhead. Pre-fabs were also built, and these and the former barracks were not demolished until the early 1970s.

Mrs Joyce Wharton, newferryonline.org.uk/1940-1949, 14 October 2009

In an attempt to protect the approach to the Mersey, and to a provide a first line of defence from enemy air attack, a system of forts, supporting much larger anti-aircraft guns, was positioned out in Liverpool Bay off the Formby coast in 1943. Devised by civil engineer Guy Anson Maunsell, a system of seven towers linked by catwalks was planned, with a control tower at the centre that operated the radar, surrounded by four towers with 3.7-inch guns, plus one tower with two Bofors guns. A seventh tower, further away from this core arrangement, was mounted with searchlights. Thirty-eight towers had originally been planned, but only twenty-one were built (three forts). Preparation work began in Bromborough docks under a veil of secrecy in October 1941, and construction by Cleveland Bridge & Engineering commenced in February 1942. Pillars of reinforced concrete, 85 feet in length, were laid in cruciform pattern on the Bromborough foreshore. On this base the slanting stilts were fixed into position, and on the top were built steel houses. When completed, they were deployed in the Mersey Estuary between 7 October 1942 and 25 July 1943. At low tide, long pontoons were eased beneath the concrete bases. These lifted with the ebb tide, and the slow procession downriver, escorted by tugs, must have presented a very strange sight. Once out in the bay, each tower was skilfully 'dropped' overboard, and the heavy concrete bases settled easily into the seabed. Queen's Fort was positioned near the Bar Lightship anchorage,

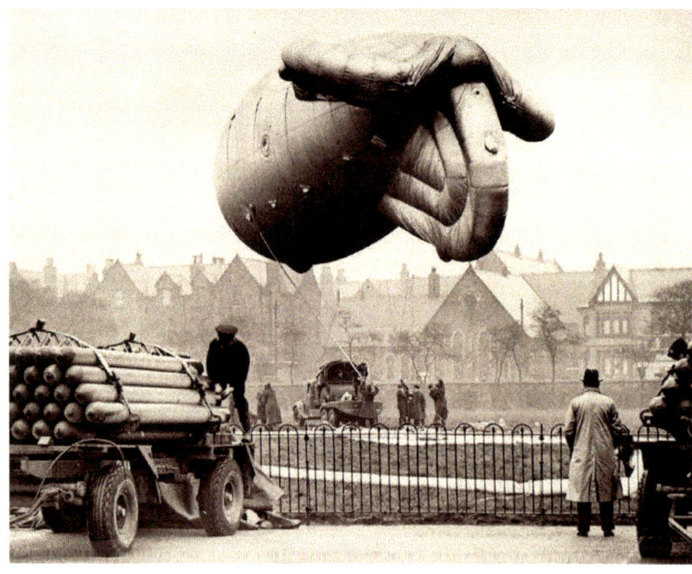

Barrage balloon site.

Burbo Fort was positioned south of the Bar, and Formby Fort to the north of the Bar. Personnel of each fort was made up of 130 officers and men, representing almost every technical branch of the Army. Men of the Royal Artillery manned the guns and searchlights, sappers of the Royal Engineers had charge of the mechanical equipment, and REME technicians were responsible for the technical apparatus. There were radio men from the Royal Signals, bakers from the RASC, cooks from the Army Catering Corps, and nursing orderlies from the RAMC. A large percentage of the men came from Merseyside, who were expected to do a month's turn of duty, and then return to a shore camp for a fortnight. For inter-communication purposes, each fort was provided with its own motor boat. A larger vessel made a weekly call for provisioning.

Despite them being clearly visible from the Crosby-Formby shore, their existence was not acknowledged until late 1944 due to national security. By that time, the war had turned; there was little risk of air attack. Not a single shot in anger was fired from the forts, but they were believed to have been an effective deterrent to any enemy mine-laying aircraft attempting to make for the river. After the war, various schemes were thought up on how to use the redundant forts, but all came to nothing. Demolition commenced in the 1950s, as they were by then regarded as a hazard to shipping, and all three had been removed by 1955.

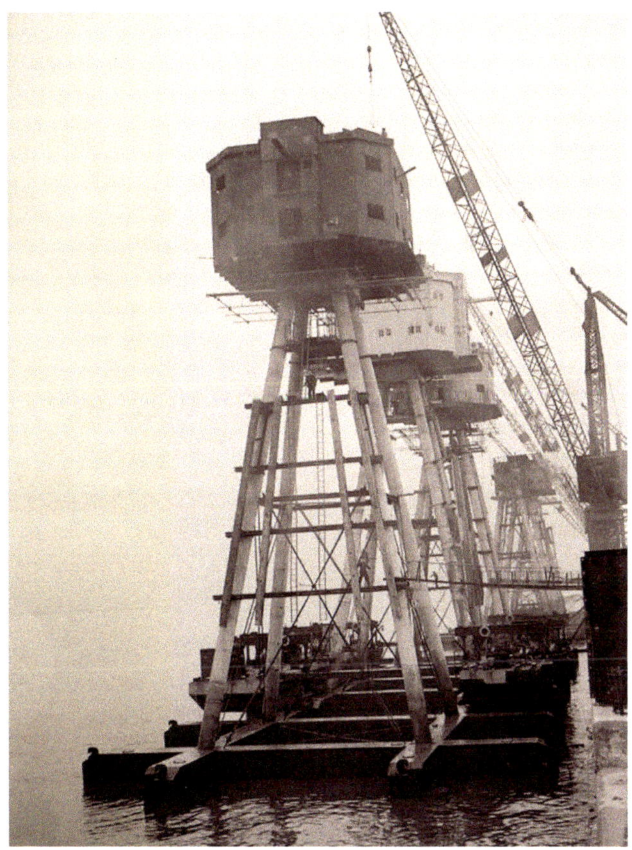

The construction of 120-foot Maunsell anti-aircraft forts for use in the Mersey estuary, Bromborough Dock, photographed on 8 December 1943. (Imperial War Museum)

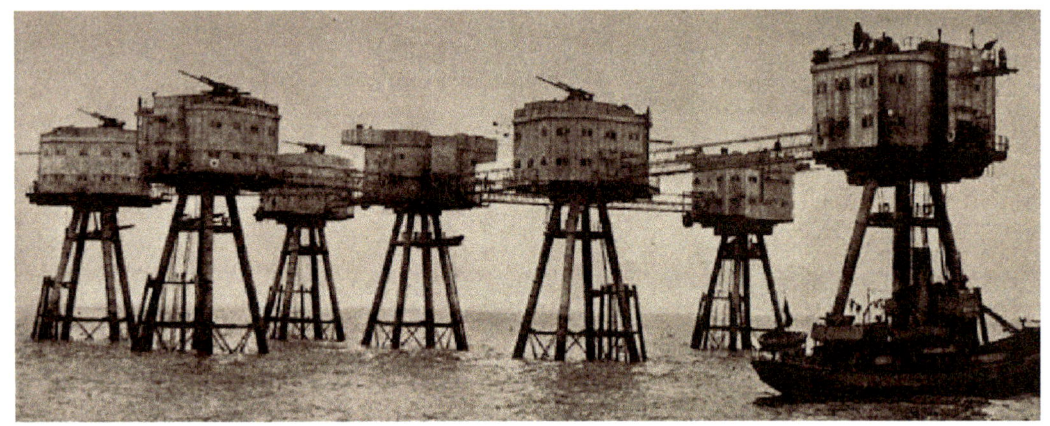

One of the Maunsell Forts in Liverpool Bay.

In January 1940, a national programme of air-raid 'decoys' was introduced designed to deflect enemy bombing away from enemy target zones. By the end of the war, there was an elaborate network of dummy airfields and hundreds of decoy sites, 237 in all, protecting eighty-one towns and cities around the country. Remnants of the decoy programme still lie scattered across the countryside, with their wartime bunkers buried in roadside hedgerows or hidden away in undergrowth in the corners of farmers' fields, with few realising their original function.

Using four main methods it developed into a complex strategy of deception, with day and night dummy aerodromes (the 'K' and 'Q' sites); diversionary fires ('QF' sites and 'Starfish'); simulated urban lighting ('QL' sites, built as part of the 'C-series' of civil decoys); and dummy factories and buildings. Across the country, the Q sites were especially effective, drawing something like 440 attacks – an enormous amount of wasted Nazi effort – and deflecting well over 2,000 tons of bombs, saving untold lives during the course of the war. The urban decoy fires were known as 'SF' for 'Special Fires', later commonly known as 'Starfish', and to distinguish them from the smaller QF installations. These were the most technically sophisticated of all the types, consisting of complex light arrays and fires laid out to simulate a fire-bombed town, with the fires differing in appearance, intensity and duration. This would replicate the fire effects an enemy aircrew would expect to see after incendiaries had taken effect. Controlled from a nearby bunker, the fires differed in their ignition and appearance by burning coal, oil or paraffin at delayed times. Many sites had an infrastructure consisting of access roads, firebreak trenches and wiring systems linked to the remote bunker. In all, some 839 decoys are officially recorded for England, constructed on 602 sites. (Some sites had more than one type of decoy.)

The sites for the Merseyside region were commissioned in December 1940, with the first civil decoys in place by the summer of 1941. Civil bombing decoy sites were also constructed in the Wirral at Brimstage, Moreton, Hoylake, Heswall, Little Hilbre, Burton Marsh and Gayton, some of which were Starfish decoys. For enemy raiders approaching from the southern Dee Estuary, they would first engage the 'permanent Starfish' decoy site at Burton Marsh, designed to replicate Garston Docks. According to English Heritage,

> Burton 'Starfish' decoy was operated by lighting a series of controlled fires during an air raid to replicate an urban area targeted by bombs. It is first referenced as being in use in 1942 and was possibly commissioned in response to the Luftwaffe's Baedeker Raids. Also in 1942, a 'QL' decoy was incorporated into the site as part of the 'C-series' of civil decoys to protect Garston Docks. The 'QL' decoy displayed lighting to simulate the railway marshalling yards and factories associated with the dockyard. The site is referenced as being in use up until 1943. Aerial photography from 1948 shows a series of over fifty structures, rectilinear features and associated trackway at the decoy site, although these seem to have gone by 1971. A control building, which would have housed an operations room and provided the decoy crew with shelter, is still visible and this site is probably associated with the bomb craters to the immediate east and south.

The site is a few hundred yards west of Denhall House Farm into the marshes. The trackway and rectilinear marks can still be seen on online satellite map images. Locals can also remember seeing a dummy ship in the 'dock' constructed from wood and canvas.

Smaller defences also began to appear across the Wirral in the form of small pillboxes, anti-tank trenches and concrete blocks, to prevent or slow down invasion, both on the coastline or further inland. Pillboxes were installed at Leasowe on the north Wirral coastline, and inland at sites such as Brimstage, Bromborough Pool and around Hooton Airfield, while pyramid-shaped concrete blocks, nicknamed 'Dragon's Teeth', littered the coastal shore, as well as inland defence works.

Air defence of the Merseyside area remained the responsibility of RAF Fighter Command's No. 12 Group (later No. 9), with night-fighter defences provided by Speke, Blackpool (Squire's Gate), Cranage (near Middlewich), Tern Hill (Market Drayton),

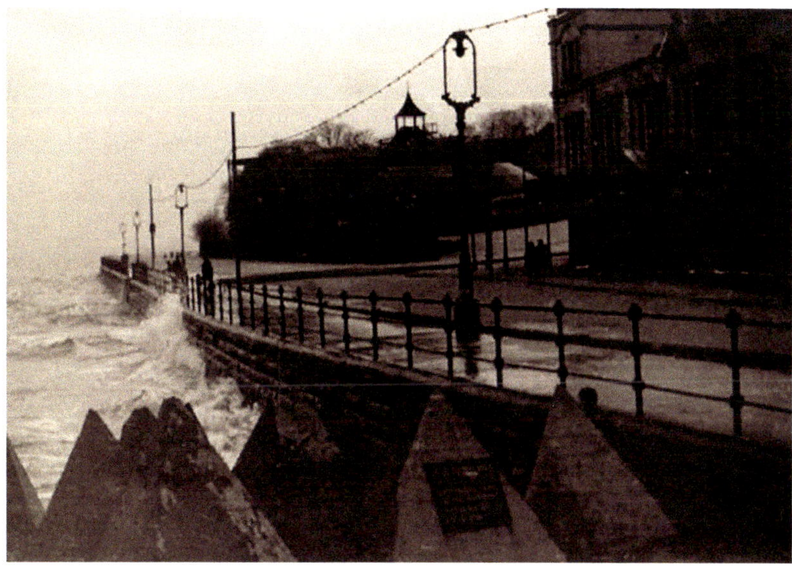

'Dragon's teeth' defences at Tower Promenade, New Brighton.

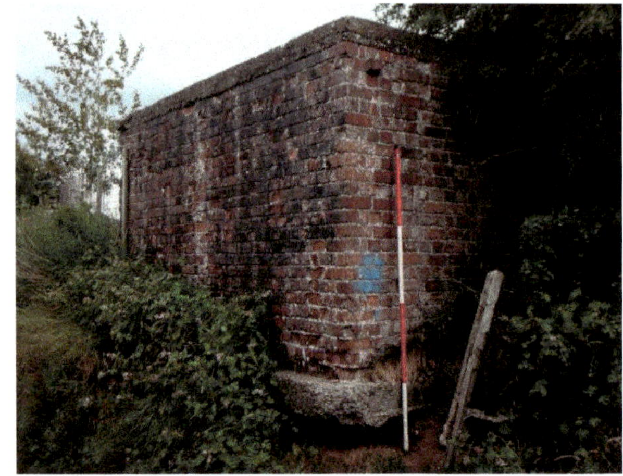

Left: QL/SF Bombing decoy control building, near Denhall House Farm, on the edge of Burton Marsh. (North West Rapid Coastal Zone Assessment, English Heritage)

Below: Four of the numerous Second World War pillboxes still to be found in the Wirral. *Clockwise from top left*: Station Road, Parkgate; Mockbeggar Wharf; Brimstage Lane; Bromborough Pool A41 bridge. (Photos: Mike Searle collection. www.geograph.org.uk)

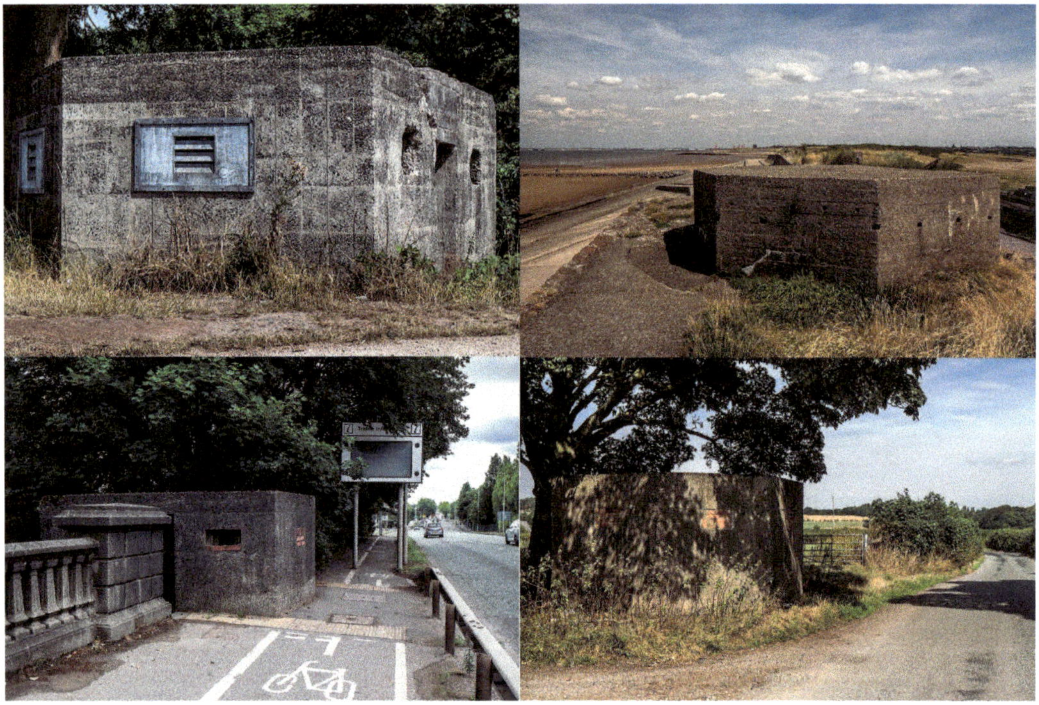

High Ercall (near Shrewsbury), Borras (Wrexham) and Valley on Anglesey. The most common fighters used were Hurricanes, Defiants, Blenheims and Beaufighters.

RAF Hooton Park was originally built for the Royal Flying Corps in 1917 as a training aerodrome for pilots in the First World War. The aerodrome continued in use after its purchase in 1927 by aviation enthusiast Mr G. H. Dawson, and from 1930–33 Hooton operated as 'Liverpool Airport' until the airfield at Speke was opened on 1 July 1933, although continued to operate commercial flights. On 10 February 1936, No. 610 (County of Chester) Squadron was formed at Hooton as a light bomber unit in the Auxiliary Air Force, flying Avro Tutors and Hawker Harts when flying commenced in the May of that year. By January 1939 the airfield was redesignated as a fighter unit with Hawker Hinds, Fairey Battles and Hurricanes, soon replaced by Spitfires. At the outbreak of war, the squadron was mobilised and sent to RAF Wittering for training. During the war, Coastal Command used Hooton when operating patrol flights over the Irish Sea from South Wales to Cumbria and to cope with wartime demands the grass airfield was upgraded in 1941 with the construction of a 5,400-foot concrete runway.

Meanwhile, Martin Hearn, an aircraft services provider, was contracted by the Ministry of Aircraft Production to maintain Avro Ansons, followed by De Havilland Mosquito fighter-bombers. Now operating as No. 7 Aircraft Assembly Unit, they also undertook work to assemble some of the American aircraft arriving at the Mersey Docks, including P-51 Mustang, P-38 Lightning and P-47 Thunderbolt fighters, A-20 Boston/Havoc and Canadian-built Handley Page Hampden bombers, and Harvard (North American T-6 Texan) trainers. Redundant aircraft were also dismantled and scrapped at Hooton. RAF Hooton remained fully operational after the war until its eventual closure in 1957, following which the site was sold to Vauxhall Motors in 1962. Either side of the Dee at Queensferry, RAF Sealand and RAF Hawarden were also operational during wartime, giving added protection to the peninsular.

At the beginning of the Second World War, the RAF also set up a camp near West Kirby. Located just 3 miles to the east at Larton, on the Saughall Massie Road,

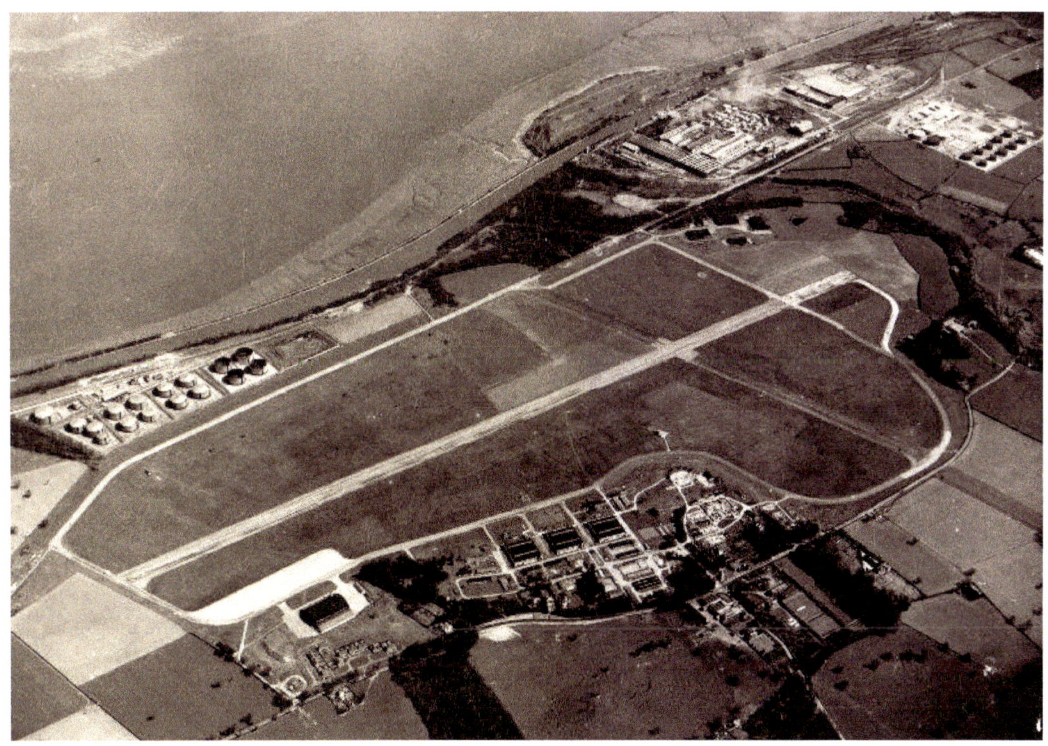

RAF Hooton Airfield. Today a small part of the Hooton runway and taxi-track on the north-west side remain intact, as well as hangars and associated buildings under the care of Hooton Park Trust.

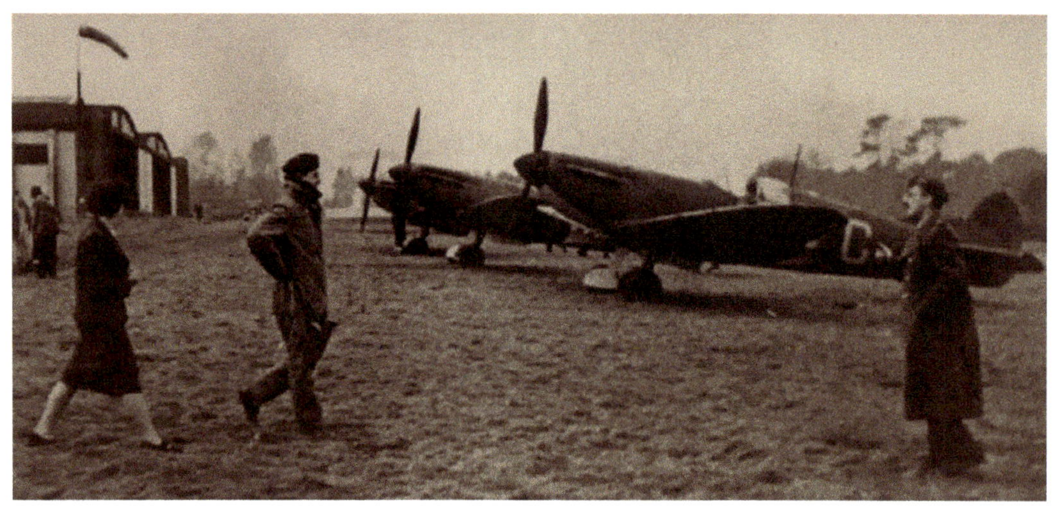

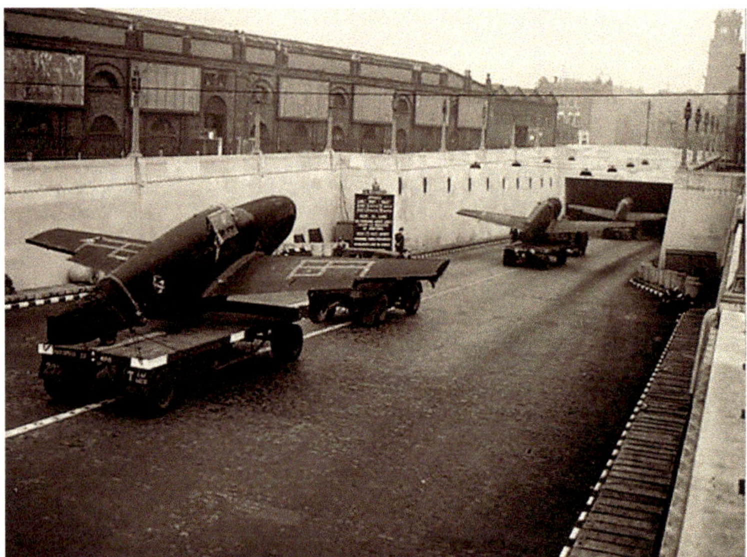

Above: Spitfires at RAF Hooton. (Photo: Michael Lewis)

Left: Convoy of P-51 Mustang aircraft on eight-wheel trailers in transit from Hooton to Speke entering the Mersey Tunnel, Birkenhead.

Below: RAF West Kirby.

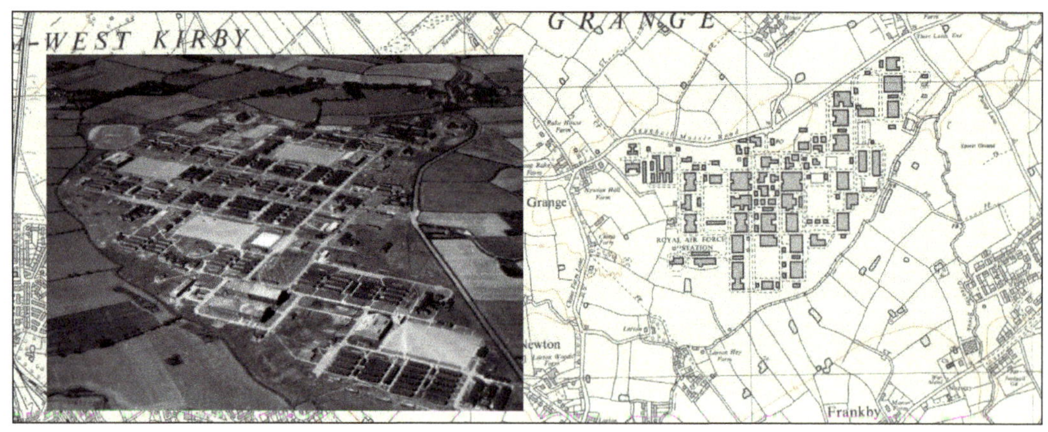

its function was to provide around two months' basic training in physical fitness, parade drill, rifle practice and ground combat and defence, before recruits were posted elsewhere. Due to this role as a primary basic skill camp, a runway and airfield were never constructed. Accommodation was provided in wooden barrack huts each housing around twenty recruits. After the war, the camp remained in service, training new recruits for National Service. The final passing-out parade took place on 20 December 1957, the camp closed and the land returned to agricultural use leaving little trace of the camp. If it wasn't for the memorial standing at the site of the former entrance it would be easy to pass by and not realise what had once been a hive of activity here for two decades. (One of huts can still be seen in the grounds of St John's, Frankby, where it was relocated after the camp closure.)

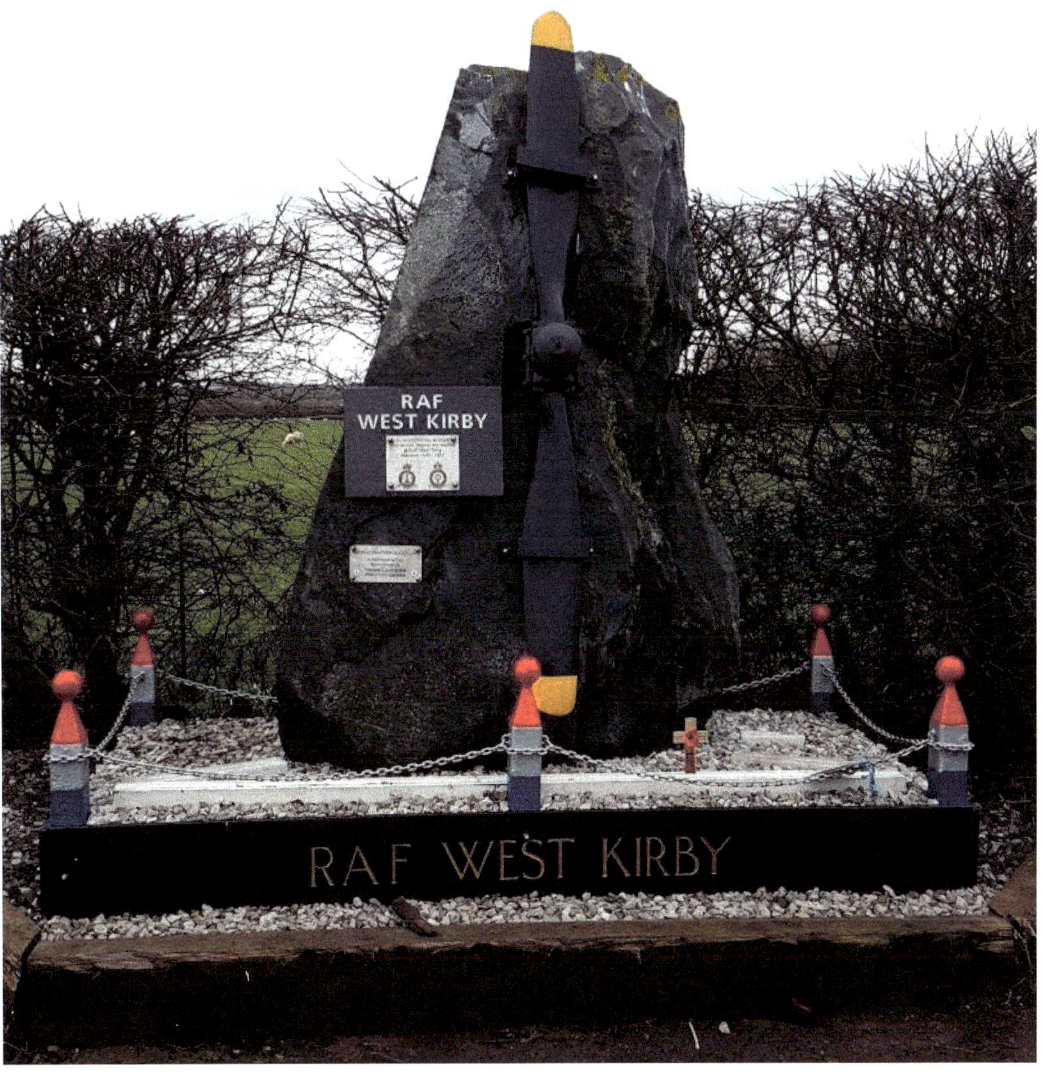

RAF West Kirby Memorial.

Chapter 8

The Blitz of 1940/41

Following the Nazi invasions and occupation of Holland and Belgium, together with the Allied retreat and Dunkirk evacuation, enemy attention began to focus on the country's major cities and ports. Liverpool being a major target resulted in Merseyside becoming the most bombed area outside London during 1940 and into 1941.

The first bombs on the Merseyside area landed near a searchlight post at Altcar on the night of 28 July 1940. At 2.55 a.m. on 29 July a stick of bombs was scattered across the Thurstaston–Irby–Neston area, but all fell in fields and no damage was done, nor were there any casualties. Just a few days later, on 9 August, bombers claimed their first Merseyside victim. The first bombs fell in the garden of the house of Captain Alan Layfield, a chief officer of the special police, who was on duty in Birkenhead Town Hall at the time. His wife and three other people indoors had a narrow escape. However, the second bomb, dropped at three minutes past midnight, scored a direct hit, striking the roof of a house a few hundred yards away, at 14 Prenton Lane, Birkenhead, killing the occupant in an upstairs room.

Air Raids in the North West
Maid Killed in Upper Room

Of six bombs which fell in a North Western area, one penetrated the roof of a large house at the top of a hill and killed a maid – Johanna Mandale aged thirty-four – in one of the upper rooms. The majority of the residents of the district were in their beds at the time of the raid. The first concussion was immediately followed by five others, but fortunately no other casualty of any kind occurred. An empty house, vacant for five years, was partially demolished, and one bomb fell in the garden of the commandant of a force of special constables. The dead maid was in the top room of a corner house. The bomb apparently struck the purling and exploded and killed her instantaneously. In the room below were the owner and his wife, Mr and Mrs W. Bunney, also in bed, and they were buried under a tremendous heap of debris from the fallen ceiling and the roof timbers. They managed to escape from the bed and were not injured. The house has surprisingly escaped complete destruction, and this is believed to be due to the fact that when the bomb struck the purling it took a glancing direction and exploded. The next-door house also had the eaves damaged and a large hole rent in the roof and many windows smashed. Enemy planes also dropped twenty bombs in fields in an agricultural area in the North-West of England early yesterday. The only damage reported is that of broken windows in a few houses in the vicinity.

Liverpool Daily Post, 10 August 1940

The following night, Wallasey was hit for the first time in the area of Strouds Corner–Cliff Road–Mill Lane, where four people were killed and several seriously injured. Another raid followed on 19 August, but the bombs fell harmlessly into the fields of Thingwall and Landican. So far, the raids had been no more than armed reconnaissance operations and not full-scale air raids. This was to change over the next few nights as the intensity was racked up. On 28/29 August, Liverpool, Wallasey and Birkenhead were attacked by 150 bombers, with waves of incendiaries lighting up the target areas for the high explosives that followed. However, many failed to arrive at their targets, falling in nearby fields, but those that did get through hit a number of houses, while the city centre escaped.

The night of 31 August saw the heaviest bombing so far, with over 100 fires lighting up both sides of the Mersey. Wallasey Town Hall was seriously damaged and its valuable organ destroyed, while at Cammell Laird six bombs struck the shipyard, one of which exploded between the quayside and the cruiser HMS *Prince of Wales*, bursting the hull plates and causing her to list. The Birkenhead fire brigade arrived to pump out the water and together with the men of the shipyard, it took two and a half days before she was patched sufficiently to move her to a dry dock for repair. She had yet to be re-commissioned, and was about to undertake sea trials when she was hit. The damage was never reported and remained a well-kept secret. After repair and launch, she took part in the sinking of the *Bismarck* in 1941, before her own sinking by the Japanese off Malaya in December 1941.

Moving into September, the raiders returned night after night, as it became very clear that Hitler intended to disable the port. In Noctorum, the Keilberg convalescent home for children was damaged on the 4th, but thankfully there were no casualties, the children having already been evacuated by ARP wardens.

There was a particularly long week of nightly air raids when the moon was full. My father was working away from home. Jackie was doing his Home Guard duties and my mother, brother George and I were on our own. The sirens went and almost immediately the anti-aircraft guns were blazing away and search lights probed the sky, and we stood on the kitchen steps watching. When the whistle of bombs dropping was heard, we went into the cellar and not into the air raid shelter, because a street shelter had been hit by a bomb nearby and mother thought we would be safer in the cellar. The throb of aeroplane engines droned on for what seemed like hours, and the guns pounded the air as bombs whistled towards the ground. Another sound, like the regular whoosh of a steam locomotive starting, was

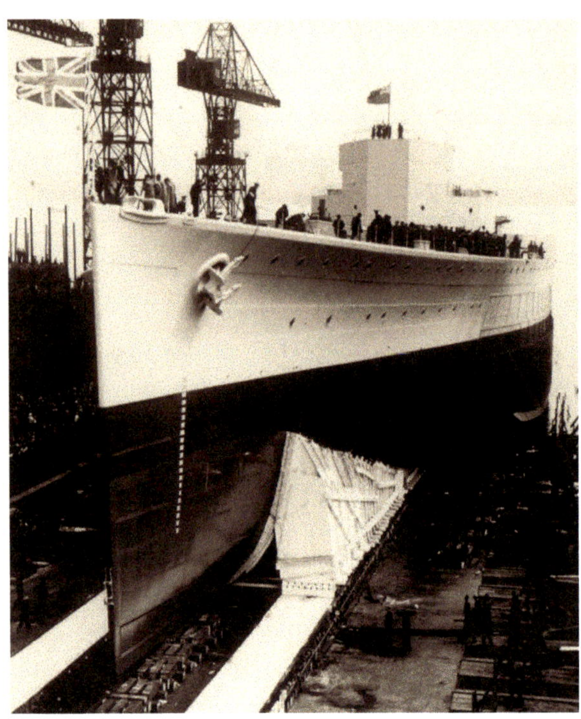

HMS *Prince of Wales* – launched at
Cammell Laird 3 May 1939.

made by bombs attached to parachutes as they glided to earth. The sounds of the explosions
were very frightening. Even the large battleship *Prince of Wales* being constructed at Cammell
Lairds used its available guns to fire at the enemy planes. Jackie came home in the thick of the
air raid saying that he had helped to put out an incendiary bomb. My mother did not like the
idea of him being so close to danger.

At night the smoke screen vehicles pumped smoke into the air to try and confuse the position
for the bombers to bomb their targets. Each day dawned, and the bomb damage seemed to be
everywhere. It was a way of life and parachute cord and silk from the parachute bombs was
much sort after by children for swops as well as other collectable items. Bombed houses were
flattened into piles of rubble, or left standing with floors and walls precariously balanced.
Areas that I had known were gone, including parts of Exmouth Street, Oxton Road and
Borough Road. There was a distinct smell of rubble dust and smouldering wood. The raids
became almost routine, and in anticipation of yet another raid, we went to Hamilton Square
underground station with lots of others for one night, thinking that it was safer and less noisy
than being at home. It was very crowded, and we did not go there again.

David Millar, *BBC WW2 People's War,* 14 November 2003

On the night of 26 September, the heaviest formation of enemy bombers yet to
attack Merseyside subjected the district to its most severe raid of the war so far.

The raid began in daylight, when small formations of three or five planes followed each other
in a determined effort to get through the defences. Some of the machines came low but were
forced up again by the balloon barrage. After 'hedge-hopping' the balloons for some time, two

of the planes, in an effort to clear a way for those following behind, turned their machine guns on the balloons, but without success. Ignoring the danger from falling bombs and flying shrapnel, people stood in one of the main shopping streets and cheered as they watched shells from the anti-aircraft batteries bursting all-round the centre plane in a group of three. Suddenly the plane seemed to rock and lost height. 'They've hit him,' people roared excitedly, and began to cheer; but the pilot steadied his machine and climbed again. People in another area believe that one man said he saw the plane come down in a spiral, but there is no official confirmation of an enemy loss. The first raiders were evidently intent on starting fires as beacons for those expected in the area after darkness. The fire casualties in one of the areas included a theatre. The glow from the scattered fires lighted the sky for a considerable distance. Following close behind the fireraisers came relays of bombers, who dropped high explosive in a number of areas, chiefly among residential property, although fire fighters had to carry on while bombs fell around them.

Liverpool Evening Express, 27 September 1940

The theatre was the much-loved Birkenhead Argyle Theatre, which took a direct hit, leaving a gutted and still smouldering shell the following morning. The nearby Public Assistance Office and the Argyle Street Income Tax Offices were also seriously damaged. Birkenhead Docks also came under fire, but the most serious situation developed when incendiaries fell on the GWR goods station between Morpeth and Wallasey docks, where buildings and wagons were set alight. Driver Ivor Davies and Fireman Frank Newns were quick to act and shunted their engine and trucks with their endangered RAF shipment of HE bombs and petrol to a cutting near Cleveden Street bridge. Together with Norman Tunna, who continued to put his life at risk, the extraordinary bravery of the three men prevented a catastrophic explosion and loss of life. Norman Tunna was later awarded the George Cross, the highest award for courage in a situation where the enemy is not present. He was one of the first recipients as it had only been instituted by the king two days earlier on 24 September. (A Victoria Cross can only be awarded in the presence of the enemy.) Ivor Davies and Frank Newns were also recognised, with the award of the George Medal.

Reading about Birkenhead's Argyle Theatre brought back memories of the night in 1940 when it took a direct hit in an air raid in the early days of World War Two. It was Saturday, 25 September. We lived in Abbey Buildings, a block of three-storey flats 200 yards from the Cammell Laird shipyard. It was about 8.30pm and we could see right over into Laird's yard. I got out on the verandah and saw fire bombs - there was no warning. I was a plater at Laird's and immediately went to the yard. There was a destroyer in Dry Dock No 5, and the sailors were on the dockside putting the fire bombs out. After sheltering under a gun platform, I ran out of the yard and the first thing I saw in Abbey Street was a house that had taken a direct hit. It was owned by a Mr Williams. Also hit in the raid was the battleship HMS *Prince of Wales*. It was damaged on the portside and listing. The platers' shop where I worked received a direct hit, too, as well as the power station.

Mr N. S. Grey, New Hey Road, Woodchurch
Wirral Globe, 12 February 2002

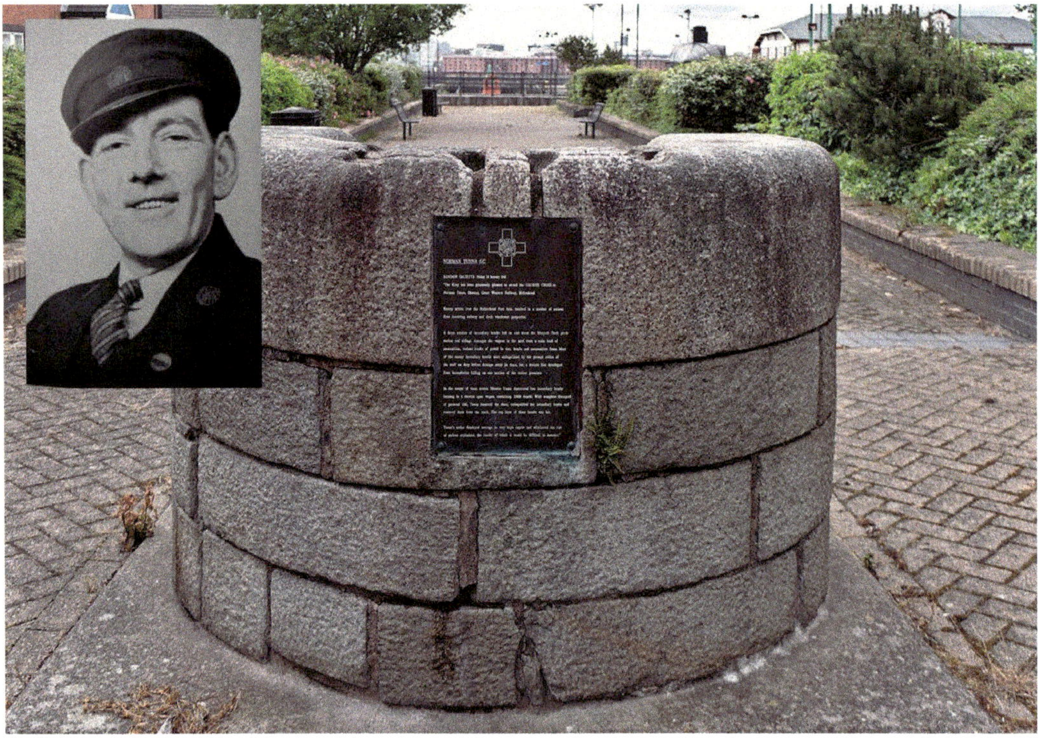

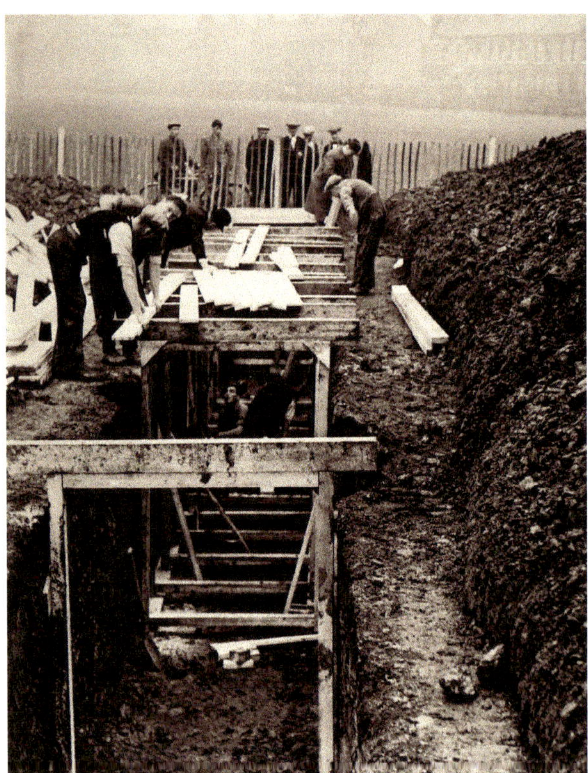

Above: Norman Tunna GC and his Woodside memorial.

Left: Timbering up the deep trenches in Birkenhead Park during construction of bomb shelters, 28 September 1938.

Below: Members of Hoylake and West Kirby Home Guard undergoing rifle and bayonet training, *Liverpool Evening Express*, 20 June 1941.

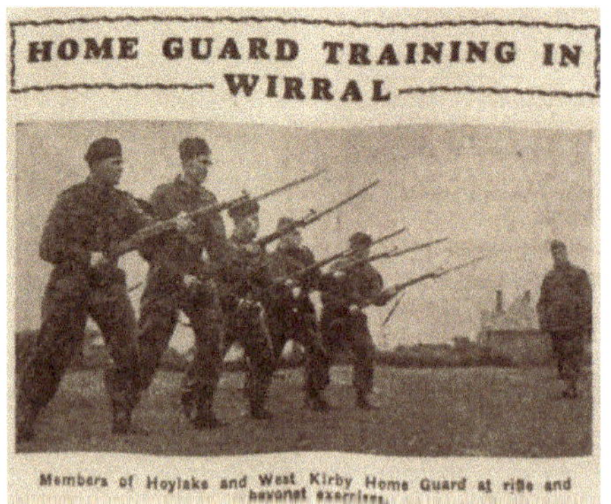

On 8 October 1940 RAF Speke was alerted that an enemy raider was heading towards the Mersey. Three Hawker Hurricanes of No. 312 (Czech) Squadron were immediately scrambled led by Flight Lieutenant Denys Gillam. He was immediately confronted by a Junkers 88 crossing his flight path, which he swiftly engaged and shot down. It happened so quickly that his undercarriage was still retracting, and the whole attack from take-off to landing took little more than twelve minutes. It is regarded as the fastest air-to-air combat kill in the Battle of Britain, and possibly of all time.

During the engagement, the Ju88's starboard engine was damaged in a hail of bullets which also killed the observer/second pilot Leutnant H. Schlegel. Accurate fire was returned from the Ju88, which hit all three Hurricanes. As the Ju88 went down, it glided past Bromborough Church, smoke billowing from its damaged engines, as it headed towards Bromborough Dock, where it crashed-landed on the reclaimed land, undercarriage retracted and two bombs still in their racks.

Harry Gill, gateman at Bromborough Dock dashed to the scene:

I was on duty at the South Gatehouse at Bromborough dock, when a twin-engined aeroplane plunged out of the clouded sky and crashed about 200 yards away on land reclaimed from the River Mersey. I ran towards it and half way there I looked up and saw a swastika on the tail fin. Two men were scrambling out of the cockpit and ran behind the damaged wing. The two Germans, who were tall and well-built, were bending over a third airman lying at their feet. I sized them by the epaulettes of their uniforms and demanded their guns, which they surrendered without argument.

Mr Rand and Thompson then appeared at my side.* Mr Thompson took charge of one of the Germans and escorted him to the Dock Gatehouse to be kept in custody until the military authorities arrived. One of the crew was found to be dead at the controls. Alongside the Ju88 was a fully inflated dinghy. Two unexploded bombs, which had fallen from the aircraft as it bounced along the ground, were lying near the smoking port engine.

Colin Schroeder, *The Bromborough Dock Ju88 Incident 8 October 1940* (**2010**)

[*Two Unilever employees from the adjacent factory; Mr. W.A. Rand from the Electrical Department and Mr. Rob Thompson, Assistant Manager of the Fuel & Steam Department].

While waiting for the military to arrive and take charge of the crash site, men from the Local Defence Volunteer (LDV) units of Unilever and Fawcett Preston were soon on the scene to control the growing crowds. The two men who had scrambled from the cockpit were the pilot Oberleutnant H. Bruckmann, and Unteroffizier H. Weth, the wireless operator/gunner. Rear gunner Sonderfuhrer H. Lehmann, who had been in the ventral gondola under the cockpit, was lying injured nearby. Once the prisoners were taken into the care of the authorities, Harry Gill was able to look inside the wreckage where he found maps of Merseyside, clearly detailing the buildings and storage tanks in the Port Sunlight factory and Bromborough Dock.

In 1990, Dougie Darroch, local aviation historian, successfully tracked down pilot Helmuth Bruckmann to his home in Munich and arranged for him to revisit the scene on 1 November 1991, and to be greeted by the mayor with a civic reception to follow.

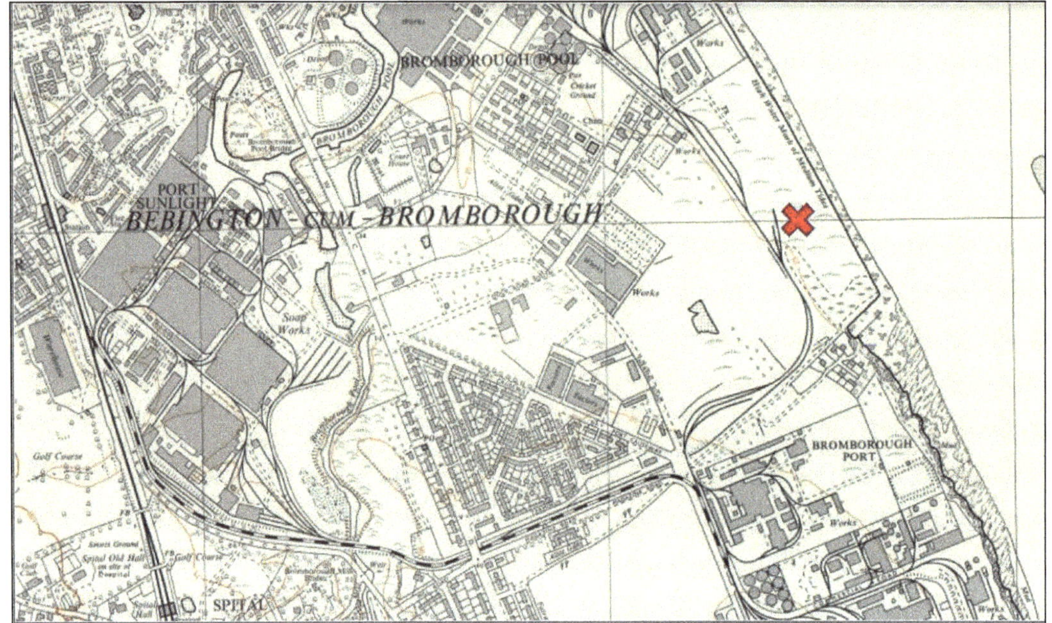

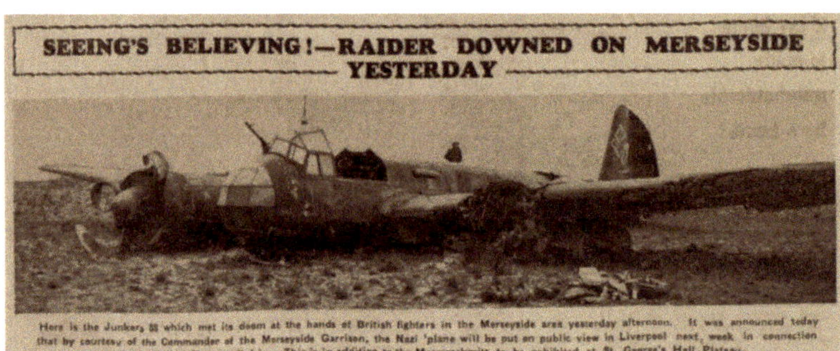

Above: Ju88 crash site, Bromborough.

Left: Ju88 to be put on display. (*Liverpool Evening Express*, 9 October 1940)

As for the Ju88, the aircraft was eventually moved and exhibited in several locations to encourage donations to local Spitfire Funds (each area was in competition to 'purchase' a Spitfire in the war effort) and a charge of *6d* an adult and *3d* a child was made to view the aircraft. On 18 October 1940, the Ju88 was paraded through the streets of Liverpool as part of the 'War Weapons Week' fundraising programme, and then displayed at St George's Hall Plateau alongside a recently downed Messerschmitt Bf.109. The aircraft was then returned to the Wirral and exhibited at the Port Sunlight Recreation Ground in Bebington. In November, the Ju88 was transported to Parkgate, where it was placed on view in a field off Bevyl Road, adjoining the Parade. Maurice Jones went to see the aircraft:

There were plenty of people there and it poured with rain. It was a very miserable day. Corrugated sheets had been put on the ground round the plane, as it was so wet. A wing had come off the plane but was laid out as it should have been. There was a long line of people waiting to go in, and you went in through the door the crew had used. It was the first German object of war I had ever seen. I went in and sat in the pilot's seat and I can remember a lady saying 'they needed terribly long legs to reach the pedals.

Eddie Scott remembers the role played by the Home Guard:

The Little Neston company of the Home Guard was charged with the responsibility of protecting it from the depredations of souvenir-hunters. Half-a-dozen of us, detailed for the task, made our way to the rendezvous, an empty house behind what is now the Parkgate Hotel, and mounted a patrolling guard in pairs for the standard two hours on and four off. I remember the four off particularly for the hardness of the bare floor and the inadequacy of the single blanket, and the two on for the inky blackness of the night.

Colin Schroeder, *ibid.*

By the end of the Parkgate exhibition, over £600 had been raised, including an anonymous donation of £50, and they were well on their way to their £1,000 end-of-year target. From 15 December 1940 it was exhibited at New Brighton Cricket Club in Rake Lane, where it helped to complete the £5,000 target for Wallasey's first Spitfire. Eventually the Ju88 had completed its role to help re-equip the RAF and it was taken to RAF Sealand to be scrapped.

The raids on Merseyside continued throughout late 1940, with one of the heaviest attacks on 21/22 December, when over 150 bombers struck in two waves from 7 p.m. until 5.15 a.m. Reinforcements from other cities were called in once again to help with firefighting. Fires were still burning from the previous night as hundreds more incendiaries were dropped to guide the bombing waves to follow. Over the two nights there were 132 warehouse fires alone. Despite these numbers, it could have been far worse, but for the firewatchers positioned on roofs and highpoints on both sides of the river, bravely carrying on as incendiaries fell about or on them. In Birkenhead there were dozens of casualties and considerable damage to houses, shops, the Ritz Cinema, and the Laird Street bus depot. With no time for recovery, the sirens sounded yet again on the following night, as anxious citizens anticipated yet another hammering. However, despite the raids continuing until the all-clear at 6.12 a.m., they were lighter and it was reported that the main target that night was Manchester.

Nevertheless, there were still dreadful casualties, especially in Wallasey, where the Home for Women on the corner of Manor Road and Withens Lane was destroyed, leaving few survivors as a gas main fractured, suffocating thirteen residents trapped in the rubble.

Into 1941, the raids were initially lighter and sporadic, but still the death toll increased. There was a heavy attack on 12/13 March causing serious damage in Liverpool, but it was across the river that took the heaviest pounding and Birkenhead and Wallasey experienced a truly terrifying night. A total of 264 people were killed in Birkenhead and damage affected housing and the docks where the flour mills were badly hit. In the centre of town, the roof of Birkenhead Hospital was set on fire and had to be evacuated. Wallasey suffered the highest rate of casualties for the whole Blitz period. Both boroughs had the worst of it again the following night.

In one incident in Wallasey there was a miraculous rescue of a baby buried in the debris of her family home in Lancaster Avenue. Her faint cries were heard four days later and she was rescued alive, still lying alongside the bodies of her dead parents.

In Birkenhead, rescue operations were in full flow, and when a party of Royal Pioneer Corps were searching the rubble of damaged houses in Carnforth Street at around 11.30 p.m., one of the men, Corporal James Scully, an Irishman from Dublin, located an elderly couple buried in the debris, in what was likely to have been the back kitchen. With great difficulty, he was able to penetrate to where they were lying. Followed in by party leader Lieutenant Chittenden, wood was obtained to use as props to shore up the debris, and after great personal risk supporting the debris over several hours, they were able to recover the couple. Mrs Amelia Marsh, aged seventy, survived the ordeal, but sadly her husband died. For their bravery, Scully was awarded the George Cross and Chittenden the George Medal.

By the end of April, the cumulative effects of the attacks had taken a heavy toll. Merseyside had endured almost seventy raids, of which at least five were major, resulting in 2,267 deaths. By percentage of population, Wallasey was hit hardest with 329 deaths, followed by Birkenhead with 403, Bootle 152 and Liverpool 1,263. Damage had been done to a number of docks and roads, and dozens of buildings had been destroyed. While the death toll would almost double in the terrifying days of the May Blitz, it is sometimes still forgotten that the casualty figures from August to April were higher. Nevertheless, this was over a nine-month period and it would take less than nine days in May for the death toll to reach similar numbers.

On 15 April 1941, Prime Minister Winston Churchill made an unannounced visit to Merseyside, to see for himself the enemy damage and to speak to local people and workforces. After a tour through Liverpool and a visit to the docks, the party immediately headed to the Cheshire side of the river, but by the time they arrived, word had got around and Churchill was greeted by crowds as he toured Wallasey, where the mayor escorted the party into the more heavily blitzed areas, and to meet the ARP personnel on duty. As he got back into the car, a young schoolboy ducked under the police cordon, and before anyone could catch him, he shoved his autograph book towards the prime minister, who smiled and signed his album.

Arriving in Birkenhead perched on the hood of the car, Churchill again toured the blitzed streets, and stopped to speak to first-aid nurses and men clearing the rubble of demolished homes. In Brattan Road, a kitchen table had been recovered from the damage, together with a collection of pots, books and utensils. A council official pushed them to one side and asked Churchill to sign the mayor's visitor's book. The prime minister took a gold fountain pen from his pocket and signed the book, and passed his pen to Mr W. Averell Harriman (who was serving as President Roosevelt's special envoy to Europe, coordinating the Lend-Lease programme), who added his signature. He continued his tour of the blitzed streets, before a full tour of Cammell Laird and his return to Liverpool.

During the seven-day period from 1 to 7 May, Merseyside experienced the most concentrated series of air attacks on any British city area outside London during the Second World War. On 1 May, the first bomb landed on Seacombe at 10.15 p.m.,

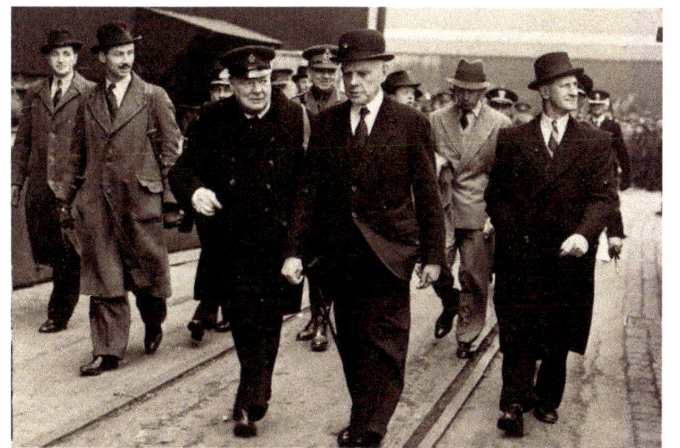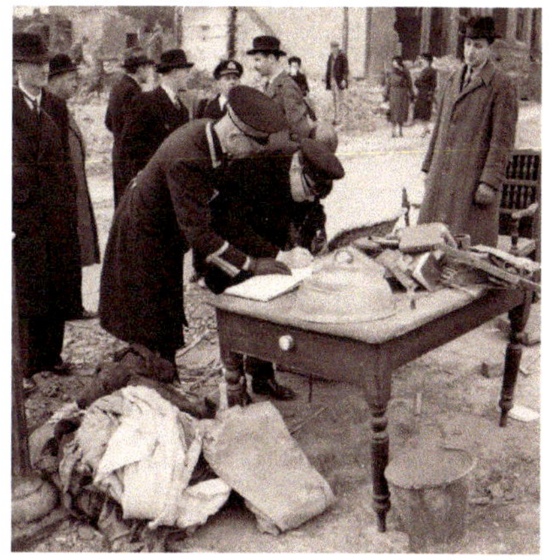

Churchill's Wartime Visit to Wirral
Above left: Prime Minister Winston Churchill touring Cammell Laird.

Above right: Churchill signing the mayor's visitor's book in Brattan Road, Birkenhead.

before almost fifty enemy aircraft had time to discharge 48 tons of high explosives and over 4,000 incendiaries. Damage was concentrated in Liverpool, but it appears the bad weather hindered the Luftwaffe's plans for a heavier attack. The following night raids were heavier and lasted four hours, with 6,000 incendiaries raining down on both sides of the river.

However, the night of 3 May 1941 will also live long in the memories of those who lived through it, and will always be remembered as the worst night ever experienced on Merseyside for the terrifying all-out assault, and the death and destruction inflicted upon an already war-weary population. The raids lasted for six and a half hours, from half past ten in the evening of the 3rd to five o'clock the following morning. Three hundred enemy aircraft invaded the skies and dropped an estimated 50,000 incendiaries, lighting up a clear path for the 360 tons of high explosives to follow. Few areas were untouched either side of the river, with over 300 reported incidents. The damage and loss of life were the heaviest of the war.

Nora Gauterin (née Gopsill), born in 1919 and raised in Birkenhead, was working as a typist in the Old Hall Street, Liverpool office of John Moores and his growing Littlewoods Mail Order empire:

It was May 1941 and I was living in Birkenhead with my parents, gran aged 87, Nell my sister, and my little brother Jimmy who was six. Jack my brother, who was out on air raid warden duties, also lived in Birkenhead, while my oldest brother Ted was away in the army. On this particular night, I had got home from work in Liverpool - it would be about 6.30pm - I had my evening meal, and we sat in the kitchen listening to the radio, hoping that the air raid sirens would not sound and we could spend our night at home, instead of in the communal air raid centre which was in the next street. However, the noise of the bombs, and the bombers got louder, and of course the sirens went, so we were just preparing to go to the air raid shelter when a furious knocking at the door proceeded a voice shouting to get out as quickly as we could as a land mine had come down at the other end of our street and was tangled in the telephone wire overhead.

Stumbling up the street, whilst wardens yelled at us to hurry - mum carrying Jim and Dad trying to help Gran, and Nell and myself carrying as many of our belongings as we could. We were on our way when we saw that Granny had no shoes on, she had had no time to put them on before we went into the shelter and hadn't said anything, walking over glass and rubble without a word. Nell and I didn't hesitate, we dumped our things and went back to Horatio Street. Dodged the ARP wardens, and dashed into No.11, found Granny's shoes and fled back up to the Roxy, to great shouting from the Wardens, we were very scared but safe. The bomb could have gone off at any moment, but we never even thought about it.

We went first under the Roxy cinema - there were lots of people there in the cellar, mostly women and children and older men who were not in the forces as most of the younger men had gone. There was nowhere to sit down, everyone was standing. Finally, we settled for a while, and we were wondering if we would have a home to go to when morning came. Then came an almighty crash. It was deafening, women shrieked, children screamed, and men shouted their terror. Then a policeman ran down the steps and told us to get out, as there was an unexploded bomb which had fallen over the road. Wardens appeared, trying to calm us but had to tell us the cinema was on fire overhead. We had to be very orderly, march out as quickly as possible and not to panic. We didn't panic, which was wonderful really, we did as we were told, and were soon out - there must have been over 100 people there, mostly women and children with some older men and women.

We all scrambled out as quickly as we could, amid the debris which was all around since a bomb had demolished the bottom end of the street. It was like an inferno in the street and there was confusion then. The warden said 'Go up to Beechcroft!' - this was a big old house in Whetstone Lane where I used to attend girls' clubs, while the hall was used for concerts, lectures, plays etc, so I knew it had huge cellars there where we could shelter. It was quite a walk away, but I told Nell, and she and I got our family together and we all started off for Beechcroft. I will never forget that walk, not too far, but what with the bombs, the fires and the people all trying to find shelter - it was a nightmare.

Fortunately, there were places for us at Beechcroft - at least we had chairs to sit on, so we made ourselves as comfortable as we could, and sat the night out still listening to that awful bombing. We passed the rest of the night sitting there tensely quiet - wondering what was happening and flinching with fear every time another bomb dropped. The old people who were there I felt so sorry for them, they had been through one war, they never thought they'd see another.

In the early hours of the morning, and after what seemed an age, the all clear went, much to our relief, and we made ready to leave. So Mother said to me 'Have you got your handbag?' Of course I did, I never went anywhere without it. 'Well you'll have your fare. Right, off you go, you're going to work.'

So, off I went through the rubble down to the tube station, wondering if the trains would run, but they did, so I managed to get to Liverpool. Got off at James Street station, I was finding my way through Derby Square so I could reach Old Hall Street where I worked as a typist in Littlewoods mail order stores. It was very early, but people were making their way to work picking their way over the rubble and the still smoking buildings. And then out of the blue a rich Liverpool voice said 'Wanna cup of tea love?' and I looked up and there was this little small plump Salvation Army lady behind an improvised table with a tea urn would you believe it, and 'would I like a cup of tea?' She said 'I haven't got any mugs left, will you have it in a jam-jar?' Well, I wouldn't have cared what it came in, I really wanted that cup of tea, and do you know it was the best cup of tea I've ever had, I couldn't thank this dear lady enough.

That was the worst night we had ever known, and Jack told us later that he and his mate - both on ARP duty - had decided to split and tossed a coin - one going up the street and Jack down the street. His mate was to blown to smithereens, since his end of the street got a direct hit. We were so grateful that it wasn't Jack, and it was a very sobering moment for us. However, life had to go on, I went to work as usual, Jim went to school and our everyday routine carried on as normal.

Every night the air raid sirens went, and we got used to going to the communal air raid shelter to try and sleep, it was terrible. And I have to say that my Mother was so strong and coped brilliantly, as most of the women did in those dreadful harrowing days. It seems incredible to me now, but then - in those awful dark days - we just got on with things, we had no time to be really frightened, we had to beat the Germans and we had to work hard to do so. Life was grim and very frightening, but the most wonderful spirit pervaded us all. It was uplifting - we helped each other willingly and happily, sharing all we had and offering shelter to those who had nothing. No one questioned it, we knew it could be us next - so we were happy to do what we could and stick together.

Nora Gauterin, unpublished Memoir and interview, November 2016

[Nora, still going strong, fiercely independent living at home, although with regular support from her family, celebrated her 102nd birthday in October 2021.]

Lying on the west coast of the Wirral, Heswall was regarded as relatively safe, despite its proximity to Liverpool and Birkenhead docks. However, this changed once the bombing decoys came into action off the coastline from Hilbre to Burton Marshes. Nevertheless, it was not until 31 May 1941 before Heswall suffered its first raid. Three people were killed when their house and the two neighbouring houses in Village Road received a direct hit. Two more people were killed in the School House, which was then in School Hill. The following night more casualties occurred in Telegraph Road. Many other buildings in the path of the bombs were destroyed and Heswall Council School on the Puddydale was damaged.

Across Merseyside during the month of May 1941 alone, 681 bombers had dropped around 870 tons of high-explosive bombs and over 112,000 incendiaries, causing over 1,800 deaths and 1,200 serious injuries. Half of the Liverpool docks were put out of action, 500 roads were closed to traffic, railways and tramlines were badly damaged, over 700 water mains and eighty sewers were fractured or destroyed; gas, electricity and telephone services were badly damaged, and 400 fires were attended by the fire brigade on the night of 3 and 4 May alone. Throughout the whole period of attacks, more than 4,000 people died, with many areas laid waste, a number of well-known buildings demolished and essential services destroyed or

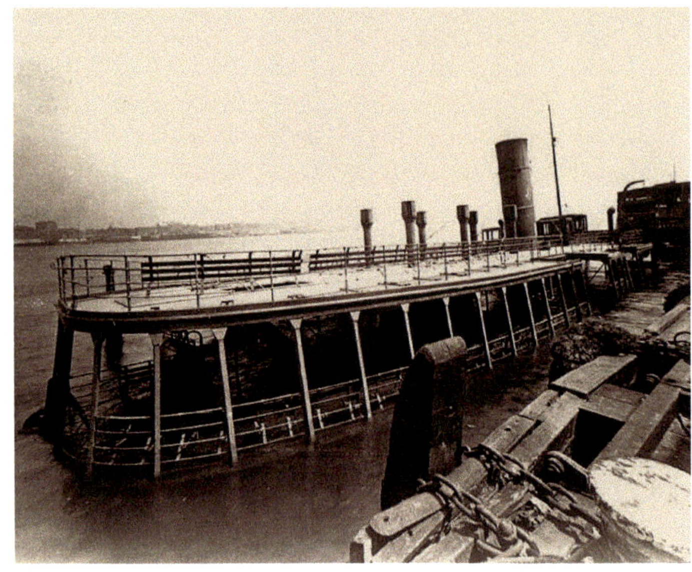

The Blitz on The Wirral
Left: *Royal Daffodil II* sunk at her berth, May 1941.

Below left: 33 Henry Street, Birkenhead.

Below right: Brougham Road bomb damage.

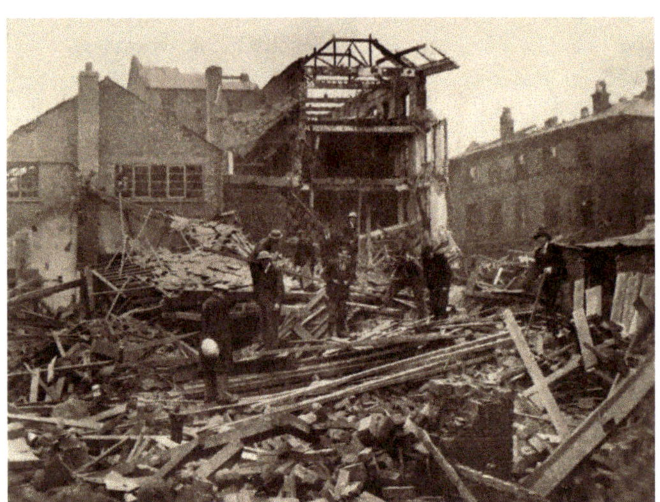

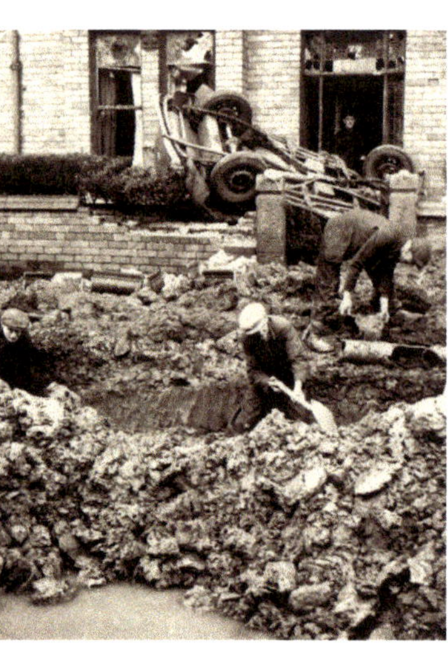

disrupted. Some 10,000 homes were lost, 16,400 seriously damaged, and 45,500 slightly damaged, which resulted in well over 75,000 people being made homeless. In the clear-up that followed, 9,000 workers from outside the city were drafted in, plus 2,700 troops deployed to help to remove debris from streets. The raids on Wallasey and Birkenhead destroyed 3,229 homes and damaged a further 43,000, 18,156 of which were in Wallasey. In Birkenhead 78 per cent of housing was affected.

There were countless acts of heroism throughout these testing times, to save lives and alleviate suffering. Many went unreported, especially among the emergency and support services, as they were 'only doing what was expected', and there were so many others who rushed to help wherever they could; to hold the hand of trapped victims, to burrow in the rubble, to lift crashed beams, calm those who were terrified – such endless acts of humanity. Many were officially recognised:

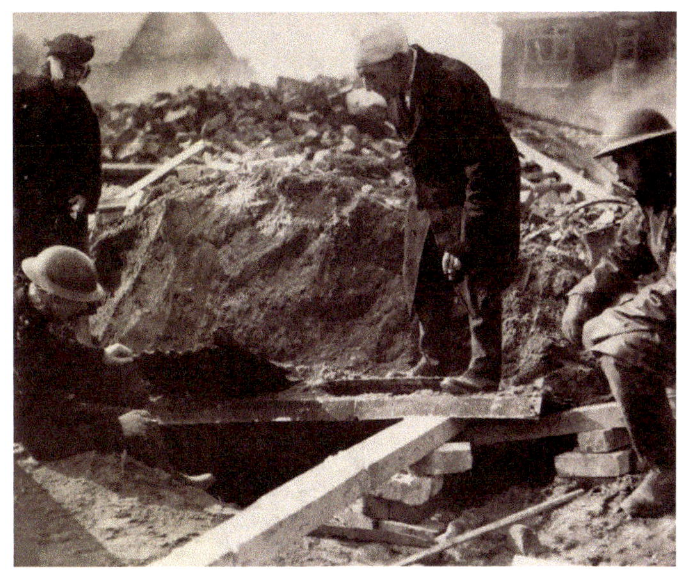

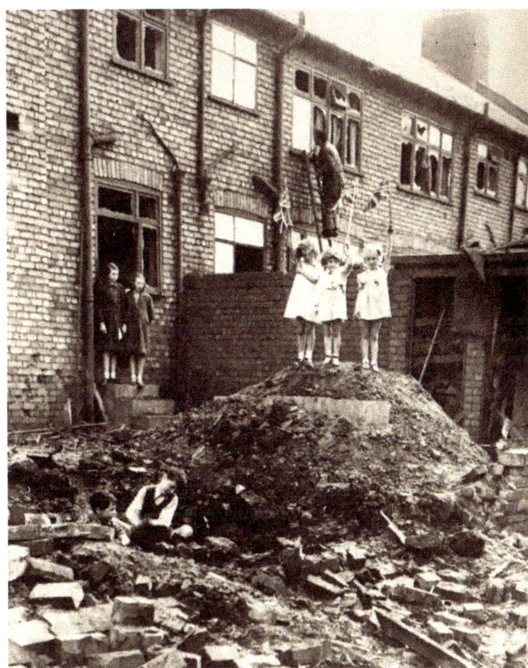

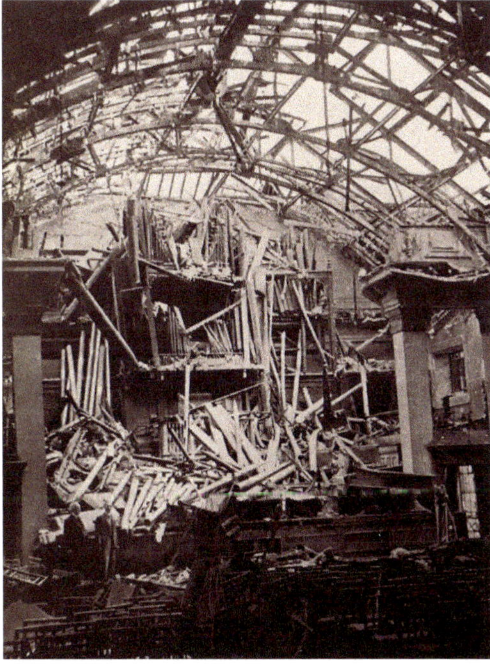

by the end of the conflict there were five George Crosses awarded for bravery on Merseyside, two incidents of which were in Birkenhead including Norman Tunna, the first ever recipient of the award.

The final German air raid on Merseyside took place on 10 January 1942. Despite the bombings, the port remained open and working for most of the war, handling over 70 million tons of cargo. Hitler's campaign to hammer Merseyside into submission and to stop the port from functioning had failed.

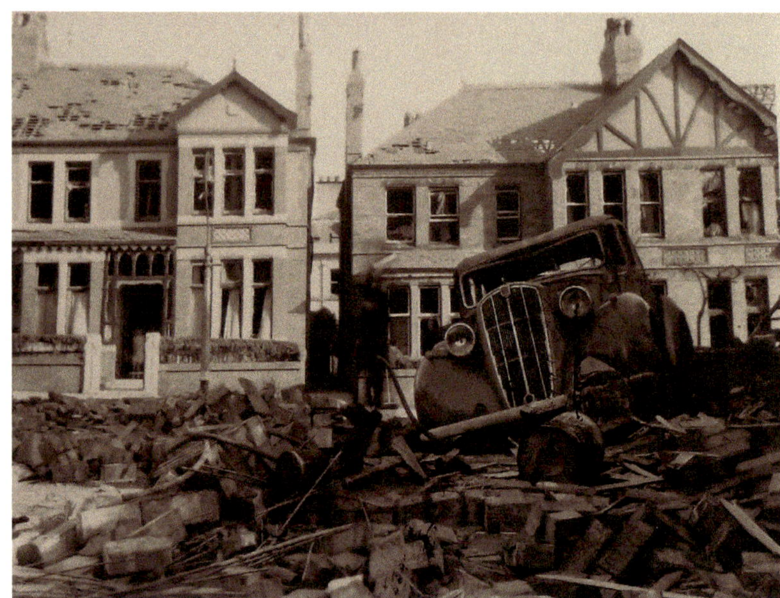

Left: Stoneby Drive, Wallasey garage.

Below: Wallasey blitz memorial.

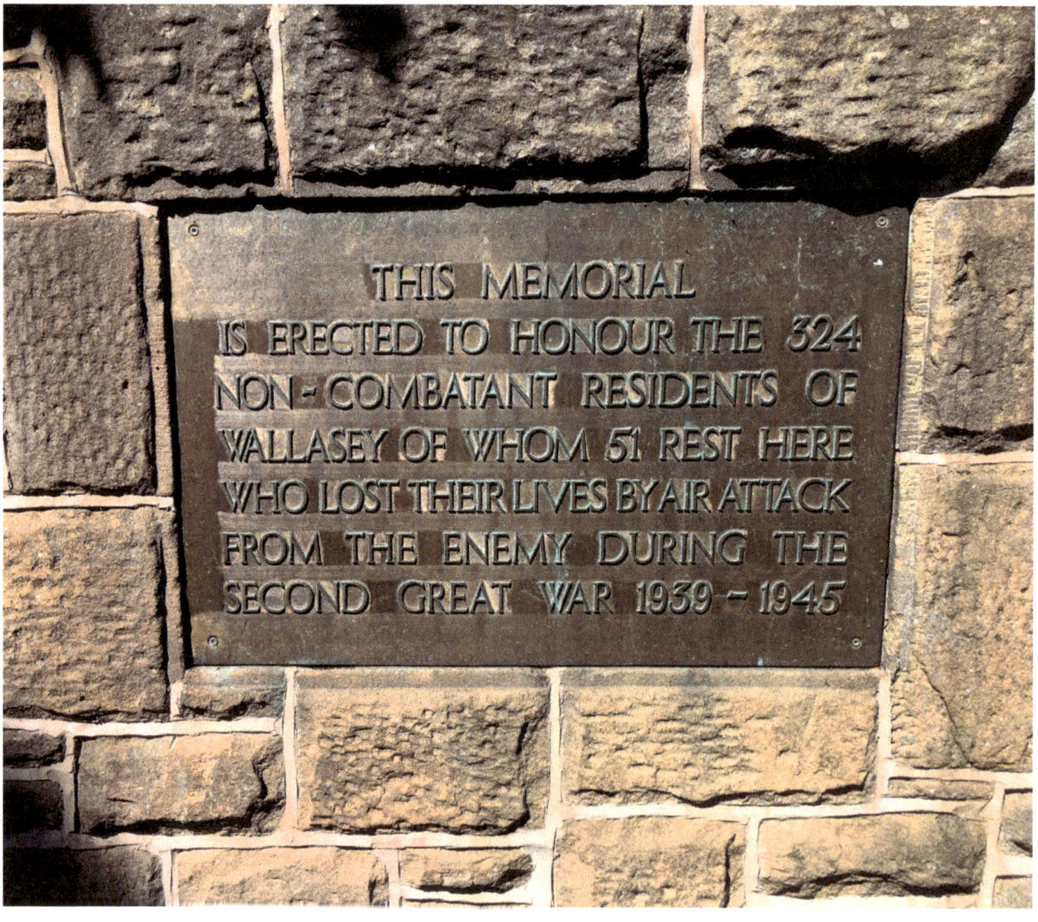

Chapter 9

The Home Front

It was soon apparent in the days and weeks following the Blitz that many of those serving overseas no longer had a home to return to, nor did their families. One of the support agencies working to help was the armed forces charity SSAFA (Soldiers, Sailors, Airmen and Families Association), which immediately provided £500 funding and set about securing accommodation. Supplemented by substantial contributions from the Lord Mayor of Liverpool's Air Raid Distress Fund, and the British War Relief Society of America, the former preparatory school of St Fillan's in Riverbank Road, Heswall, opened in late May – only two weeks after the bombings – as an emergency home for Merseyside families of soldiers serving abroad. St Fillan's not only provided shelter for young children but also their mothers, meaning families could stay together for the duration. Through wartime the new home admitted over several hundred women and children and there was a long waiting list, prompting the opening of further emergency homes and children's homes across the country.

Nancy Batten, daughter of Sir Ernest Royden of Hill Bark, Frankby, was a voluntary worker for the SSAFA from 1937, before her appointment as a Honorary County Secretary in 1945. This was a family team as her husband, Lieutenant-Colonel J. F. Batten MC, joined the SSAFA in 1942 following his retirement from the army. He became the Director of Overseas Department of the organisation and was awarded the OBE for his work with the charity in 1950.

In the months following the last bombing raids on Merseyside in January 1942, life assumed a routine of perseverance through various hardships: the rationing of food, clothing, and many other essential items; coping with the upheaval of lost homes or workplaces through enemy attack; and worst of all, the loss of family members. Birkenhead and Wallasey had borne the brunt of the Blitz, and many buildings lay in ruins or were boarded up, and others were simply fenced off. Dockers worked night and day to keep the war supplies coming through, and heavily laden horse-drawn

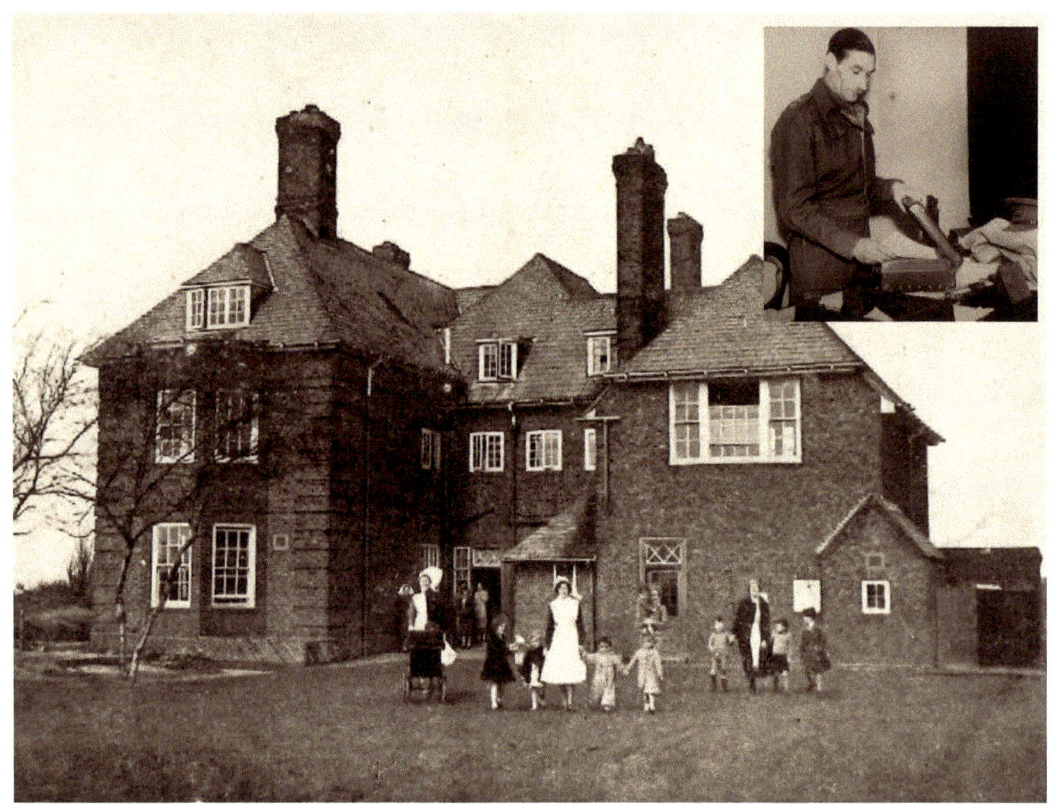

St Fillians Emergency rest home, Heswall. *Inset:* Lieutenant-Colonel J. F. Batten, OBE, MC.

carts were still a normal sight due to petrol rationing. The same streets were frequently crowded with servicemen on leave or on duty, many from abroad joining with the Allied cause, and thousands more arriving after 1942 with America's entry into the war. Occasionally there would be Home Guard military exercises, which would often create interest and draw spectators, who would be able to witness first-hand our soldiers 'in action'.

It was about this time that another incident occurred which I saw. A Spitfire came flying over our house quite noisily and low, then it seemed to climb, banked, and came hurtling towards the ground. There was a tremendous thud then silence. Word soon got around that the plane had crashed, narrowly missing houses in Claughton Road, and had nosed dived into the park. My brother George and I went to see where it had landed. There was a huge crater and chunks of metal around it. Apparently, the pilot had bailed out after setting the plane to fly out to sea, but something went wrong. The pilot landed safely.

David Millar, *BBC WW2 People's War,* 14 November 2003

On 14 October 1942 an American pilot, Flight Sergeant Douglas Cooper Goudie, flying for the Royal Canadian Air Force, had taken off from RAF Hawarden on a test flight in a Mark 2A Spitfire P7533. While over the Mersey he got into difficulties and bailed out, landing in the Dingle in Toxteth, where he suffered just a sprained ankle. The Spitfire, however, continued towards the built-up areas on the Wirral side of the river, but crashed safely without causing injuries, in Birkenhead Park, near Park Road East, in a field known as Night Pasture. In the late 1970s the Warplane Wreck Investigation Group (WWIG) made an attempt to recover the Spitfire, but their focus was at least 20 metres away from the actual crash site and nothing was recovered. However, in December 2005 a further search by the WWIG using UXB metal-detecting magnetometer equipment revealed the correct site. Consequently, in 2007 an excavation took place which revealed the remains of the heavily fragmented and compacted Spitfire wreckage, including the engine block, so crushed that they confirmed the aircraft had crashed at a steep trajectory, as reported by several eyewitnesses at the time. The artefacts are now on exhibition in Fort Perch Rock, New Brighton.

As the war progressed, the war effort began to take on many facets, and lives at home were affected in a variety of ways. As the government responded to unfolding shortages, there were constant drives to boost the war economy and to ensure the war machine was well supplied. Factories were requisitioned for war work, rationing was stepped up, and women were mobilised to an unprecedented degree. Drives for recyclable materials were introduced, which provided morale-boosting work, making those involved feel they were making a difference and part of the war effort. There were opportunities for children too, usually through their schools, fundraising and recycling materials, eager to make a contribution.

Food rationing commenced in January 1940, when bacon, butter and sugar were rationed, followed by meat, fish, tea, jam, biscuits, breakfast cereals, cheese, eggs, milk and canned fruit. Ration books with coupons were issued to every man, woman and child, and adults had to register with particular retailers. Fresh fruit and vegetables were never rationed but were often in short supply, especially tomatoes, while petrol was rationed from the start of the war. Other key commodities were also rationed, such as clothes from June 1941, and soap in February 1942. Also in short supply were cigarettes and alcohol, despite them not being rationed.

The Ministry of Food bombarded the public with poster campaigns, leaflets and cinema adverts, giving advice and guidance, while cooking tips and recipes regularly featured in the local press. Alternative ingredients in mock recipes became the norm, such as 'cream' made from margarine, milk and cornflour, and carrots replacing sugar in tarts. Powdered egg and Spam kept many a family going. Large areas, especially local parkland, were given over to allotments in the 'Dig for Victory' campaign.

As hardship began to bite regarding the clothing rations, the 'Make Do and Mend' campaign was introduced with numerous hints and tips on how to recycle domestic materials:

To encourage the War Effort people were encouraged to grow their own vegetables, and my father obtained a plot near to Tranmere Rovers Football ground just off Borough Road. We grew vegetables and marrows and even loganberries. It was quite a distance to get to the allotment and when part of Birkenhead Park was opened up for allotments we went there instead. We built a tool box, a compost heap and grew lots of vegetables. I learned about double digging, sowing seeds, transplanting and the importance of horse manure, watering and spraying derris powder as an insecticide using a brass hand pump. I often went around with a small handcart my father had made to sweep up after horses, or went to the stables in the docks and filled the cart with well-rotted manure and took it to the compost heap, where it steamed. I remember planting drumhead cabbage seeds that my father had been given to him when he had been working in Bangor in North Wales, and how well they grew.

David Millar, BBC WW2 People's War, 14 November 2003

We got used to rations too, though it was the mothers who had the hardest task trying to make them spread out and concoct meals from what there was. There were no eggs, fruit, cakes, biscuits, sweets etc. They were the luxuries and we could live without them. But even the essentials were in short supply. Very little meat and if the queue at the butcher's shop was long, and you were at the end, then you would find your meat ration for the week consisting of a lump of corned beef. This went on for years after the war, but by then we were so used to it that we took it all as normal. Queues became part of our life. If you saw one, you automatically joined it - if you had time. It didn't matter what it was for, you just joined it and hoped that it was for something edible. Half your life was spent queuing for something and oh, the triumph when you got to the counter and managed to buy whatever it was that you had waited for. I remember bringing home a lemon - great luxury - after queuing for hours. Mothers came up with marvellous recipes to make sustaining meals on what we got.

Clothes also went on ration. We had an issue of clothing coupons twice a year, and you had to manage with them. So, you looked after your clothes, you darned and mended and patched - hence the expression 'Make do and mend'. Goodness, we learned to do that alright. Every last thing was in short supply or else rationed, but there was always the 'black market'. There was always someone who could get something and know how to make money selling it to those who didn't have. I often wondered how the 'spivs', as we called them, obtained goods that were really on ration, but those who bought never questioned it, and there were not too many people who could honestly say they had never bought anything off the 'black market'. I think an awful lot of people got rich in those years.

Nora (Gopsill) Gauterin, unpublished memoir and interview, November 2016

One night, out of the blue, Nora's young brothers, Jack and Jimmy, arrived home. They had been desperately unhappy living with their evacuation hosts in Western Rhyn and decided to pack their bags and return home, much to everyone's surprise when they walked in unannounced after being dropped off by a friendly lorry driver who had stopped to give them a lift. At fourteen Jack joined the ARP and became an air-raid warden, while also serving in the sea cadets. He eventually joined up in 1944 and served with the Royal Engineers in Palestine. After the war, young Jimmy was called up for National Service in 1950 and served in the Cheshire Regiment. Sister Nell was in the Women's Land Army, while older brother Ted joined the King's (Liverpool) Regiment on the outbreak of war. He had already been given an award for bravery when he dived into the Mersey to rescue a boy from drowning. In 1942 he was commissioned as an officer into the 1st King George V's Own Gurkha Rifles (The Malaun Regiment), and served with the 3rd Battalion in Burma. At the

110

age of twenty-three, he was awarded the Military Cross in 1945 while fighting in Cochin-China (now Vietnam). He continued to serve in the Far East with great distinction after the war, and was awarded the DSO for exemplary bravery while in command of the 7th Gurkha Rifles during communist insurgency in Malaya in December 1949. He founded and trained a new regiment, the 1st Malayan Rangers, and became chief instructor at the Brigade of Gurkhas Training Depot. In 1965 he was awarded the OBE for services to the Malayan Armed Forces. Long into retirement he never forgot the Gurkhas, and was instrumental in the campaign for a memorial to mark the 200th year of their service in the British Army, later unveiled by the Princess Royal at the National Arboretum in Staffordshire.

The man whose idea it was to create a memorial was Lieutenant Colonel Edward Gopsill, a veteran of the unforgiving jungles of Burma and Indochina in the Second World War. Mr Gopsill said: 'It is absolutely wonderful to have Princess Anne here, and also to remember the sacrifice of these men. We owe so much to the Gurkha - there's a great danger they could be forgotten.' He also paid tribute to the men's fighting ability on the battlefield and their kindness off it. 'We were in Burma, Indochina, the Dutch East Indies - the fighting and killing, it seemed like it would never stop, but eventually it did, and we came back for a bit of peace and quiet,' he said. 'But with the Gurkha, you got a real person wherever you went. I took my wife to Nepal where they live, and the family matters enormously to them. It is a hard life for them, but they are the most joyous and kind people I have ever met.' Mr Gopsill, who also fought in the Malaya Emergency, said, 'I think the messages will go back from the Gurkha here today, when they are on leave in their villages, and they will tell them about it. The people there will be thrilled that we are thinking of them here.'

TV interview – Lieutenant-Colonel Edward Gopsill DSO, OBE,
MC speaking at the Gurkha memorial unveiling at the
National Memorial Arboretum, 23 September 2014

Lieutenant-Colonel Edward Gopsill DSO, OBE, MC, this unsung Wirral hero, died on 25 July 2016, at the age of ninety-four.

Cinema played a valuable role in keeping civilian morale high – as well as keeping people up to date with the latest Pathé news reels on the war effort. Most of the local population went a least once a week, with Saturday mornings the preserve of children, who would queue excitedly around block in the 'Tuppenny Crush' waiting to see the cartoons or the latest Roy Rogers cowboy film. Adults could escape in the lavish drama of *Gone with the Wind* (1939), or classics like *Rebecca* (1940) while dramas about the war featured too of course, reflected in *Casablanca* (1942) and *Waterloo Bridge* (1940). Life on the Home Front in Britain was echoed in films like *And Millions Like Us* (1943). For the fit and energetic, and the urgent sense of living for the day, the local dance hall was the popular way to forget the war for a few hours, and there were plenty across Merseyside, especially the Tower Ballroom in New Brighton and the Ritz in Birkenhead.

Radio was the popular lifeline for most, and for many listeners it was the comedy of two stars from Toxteth that kept morale up, while introducing a host of new

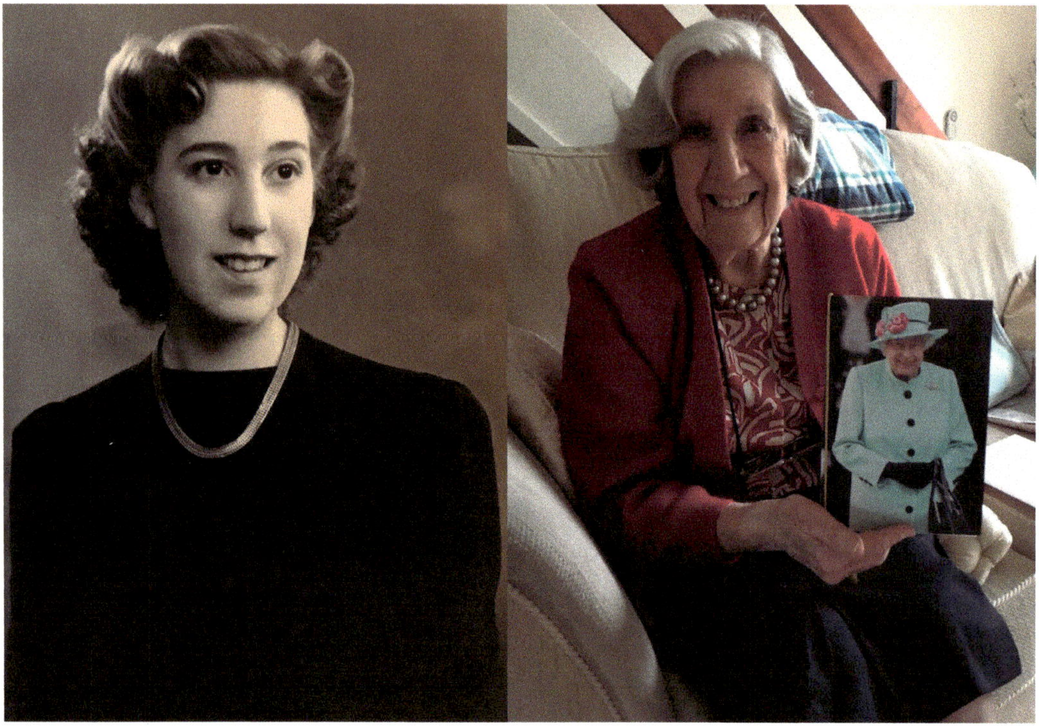

Left: Nora Gopsill at the start of the war. *Right*: Nora Gauterin in October 2019 on the occasion of her 100th birthday and her message from the Queen.

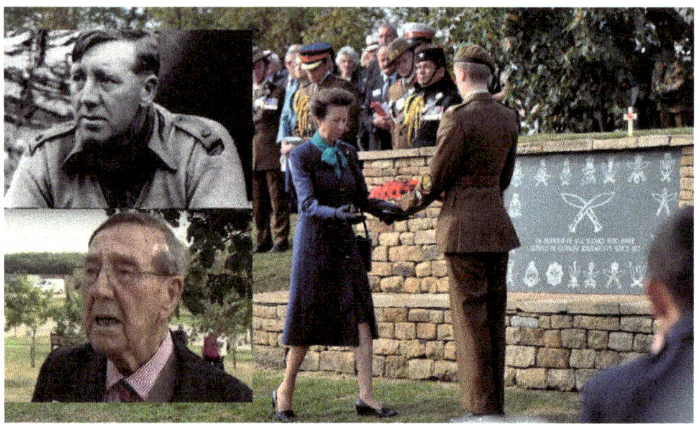

Above left: Princess Anne at the Gurkha memorial. *Insets*: Edward Gopsill with the Gurkhas, and at the Gurkha Memorial.

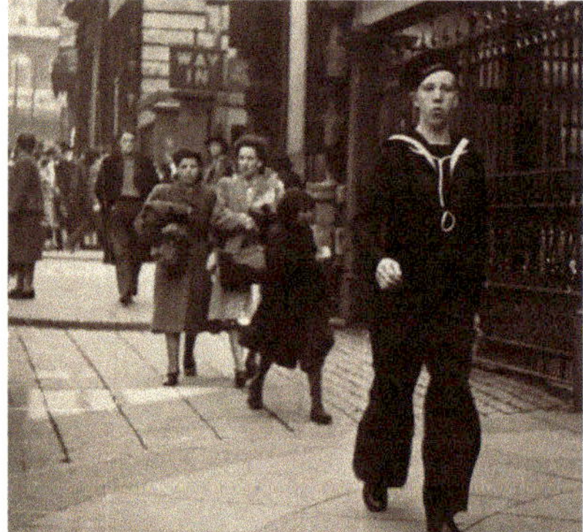

Above right: Jack Gopsill in his cadet uniform passing Liverpool Central Station.

catchphrases into everyday language. Arthur Askey was the star of *Band Waggon*, a groundbreaking series that took listeners into comedy fantasy. While Tommy Handley starred in *ITMA* – 'It's That Man Again' – together with cast member Deryck Guyler and scriptwriter Ted Kavanagh, also from Liverpool. One of the characters, played by Horace Percival, was *The Diver*, a caricature of a well known real-life figure on Merseyside. Frank 'Peggy' Gadsby was a one-legged diver who entertained thousands of visitors to the open-air pools at Hoylake and New Brighton with his daredevil high dives. His appeal for donations after his performance also became *The Diver's* catchphrase on *ITMA*: 'Don't forget the diver, sir, don't forget the diver. Every penny makes the water warmer!'

Yet for many, this escapism was brief, as more people began to be called up. Many women, some of whom were already contributing to the war effort by working as volunteers in various supporting roles, now found their services were required in the factories or the military.

It was announced that all women over the age of 18 had to register for war work. So I did this, and was told I had to leave Littlewoods and do proper work. If I couldn't find something myself within a certain time, I would be directed into a munitions factory or something similar. So, I wrote to Martin Hearns, the aircraft factory in Hooton, and after an interview I started work there as a typist. The money was not much better than what I was already earning, but the work was harder and duller. At Martin Hearns, training planes were repaired and maintained, and my job was to type out all the repairs that had been done. As it was all technical, it was not at all interesting. The offices were situated in an aircraft hangar which were very stark and cold, and we had to travel to and from Birkenhead by bus, so it took a long time. But I felt myself to be lucky, I was still living at home. The eldest of my brothers, Ted had, by then, joined the Kings Regiment (he told a lie about his age). He was somewhere in England, no one ever knew where their menfolk were, it was all strictly hush hush. Even letters gave no clue. My younger sister Nell had joined the Land Army. She looked lovely in her uniform and was full of fun and laughter, but only she knows the sheer drudgery and back breaking work she had to do. She was in the Scilly Isles and didn't get home often, but there was always a giggle when she did come home and relate some of her experiences.

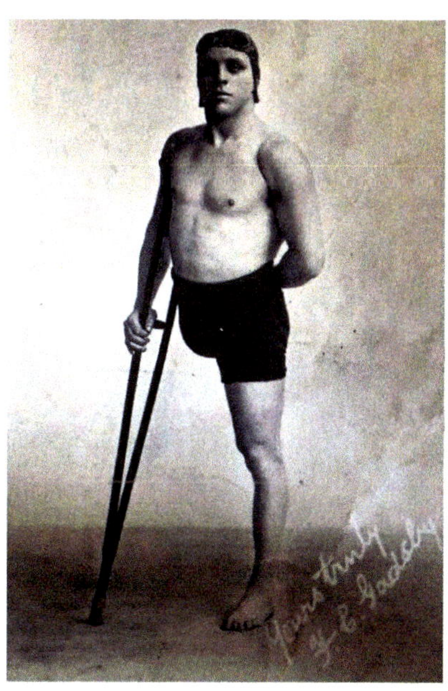

Frank 'Peggy' Gadsby.

I received a letter from the War Office, saying I had to present myself at Central Hall in Liverpool for a medical regarding entry into the Armed Forces. I was quite scared really, but anyway, I duly presented myself at Central Hall, and waited and waited and waited. There were scores of women there, and we were shunted around from room to room where harassed and short-tempered NCO's gave us various tests, oral, mental and practical. As I was a good typist I was to go into the Royal Signals – but to go home first and await further instructions.

Then came the day when THE letter came, I had to report to Queen Ethelburgha's School, Harrogate, to train as a teleprinter operator with the Royal Signals. At Lime Street Station, there were about six girls getting the same train, so I presumed they too were going to Harrogate. I got talking to one of the girls and yes, she was going to Harrogate to train too. Her name was Phyllis Hayes and she lived in Rock Ferry. We both admitted that we were very apprehensive and scared, since we had no idea what lay ahead of us. We soon found out. Met at Harrogate by a sergeant, a woman built like a tank with a voice to match. She ushered us to the front of the station and told us to wait. There were other girls there, having been met from the other trains and obviously we were all going together. Finally, we all seemed to be assembled and two lorries came and off we went. That was the first time I had ridden in an army lorry and very uncomfortable it was too. We couldn't see very much of where we were going, but finally we arrived and out we got, wondering what was in store for us.

Nora Gauterin, *Unpublished Memoir,* **November 2016**

[Nora and Phyllis completed their training and were posted to Chester where they served in the bunkers below Western Command overlooking the Dee.]

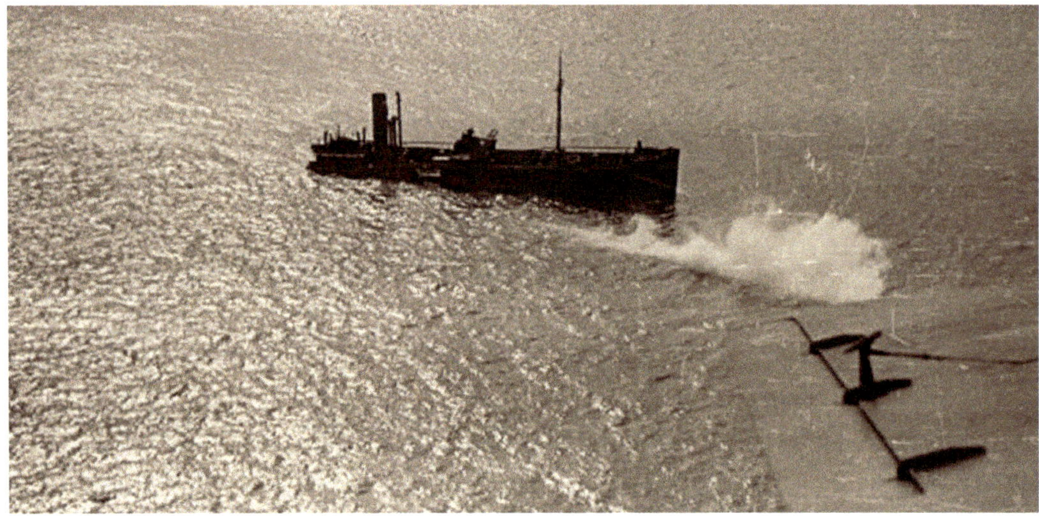

The wreck of the Greek steamer SS *Nestos*, which had run aground and was abandoned on Hoyle Sands off Hoylake in April 1941 while trying to avoid an enemy attack, became instrumental in the development of radar. Test flights from RAF Valley on Anglesey were directed to the Dee estuary and the vessel made an ideal target, as the wreck varied from being almost totally exposed at low tide, to being almost covered at high tide. This offered a range of different target profiles for radar trials. The remains of the wreck can still be seen today.

A FAMILY AT WAR

Bebington Roydens

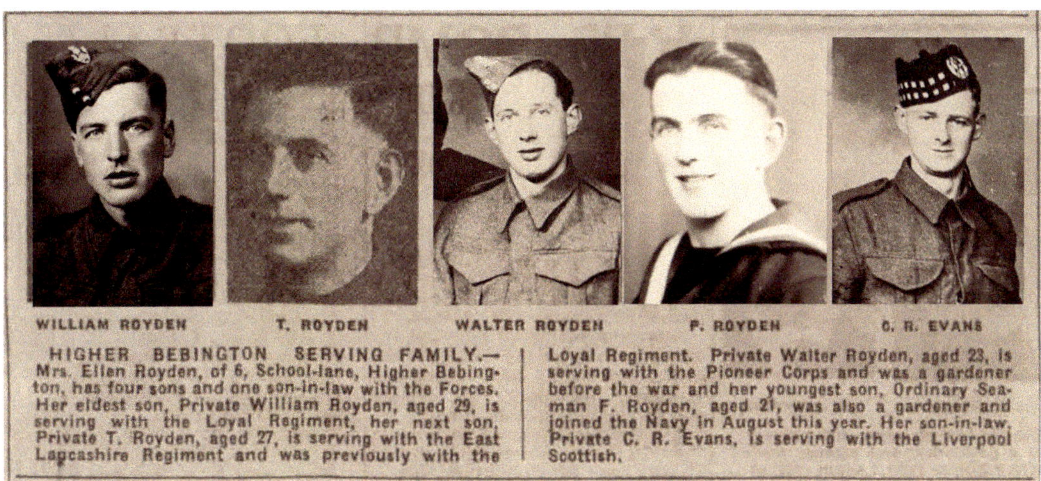

HIGHER BEBINGTON SERVING FAMILY.— Mrs. Ellen Royden, of 6, School-lane, Higher Bebington, has four sons and one son-in-law with the Forces. Her eldest son, Private William Royden, aged 29, is serving with the Loyal Regiment, her next son, Private T. Royden, aged 27, is serving with the East Lancashire Regiment and was previously with the Loyal Regiment. Private Walter Royden, aged 23, is serving with the Pioneer Corps and was a gardener before the war and her youngest son, Ordinary Seaman F. Royden, aged 21, was also a gardener and joined the Navy in August this year. Her son-in-law, Private C. R. Evans, is serving with the Liverpool Scottish.

Several of the Bebington Royden family served in the war. Their younger brother Charles also served – in the Navy after lying about his age. (Their father's brother was Alfred Royden who lost his life in the First World War, described in Chapter 3.) All survived the war. (*Liverpool Evening Express*, 20 December 1941)

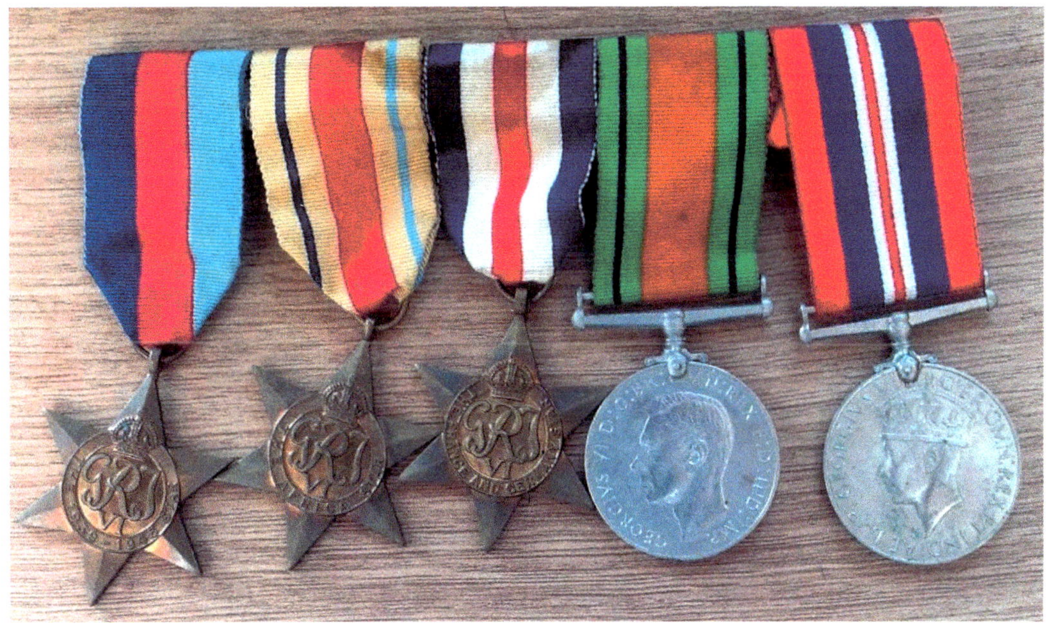

Medals of Private William Henry Royden, Loyal Regiment (North Lancashire), of Bebington. *Left to right*: 1. 1939–45 Star, 2. Africa Star North Africa 1942–43, 3. France and Germany Star 1944/45, 4. Defence Medal Civilian Service, 5. Second World War Campaign Medal 1939–45.

Chapter 10

The End of the War

By the time Winston Churchill announced on a radio broadcast at three o'clock in the afternoon on Tuesday 8 May 1945 that Victory in Europe would be official later that evening when surrender terms were ratified in Berlin, crowds had already been on the streets from late the previous evening. The BBC radio newsflash at 11 p.m. on the 7th announced that the next day would be Victory in Europe Day and a national holiday, but after six years of war, there was no way people were going to obediently wait to be told when they could celebrate, and within minutes of the newsflash streets were full of revellers enjoying themselves, lighting bonfires and singing and dancing.

Consequently, the following day, the official VE Day, the British public were ready for a full celebration. Flags and bunting fluttered triumphantly out of household windows, while fixed and touring loudspeakers relayed speeches and music for dancing, In Birkenhead, a massed procession took place, with detachments representing every branch of the town's war service taking part. Cheering crowds lined the route to Hamilton Square, where the mayor was waiting with the mayoress to take the salute. More speakers blasted out the prime minister's speech as the procession reached the Town Hall, before a formal church service and a minute's silence in commemoration of the fallen, while a Salvation Army Band provided the accompaniment to 'Now Thank We All Our God' and the national anthem.

In Bebington, the Mayer Hall was given the added touches of fairy lights for the evening's celebrations, and a procession was planned for the following morning to St Andrew's. In Wallasey, there were few streets without a display of some sort, with illuminations and bonfires lighting up the evening. Organised dancing was everywhere: West Kirby, Hoylake, the local parks, and New Brighton Promenade, where the specially erected speakers blasted out the music outdoors while local halls were packed to the rafters.

There were similar scenes, processions and church thanksgiving services across the Wirral with speakers erected at local vantage points for the relaying of speeches by the king and the prime minister.

Celebrations were rather muted at first due to the lashing rain, but the wet weather gave way to an afternoon of glorious sunshine as the crowds re-emerged, and the revelries picked up once more. Victory chimes rang from city churches and municipal buildings, while on the river, ships, tugs and ferry boats on the crowded water displayed flags and banners and sounded horns, which at 3.08 p.m. turned into a great cacophony at the conclusion of Churchill's relayed speech, with the ferry boats trying to drown out the rest with blasts of the V-for-Victory note.

I remember when VE Day was announced by Winston Churchill, there was great relief and rejoicing. I was 13 at the time and my friend and I danced in the park. The biggest thrill was the end of the blackout. No more putting up the blackout frames on all the windows every night! The local Council had installed new electric lights for the occasion (some of the side streets still had gaslights up to 1939). We all went to the village, especially to see the lights turned on at last. No more fumbling in the dark with a dimmed-out torch!

There was a Victory Parade through the village and we watched the men and women of the army, navy and air force, with allied personnel included, march past. We felt very proud. The golf links had been mined at the outbreak of war to stop the enemy landing on our beach nearby. These mines were detonated one day and we heard one explosion after another. Rationing did not end with the war, and the food situation got worse for a while. Eventually various foods came off the ration over several years, after the war. The last thing to come off the ration was butter - in 1954! By this time, I was on a Buff Ration Book and I kept my last one as a souvenir!

There were memorable times I lived through, and I am one of the lucky ones to survive to tell the tale.

Ann McKay, Hoylake (2005), *BBC WW2 People's War*

Just like old times isn't it? Just, except that the ice-cream may be in a wobbly paper baking-case, or may taste like sweetened soap suds; that the dinners advertised don't include ham and eggs or steak and chips; and that there is a curious dearth of daddies in the crowds sitting on the sands. Well, a day at New Brighton is much the same as it ever was, so far as a treat for the children is concerned. The sand is still there, tons of it, and the prom, and the pier and the bell they ring for the ferryboat. The donkeys are yet to come, but the merry-go-rounds are getting polished up. Whether you just go for the sail and back again, or whether you go for a snooze on the sands and a bobsworth of 'Tell-your-fortune-lady', there are worse ways of spending a fine day. Only one thing is missing - perhaps that is still to come. Let's hope so - for somehow you can't forget the Diver!

Sara Power, *Liverpool Echo*, 8 May 1945

This real sense of getting back to normal continued just days later on the May Bank Holiday. The previous day had been the wettest Bank Holiday Sunday recorded since 1900, so there was a real eagerness to take advantage of the improved forecast. The misty start to the day gradually saw the sun emerge, creating pastel blues and greens that made the Mersey a very pleasant sight. By 10 a.m. there were already large crowds gathering on the Princes Landing Stage ready for the ferry trip. The river was busy with plenty of shipping to interest the holiday crowds, while fighter aircraft were putting on a show chasing each other up and down the estuary, just feet above the water. The accompanying bombers maintained a more 'respectable' level.

The New Brighton boats were, of course, highly popular. If the war could not stop Merseysiders asserting their inalienable right to a trip to New Brighton on a Bank Holiday, the first festival of peace was certain to bring them out in large numbers and 'young men and maidens, old men and children,' most of them with parcels of food, and the children, as excited as they always are on these occasions, were soon filling these ships, which can take well over a thousand on every voyage. Many carrying packs waited at Woodside or Seacombe for buses to take them to strategic points from which to begin their hike in Wirral. Determined looking cyclists bound for Queen's Ferry also came over in large numbers.

One of the star attractions was the surrendered U-boat 532*, and as early as eleven o'clock there was a queue well over a quarter of a mile long and four or five deep.

By noon, New Brighton was already crowded, all the amusements were in full swing in the Tower and promenade pleasure grounds, and there were queues for boats on the Marine Lake. A band played for dancing on the pier. By three o'clock, it was estimated that the crowd was larger than at any time since before the war. There were queues of almost 100 yards at some of the cafes. The sands were black with people, and outside the pier it was difficult to walk about in the dense crowd.

Liverpool Evening Express, 21 May 1945

*Not to be confused with the U-boat (U-534), still on show today in Birkenhead. Submarine U-532 was later removed to Loch Eriboll and then to Loch Ryan (both in Scotland) for *Operation Deadlight* (the code name for the Royal Navy operation to scuttle German U-boats surrendered to the Allies). She was sunk out in the North Atlantic to the west of Scotland by torpedo, from the British submarine *Tantivy* on 9 December 1945.

For many, the torment was not over, as the war in the Far East would last another three months, before midnight on 14 August, when the new British prime minister, Clement Attlee, confirmed the news in a radio broadcast to the nation, and that two national holidays were declared for VJ Day – Wednesday and Thursday 15/16 August. The celebrating crowds across Wirral were no less enthusiastic as they had been in May.

Getting back to normal though was going to take some time. The end of the war saw additional cuts. Bread, for example, which was never rationed during wartime, was put on the ration in July 1946. It would be three years after the end of the war before restrictions were gradually lifted, starting with flour on 25 July 1948, followed by clothes on 15 March 1949. Rationing for canned and dried fruit, chocolate biscuits, treacle, syrup, jellies and mincemeat ended on 19 May 1950. Petrol rationing, imposed in 1939, ended in May 1950, followed by soap in September 1950. Three years later, sales of sugar and butter were finally off ration, while meat was the last item to be de-rationed, seeing the complete end of food rationing on 4 July 1954.

The port of Liverpool, together with the Wirral dock estate, remained operational throughout the war, despite enemy action, but a third of the docks remained out

118

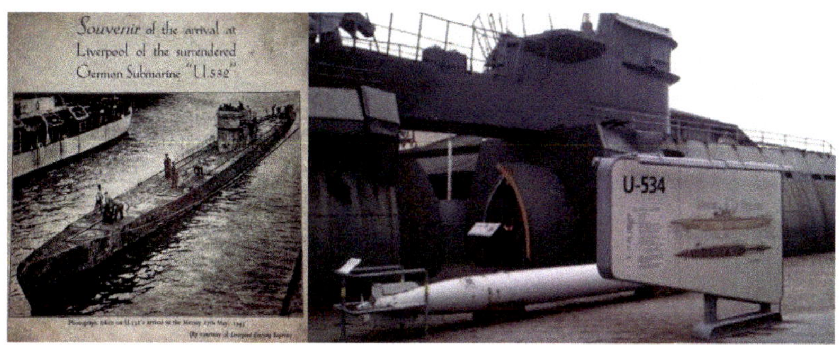

Left: U-boat *532* on arrival in the Mersey. *Right*: U-boat *534* now in sections on display at Woodside, Birkenhead.

of commission due to the damage, and recovery would also take time. While the port dominated Merseyside's economic structure, its future was far from certain, and diversification was clearly essential, especially as many of the older industries were already in decline before the war. There were tough challenges ahead.

Considering the fascination that surrounds Hitler's final hours in the bunker in Berlin as the Allied armies converged upon the city, it is intriguing to learn that one of those present in the underground refuge became a resident of Wallasey. Thirty-year-old Else Krüger from Hamburg-Altona was Martin Bormann's secretary (and, allegedly, his mistress) from the end of 1942 until 1 May 1945. Krüger was with Eva Braun, Gerda Christian, Traudl Junge, and Constanze Manziarly in the Führerbunker during the Battle of Berlin. When Hitler told them that they must prepare to leave for the Berghof, she was one of those who volunteered to remain with Hitler in the bunker. However, on 1 May, the day after Hitler's suicide on 30 April, Else was among the group of survivors led by Waffen-SS Brigadeführer Wilhelm Mohnke who made their escape. Their flight was short-lived, as on the morning of 2 May, the group was captured by soldiers of the Soviet Red Army while hiding in a cellar at the Schultheiss-Patzenhofer Brewery on Prinzenallee. While Junge was later held for several months by the Russians, Gerda Christian and Else Krüger were smuggled across Soviet-occupied territory by sympathetic British soldiers, and eventually made it to the British/American lines, where Krüger was questioned extensively about Bormann and his whereabouts. Bormann was later tried at the Nuremberg trials of 1945/46 'in absentia'. Else gave written evidence to the Nuremberg court but did not appear in person.

Her British interrogator was Birkenhead-born Captain Leslie James, with whom she struck up a relationship after the trial. By 1947 they had returned to James' Wirral home, and they married in Wallasey Registry Office on 23 December 1947. After their Christmas wedding and reception, the couple settled in Ivy Cottage in Green Lane, Wallasey, while Leslie forged ahead with an academic career. By the 1970s they were living in Cambridge where the ex-British Intelligence officer was lecturing in English. Local Wirral residents remember seeing the couple during visits home to see their family. In later life, the couple returned to Else's homeland, living in Staufen im Breisgau, in the Black Forest region of south-west Germany. Leslie suffered a stroke and passed away on 18 August 1995 at the age of seventy-nine, while Else died at the age of eighty-nine on 24 January 2005. Her ashes were laid to rest in the local cemetery, where a memorial plaque records both the names of Else and her husband.

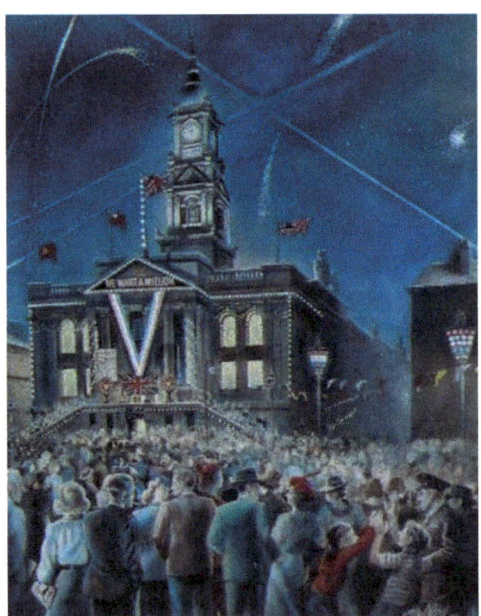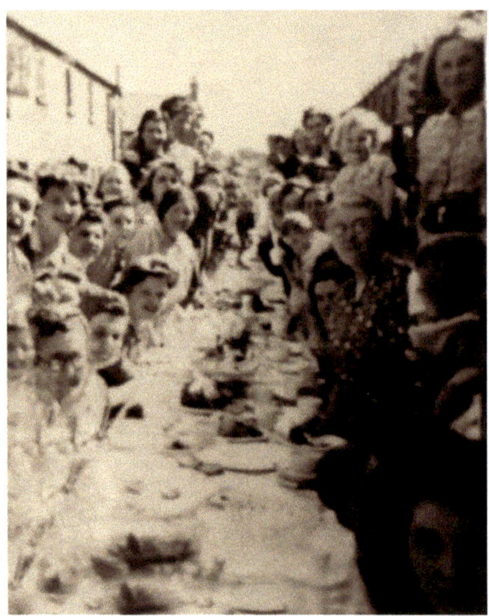

Above left: In Birkenhead a 30-foot illuminated V for Victory sign consisting of 740 blue, red and white light bulbs hung down the front of the Town Hall in Hamilton Square, where speeches were made before cheering crowds. (*VE Day* by Athol Ostell, Williamson Art Gallery)

Above right: Some of the Bebington Royden family at their VE Day street party on School Lane.

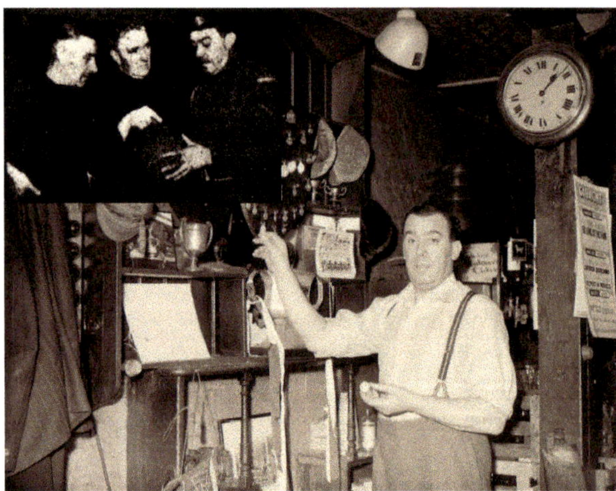

Inset: A rare photo in uniform of another of Wirral's famous sons, Dixie Dean, pictured here in October 1945 with Newcastle footballers Andy McCombie and Joe Richardson at St James' Park, where he had become a regular visitor (he was due to be demobbed the following month). Dean had been a munitions worker at Fawcett, Preston and Co., of Bromborough, before enlisting in July 1940 with the 59th Training Regiment Royal Armoured Corps, where he was a corporal and PT instructor based in Barnard Castle for almost five years. He played regularly for the Army in war effort fundraising matches, and for a variety of other sides too, even turning out for York City in the Northern League and Cambridge Town against an RAF side which they beat 15-1, Dean scoring eight. After his discharge he became the licensee of the Dublin Packet in Chester in 1946 (*main photo*).

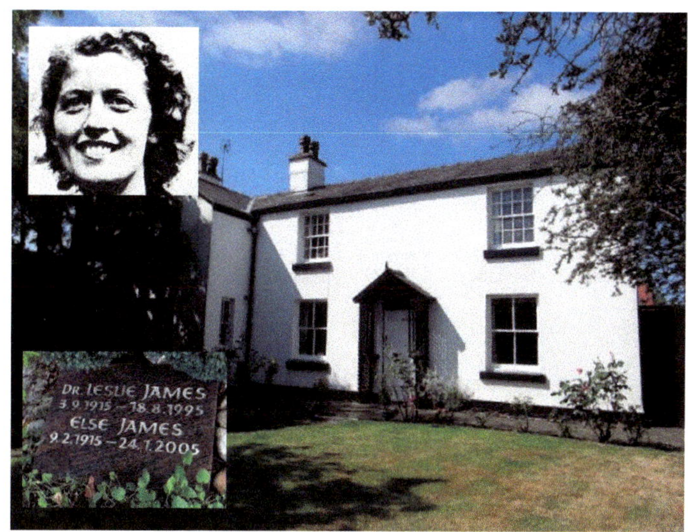

Ivy Cottage in Green Lane, Wallasey, home of Leslie and Else James after the war. *Inset*: Else Kruger James (1915–2005) and the cemetery memorial marker of Leslie James and Else James. (Robin Smith)

After she had moved to England in the aftermath of the war, Else never spoke publicly about her wartime experience, nor did she write her biography, while all requests for interviews were rebuffed. Any further knowledge of what happened in the Führerbunker, in addition to her statements under interrogation, went with her to the grave.

Unlike Leslie James and his new wife, many Wirral people did not have a home to return to after the war, and several temporary prefab estates were constructed for those needing to be rehoused. The devastation caused by the bombing raids on suburban communities led to a desperate shortage in housing, which had to be solved urgently. The spread of temporary 'prefab' estates after the war became a common sight across the Wirral, particularly in Moreton and Molyneux Road, Upton, plus the 'Tintown' estate in Rivacre, Ellesmere Port, many of which were constructed by prisoners of war before their repatriation. There was also the matter of the Woodchurch Estate, purchased from Sir Ernest Royden as long ago as 1926, which still awaited development at the end of the war. The desperate need for housing accelerated bureaucratic decisions, and many of the 2,300 on Birkenhead's council housing waiting list in July 1945 would soon be able to move in, although facilities were woefully slow to be completed.

Britain emerged from the Second World War a different country to that which had entered the conflict six long years previously. Financially ruined, physically exhausted, and facing a massive housing crisis, the problems facing the country were there for all to see. But there was also a tremendous sense of optimism in the country, a feeling that this was a chance to build a new nation, and to rectify the worst mistakes of the past. There was also an almost universal feeling, exemplified by the popularity of the 1942 Beveridge Report, that after victory the country could not go back to pre-war social conditions. Returning servicemen and women had a better chance of living in homes fit for heroes than their First World War counterparts, although some may have had to put up with temporary prefab homes first. The new housing programmes would be swiftly followed by the national legislation to aimed at rebuilding a better Britain. The 1944 Education Act was already on the statute book, but the Labour government's landslide victory in 1945 was very much about creating a new deal for returning servicemen and women, giving them a sense that their country had been worth fighting for and would support and care for them in peacetime by offering them and their families the opportunity for jobs, homes, education, the formation of the NHS and a standard of living of which they could be proud.

There were great challenges ahead, but there was a sense that if the country had got through the war, they could get through this too.

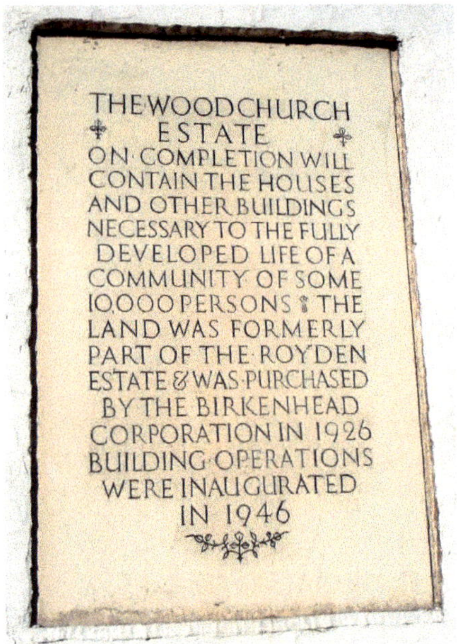

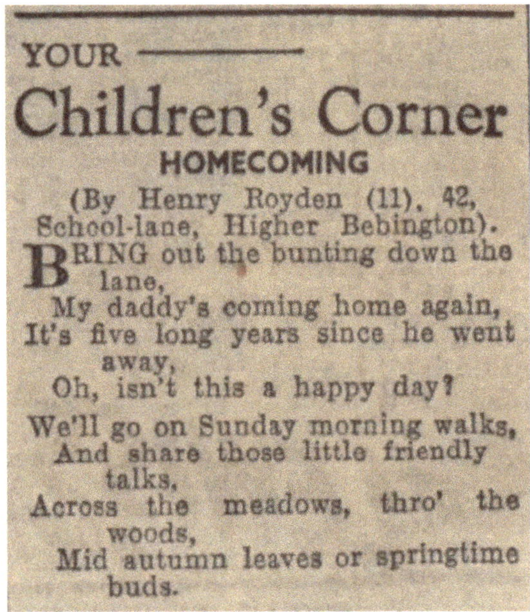

Above left: Woodchurch estate plaque.

Above right: Henry Royden poem. Henry's father was Private William Royden, serving with the Loyal Regiment and previously pictured in Chapter 9 with his brothers from Bebington.

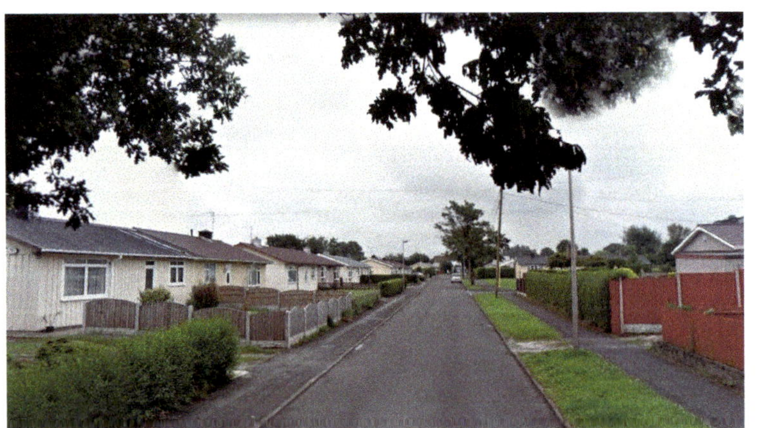

Designed to provide short-term accommodation following the devastation of housing during the Blitz, this prefab estate in Rivacre, Ellesmere Port, is still well maintained with a thriving community. It is one of the last survivors of a prefab estate in the country.

Bibliography

Birkenhead News
Wallasey News
Liverpool Daily Post
Liverpool Echo
Liverpool Evening Express
Chester Observer
Chester Chronicle
Chester Courant
London Gazette Supplements (medals/honours/citations)

FIRST WORLD WAR

Barr, Ronald J., 'The 1st Battalion 22nd (The Cheshire) Regiment and the Reasons for the Military Disaster at Mons', *Cheshire History* No. 35 (1995/96)

Chambers, Susan, *Chester in the Great War (Your Towns and Cities in the Great War)* (Pen & Sword, 2015)

Churton DSO., Lieut.-Col. W.A.V., *War Record of the 1/5th (Earl of Chester's) Battalion, The Cheshire Regiment 1914–1919* (1919, rep. 2009)

Crookenden, A., *History of The Cheshire Regiment in the Great War* (1920)

Curtis, Ann Marie, *A War-Torn Chester Parish: St Werburgh's Before, During and After the Great War* (2017)

Disbrowe, E. J. W. (Ed.): *History of the Volunteer Movement in Cheshire, 1914–1920* (1920).

Ellsworth-Jones, W., *We Will Not Fight* (2008)

Harris, Brian, *Cheshire at War, 1914–18: Chester Armistice Remembrance Week, 4–11 Nov. 1978* (1978)

Honingsbaum, Mark, 'Regulating the 1918–19 Pandemic: Flu, Stoicism and the Northcliffe Press', *Journal of Medical History* vol. 57 (2) (2013), pp. 165–185 (Cambridge University Press, 2013)

Longbottom, Frederick William, *Chester in the Great War* (1920)

McGreal, Stephen, *Moreton & District Patriots 1914–1919* (1999)

McGreal, Stephen, *Cheshire Bantams: 15th, 16th and 17th Battalions of the Cheshire Regiment* (Pen & Sword 2006)

McGreal, Stephen, *Wirral at War* (Pen & Sword 2014)

McGreal, Stephen, *Zeebrugge and Ostend Raids* (Pen & Sword 2007)

Rigby, B., *Ever Glorious: The Story of the 22nd (Cheshire) Regiment, Vol 1* (1982)

Royden, Mike, *Chester at War* (2019)

Royden, Mike, *Village at War: The Cheshire Village of Farndon During the First World War* (2016)

Simpson, F., *Cheshire Regiment; the First Battalion at Mons and the Miniature Colour* (1929)

Simpson, F., *The Chester Volunteers (3rd Volunteer Bn, The Cheshire Regiment 1914–1920)* (1922)

SECOND WORLD WAR

Ayers, Pat, *Women at War* (1988)

Bailey, David, *610 County of Chester Auxiliary Air Force Squadron, 1936–1940* (2018)

Bamford, Joe, & Collier, Ron, *Eyes of the Night; The Air Defence of North Western England 1940–1943* (2005)

Barfield, Norman, *Broughton: From Wellington to Airbus* (2001)

Barr, Ronald, *The Cheshire Regiment* (2000)

Booth, Tony, *Thetis Down: The Slow Death of a Submarine* (2009) Pen & Sword

Boumphrey, Ian, *Wirral on the Home Front 1939–45*

Boumphrey, Ian, *Birkenhead at War 1939–45*

Boumphrey, Ian, *Wallasey at War 1939–45*

Boyce, Joan, *Pillowslips and gasmasks: Liverpool's Wartime Evacuation* (Liver Press 1989)

Buckley, T. J., *Port at War 1939–1945* (Mersey Docks and Harbour Board, 1946)

Burton & Neston History Society, *Neston at War 1939–45* (1999)

Cameron, Gail and Crooke, Stan, *Battle of the Atlantic – An Anthology of Personal Memories*, Liverpool City Libraries (1993)

Ireland, Bernard, *Battle of the Atlantic*, Pen and Sword (2003)

Cullen, Stephen M., *In Search of the Real Dad's Army: The Home Guard and the Defence of the United Kingdom 1940–1944* (2011)

Dobinson, Colin, *Fields of Deception: Britain's Bombing Decoys of World War II* (2008)

Ferguson, Aldon P., *A History of Royal Air Force Sealand* (1978)

Goodall, Felicity, *We Will Not Go to War: Conscientious Objection During the World Wars* (2010)

Jager, Harold, *The Rise and Ascent of Number Two Platoon (Home Guard)* (*Liverpool Daily Post*, 1945). The story of 'A' Company, 17th Battalion Cheshire Regiment (Home Guard), based in Hoylake Wirral during the Second World War

Hughes, John, *Port in a Storm – The Air attacks on Liverpool and its shipping in the Second World War* (1993)

Irby, W. E. A., *Wirral at War* (1991)

Jackson, Richard & Hearn, David, *The Wallasey Blitz* (2020)

Jewell, Alan & Brough, Harold, *Mersey Blitz: Liverpool Under Siege* (*Liverpool Daily Post & Echo* 70th anniversary booklet) (2011)

Johnson, Arthur, *Merseyside's secret Blitz diary: A remarkable personal account of Liverpool at war* (Liverpool, 2005)

Kramer, Ann, *Conscientious Objectors of the Second World War – Refusing to Fight* (2013)

Leslie, S. C. et al, *Bombers over Merseyside, The Authoritative Record of the Blitz 1940–41 Liverpool Daily Post & Echo* (1943)

Liverpool Central Library, *Liverpool Women at War: An Anthology of Personal Memories* (1991)

Longman, Daniel K., *Merseyside War Years: Then and Now* (2012)

Lowry, Bernard, *British Home Defences 1940–45* (2004)

Longmate, N., *The Real Dad's Army: The Story of the Home Guard* (1974)

MacKenzie, S. P., *The Home Guard: A Military and Political History* (1995)

McCarron, K., *Fort Perch Rock and the Defence of the Mersey*, Merseyside Portfolios, Birkenhead (1991)

Perrett, Bryan, *Liverpool: A City at War* (1990)

Powell, Bob and Westacott, Nigel, *The Women's Land Army* (2009)

Roberts, David, *HMS Thetis: Secrets and Scandal, Aftermath of a Disaster* (1999).

Royden, Mike, *Merseyside at War 1939-45* (Pen & Sword 2018)

Royden, Mike, 'Liverpool Pals – The Caldicott Brothers' in *Tales From the 'Pool, A Collection of Liverpool Stories* (2017)

Russell, Pamela, *Liverpool's Children in The Second World War* (2009)

Smith, Noel E., *Helmets, Handcuffs and Hoses: The Story of the Wallasey Police* (Part One) *and The Wallasey Fire Brigade* (Part Two) (2002)

Starkey, P. 'Will Not Fight: Conscientious Objectors and Pacifists in the North West During the Second World War', *Liverpool Historical Studies* Vol.7, Liverpool University Press (1992)

Tyrer, Nicola, *They Fought in the Fields: The Women's Land Army* (2007)

Stevenson, Ian 'The Defences of the Mersey', *The Redan 71, Journal of the Palmerston Forts Society*, pp. 99-130 (2007)

Summerfield, Penny & Peniston-Bird, Corinna, *Contesting home defence: men, women and the Home Guard in the Second World War* (2007)

Tomlinson, N. H. C., *Walking Through the Blitz in the Birkenhead Area 1940–41* (1996)

Turner, F. R., *Maunsell Sea Forts: The World War Two Sea Forts of the Thames and Mersey Estuaries* (1995)

Wade, Beryl, *Storm over the Mersey* (1990)

Whittington-Egan, Richard, *The Great Liverpool Blitz* (1987)

Whitworth, Rodney, *Merseyside at War; A day-to-day diary of the 1940–41 Bombing* (1988)

Unknown Author, *Discovering Wartime Cheshire 1939–1945* (1985)

Defence of Britain Archive Council for British Archaeology, 2002 (updated 2006) – https://archaeologydataservice.ac.uk/archives/view/dob/

28 Days Later (Urban Exploration) – www.28dayslater.co.uk

Derelict Places-documenting decay – www.derelictplaces.co.uk

Hidden Wirral – www.hiddenwirral.org.uk.

North West Exploration Forum – http://nwex.co.uk

The history of Hooton Airfield: www.hootonparktrust.co.uk

Hooton Airfield – https://forgottenairfields.com/airfield-raf-hooton-park-1250.html

UK Invasion Defences of World War 2 – www.pillboxesuk.co.uk.

Colin Schroeder, *The Bromborough Dock Ju88 Incident 8th October 1940* (2010)

National Heritage List for England (Scheduled Monuments List): www.historicengland.org.uk

National Record of the Historic Environment (NRHE) (Historic England): www.pastscape.org.uk

Revealing Cheshire's Past (Cheshire Historic Environment Record http://rcplive.cheshiresharedservices.gov.uk/monumentsearch.aspx – *BBC People's War* – www.bbc.co.uk/history/ww2peopleswar

The Cheshire Military Museum – www.cheshiremilitarymuseum.co.uk

The Cheshire Archives and Local Studies Service Archives – www.cheshire.gov.uk

Cheshire Image Bank – cheshireimagebank.org.uk

Acknowledgements

The author and publisher would like to thank the following people/organisations for permission to use copyright material in this book:

The Cheshire Archives and Local Studies Service
Wirral Archives
Williamson Art Gallery
Cheshire West and Chester Council

Every attempt has been made to seek permission for copyright material used in this book. However, if we have inadvertently used copyright material without permission/acknowledgement we apologise and we will make the necessary correction at the first opportunity.

The author would also like to thank Nick Grant and Jenny Stephens at Amberley for their help and guidance; Tony Wainwright BEM & Peter Jones, fellow members of Everton FC Heritage Society, who have a great depth of knowledge of both wars; Richie Gillham, also of Everton FC Heritage Society, for the information and photographs regarding his great-grandfather Sergeant J. E. Williams; Mike Royden, my namesake and Wirral cousin, for information on his Bebington family during both wars; Peter Gauterin and his mother, Nora, for permission to use extracts of interviews and her unpublished memoir; and as always, my sons Lewis and Liam for all the support.

About the Author

Mike Royden has taught History for over thirty years, and has also lectured on numerous courses in local history in the Centre for Continuing Education at the University of Liverpool. He has had several books and numerous articles published, and has made regular appearances on radio and television including Radio 4's *Making History*, BBC's *Heirhunters, Who Do You Think You Are?, Blitz Cities* with Ricky Tomlinson, and two Channel 5 documentaries on wartime in Liverpool and Merseyside with Michael Buerk. He has also researched extensively into the history of the First World War and has led tours on the battlefields of France and Flanders.

In 2017 he was elected as a member of Everton FC Heritage Society. Mike Royden also runs several history websites at www.roydenhistory.co.uk.

He has two sons: Lewis, who is a photographer; and Liam, a musician.

ALSO BY THE AUTHOR

Chester at War (2019)
Merseyside at War 1939–45 (2018)
A–Z of Chester: People, Places, History (2018)
Tales from the 'Pool: A Collection of Liverpool Stories (2017)
Village at War: A Cheshire Village During the First World War (2016)
Liverpool Then and Now (2012, 2nd edition 2015)
Tracing Your Liverpool Ancestors (2010, 2nd edition 2014)
Did Adolf Hitler Visit Liverpool in 1912/13? – BBC.co.uk website (Legacies)
A History of Liverpool Maternity Hospital and the Women's Hospital (1995)
A History of Mill Road Hospital, Liverpool (1993)
Pioneers and Perseverance: A History of the Royal School for the Blind, Liverpool, 1791–1991 (1991)

FORTHCOMING

Sailing ships, Shipwrecks and Suffragists: A History of Thomas Royden & Sons, Liverpool Shipbuilders (2022)